POW Baseball
in World War II

POW Baseball in World War II

The National Pastime Behind Barbed Wire

by TIM WOLTER

McFarland & Company, Inc., Publishers
Jefferson, North Carolina, and London

Library of Congress Cataloguing-in-Publication Data

Wolter, Tim, 1957–
    POW baseball in World War II : the national pastime behind
barbed wire / by Tim Wolter.
        p.   cm.
    Includes bibliographical references and index.
    ISBN 0-7864-1186-4 (softcover : 50# alkaline paper) ∞
    1. World War, 1939–1945 — Prisoners and prisons.   2. Baseball —
History — 20th century.   3. United States — Armed forces — Sports.
4. Canada — Armed Forces — Sports.   I. Title.

D805.A2 W65   2002
940.54'72 — dc21

                                                         2001055835

British Library cataloguing data are available

Manufactured in the United States of America

Front cover: Mickey Grasso batting in an All Star game at Stalag 111B,
Furstenberg, Germany, 1944 *(Photograph by Angello Spinelli, National
POW Museum, Andersonville, GA)*

McFarland & Company, Inc., Publishers
    Box 611, Jefferson, North Carolina 28640
    www.mcfarlandpub.com

Contents

Introduction:
Time on the Bench

There was a generation of Americans, now mostly gone or playing out their last few innings, for whom baseball really was *the* national pastime. They grew up idolizing Ruth and Gehrig, playing ball on sandlots, in cow pastures, and on city streets. For these young men, and for some young women as well, baseball was a sort of spontaneous combustion. Put eighteen players on a fairly level patch of ground, toss out a few gloves, a ball, and a bat, and a baseball game would happen. In fact it would take quite a bit to prevent it from happening, surely more than the minor inconvenience of being captured and imprisoned as a prisoner of war (POW).

About 130,000 American soldiers were captured during the Second World War. There were also just under 19,000 American civilians who were interned by the enemy. The conditions under which they were held varied enormously. There were a few diplomats who were held in a strange, genteel captivity with many of the comforts of home. There were many prisoners, especially those held in the worst of the Japanese camps, who if they survived at all lived desperate lives under conditions of brutal inhumanity.

In all but the worst circumstances there was room for at least a little recreation, and one can actually use baseball as a barometer to measure the quality of life in a camp. In the best of the German stalags there were often several leagues active at a time, with dozens of teams playing games continuously during the warm weather months. In the harsher stalags and in some Japanese camps there was only makeshift ball playing. In the worst of the camps, wretched places like Camp O'Donnell, there was no energy for anything but the struggle to survive. Starving men will not play baseball. But over the course of my research, I have been surprised at how frequently half-starving men will.

World War Two was a worldwide affair indeed. As a result baseball and its lesser sibling, softball, were played behind barbed wire in all manner of places. Baseball diamonds were laid out from the deserts of Australia to an ancient caravan city in Central Asia to the frigid shores of the Baltic Sea. The crack of the bat was heard in Indonesian jungles, on the streets of Japanese cities, and in the pine woods of northern Minnesota. Americans played baseball the most, but the British, Australians, and New Zealanders modified their cricket skills to play a game that to them seemed to be a variation of "rounders." Canadians figure prominently in the story of POW baseball, as being at war two years longer than Americans afforded them more opportunities to be captured and to spend more years in captivity. Of course the Japanese have a long baseball tradition, so we find them playing the occasional game against their captives, then having to drink from the same cup, ending up as captives themselves and playing ball there. Other nationalities made brief appearances on the field: Filipinos who learned the game from Americans, Chinese who learned from Japanese, and even some German prisoners, who never seemed to get the hang of it, but were willing to give it a try.

At first glance one might wonder why prisoners of war would play baseball at all. The reasons were various. Sometimes they had no choice in the matter. There were several instances where Japanese guards "invited" their American captives to play. Under the circumstances refusal would have been at best awkward, and at worst dangerous. In some camps an organized sports program was part of the system under which ranking officers maintained morale and military discipline. Boredom, with all of its corrosive effects on the human spirit, is a universal feature of captivity, and elaborate measures to keep minds occupied and bodies in some sort of fighting trim were looked upon with favor. But mostly, baseball was an effort on the part of the prisoners to recreate on a small scale the world from which they had been separated to build what one former prisoner called "Little Americas." They succeeded pretty well. At times the world of POW baseball was a near-perfect mirror of professional baseball. There were leagues with fierce rivalries. There were controversial umpiring decisions with the heated commentary that always follows. There were allegations that some teams were stacking their rosters with ringers, brought into a barracks or hut solely for the purpose of strengthening its ball team. There were prisoner-run newspapers in many camps, each with its own sports section, often with sports columnists who wrote in a style that would not have been out of place in any newspaper back home. Some papers published sketches and biographical information on sports heroes of the week, along with lengthy statistics compiled by an official statistician. Of course, there were differences. There could be no "away" games in any usual sense, and stateside there were probably not many games postponed for the occasional air raid.

The participants were generally a cross section of their generation, young men from all walks of life. But there were a few professional players among them, and the story of the former and future major leaguers among the POW ranks is a story both odd and to date mostly untold. There were even a few female POWs for the first time in American military history, and they too played a role in the story of POW baseball.

There are a few controversies that should be mentioned up front. I have chosen to include civilian internees in my story. The lines between military and civilian captives were not always cleanly defined. Army and Navy nurses who were clearly military personnel were held in civilian camps, and civilians such as Merchant Marine sailors and construction workers on Pacific island fortifications were sometimes kept in military compounds. Furthermore, to exclude the civilian men, women, and children who found themselves behind barbed wire would be a loss to the history of baseball under these difficult circumstances.

Unfortunately there seems to exist some tension between the ranks of former military POWs and former civilian internees, who sometimes choose to refer to themselves as "civilian POWs." The military types point out correctly that the civilians in general experienced conditions that were significantly better than those in the military camps. They further point out that at least in theory the civilians were in harm's way by choice, not because they were dutifully following the orders of their country. The organizations representing former civilian internees are quite active in pursuing legal redress and monetary compensation from their former captors, notions that seem to hold less appeal for the former military men. That having been said I have decided to include the civilians, and not only for the interesting perspectives that they add. The civilians may have had less actual hardship than most of the military prisoners, but they still had plenty, especially in the later stages of the war. And they were in general less equipped mentally and physically to bear the ill treatment.

On the other hand, I am purposely leaving out one large group of baseball-playing civilian internees. Using reasoning that appears quite flawed in retrospect the U.S. government decided after Pearl Harbor to confine large numbers of citizens of Japanese descent in facilities that can only properly be called concentration camps. Japanese Americans were interned in the United States in numbers almost equal to the total of American POWs held by the Axis. Conditions for these internees were roughly on a par with the better German prisoner-of-war camps. The Japanese-American internees played baseball on a wide scale, and it played a significant role in helping hold together a community struggling under a considerable and undeserved hardship. It is a brave tale, and one that merits being remembered. Other researchers have discovered this single area of POW baseball and have begun to give it some of the recognition it richly deserves.

Some baseball purists may insist that the title and premise of this work are deceptive, as the game most often played by the prisoners more closely resembled softball than baseball. From one point of view they may be right. Probably 90 percent of the ball played behind barbed wire involved pitchers throwing underhand, and of the wide range of balls used, both manufactured and handmade, the majority were not what we would recognize as hardballs. But I think that is an unfairly narrow viewpoint. Players made do with what they had and modified the rules to fit the circumstances. The limited amount of open space within the camps often dictated use of a softer ball, as there were some understandable difficulties retrieving balls hit "out of the park." In the finest traditions of the sandlot the national pastime was altered as necessary. Rules were often hybridized: in one camp, for example, there was a former professional fast-pitch softball player. Bunting was allowed against him, for the simple reason that otherwise nobody could ever get a hit off of him. The lone exception was a fellow who ten years later found himself playing in the World Series.

The matter of baseball versus softball does not seem to have bothered the prisoners to any great extent. There is an occasional aside on the topic in some of the camp newspapers, but mostly the terms baseball and softball are used interchangeably, sometimes even in the same sentence. Clearly, to the POW, baseball was a matter more of dreams and hope than of precise rules and regulation ball fields.

A matter of greater concern must also be mentioned. There are many tales of POW baseball floating about, especially from the Pacific. Not all of them are true. One of the most stirring tales of prisoner-versus-guard baseball was related to me by a charming older fellow, who I later learned to be a notorious teller of fanciful yarns. The game he described never happened, according to several other ex–POWs from the same small camp.

Many former prisoners of the Japanese insist that the entire concept of baseball being played during their captivity is a bunch of nonsense: they never saw it, they never heard about it, and it has never been mentioned at any of their numerous reunions. It is hard to refute these arguments. On the other hand, there are also numerous credible ex–POWs who say it did happen, and with the large number of POW memoirs that have been published in the 1980s and 1990s, the number of sources to be reconciled is growing.

Whenever possible I have correlated several sources from the same camp, and given what weight I can fairly assign to their stories. Next to eyewitnesses, contemporary diaries are the most authoritative sources, and I give them considerable weight in debatable cases. Another useful tie breaker is the extensive set of reports prepared by the U.S. Provost Marshal immediately after the war. These reports were based on Red Cross inspection reports and on debriefings of returning POWs and in theory should be relatively free of the problems with which a researcher many years later is cursed: the deaths of key participants, the failing memories of survivors, and the tendency of stories to grow more and more colorful as years pass.

The POW experience in the Pacific created a higher degree of isolation of POWs, and even the most vocal skeptics of POW baseball admit that they were only able to see a small part of what was going on.

All that having been said, I have probably erred in some details, large or small. This is hard to avoid in addressing a topic where the sources of information are so diverse and where most of the participants are no longer around to either add or subtract any details.

I hope that nobody reading this story will be misled into thinking that the life of a POW was fun and games. It was at best a life of drudgery and, especially in the Pacific, was often a horrific experience indeed. My intent is only to focus on this small area of prison existence to show how baseball could be at times a reminder of life far beyond the barbed wire and on even rarer occasions could be a fragile bridge between captive and captor.

I am arbitrarily dividing this story into two main sections reflecting the experiences of POWs in German and Japanese captivity. (I have found no stories of baseball played by POWs held by the Italians.) I will deal separately with those topics that do not fit either category well, including the mysterious internment of American pilots by our "semi-ally," Russia. To get just a bit ahead of my story, The United States was allied with Russia against Germany, but Russia was neutral with respect to Japan, so American air crews that landed in Russia from the West were welcomed as comrades, while those that flew in from the East were locked up. A bit more digging would no doubt uncover evidence of ball playing among other groups of captive Americans as well, for instance, those interned by Sweden and Switzerland when their aircraft landed there by accident or necessity. But the conditions of captivity there appear to have been so posh as to be a bit out of place in a study of how Americans turned to their traditional game under the rigors of imprisonment.*

It is not my specific intent to retell the story of the prison camps. The many first-person accounts do so with a power and eloquence that nobody of a later generation can hope to match. But it is necessary to describe the camps and the POW experience in general to some extent. To attempt to tell the story of POW baseball without doing so would be an exercise in futility. You just cannot separate baseball from the times and places where it is played without reducing the game to trivial statistics and the players to superficial stereotypes. On occasion in the pages that follow, I have also tossed in a few references to the other athletic pursuits of the prisoners of war. There were just some stories I could not resist.

So far as I can determine, the full story of POW baseball has never been told before. It is not exactly as if it has been hidden, since there are mentions here and there in most first-person accounts of former prisoners of the Germans held before late 1944, and even the elusive tales of baseball in the Pacific have been in print for a while. It seems instead to be a case of having something hidden in plain sight. In much the same way, the former POWs themselves have always been around, mostly living ordinary lives and not calling much attention to their past experiences. For all the difficulties of researching events that happened over a half century ago this has actually been a good time to be asking questions of these quiet heroes. Many who have in the past been reluctant to speak out have become more forthcoming with their memoirs and more willing to talk about their captivity as they become aware that the day is approaching when there will be nobody left who can tell the story from personal experience. I have also found many second-generation stories as children of the POWs bring out diaries and photographs that have been hidden for a long time.

Some of the surviving POWs have also been, so to speak, hidden in plain sight. It was not until I was well into my research that I learned that in my little town of some 12,000 souls there was a former prisoner from Stalag Luft III. To my surprise he lived within sight of the ball diamond where I coached my son's Little League team. He did not have much new to add to my story; he had had the misfortune to be shot down while wearing a lightweight uniform designed for the Mediterranean theater and

---

Americans held in Switzerland and Sweden were housed in resort hotels, were minimally if at all guarded, and appear to have spent a lot of time skiing and in the company of local women.

recalled that the central focus of his POW experience was trying to stay warm. But he remembered ball being played at his camp, which represented the pinnacle of POW ball in terms of number of players and organization of play.

To that old soldier and all of his comrades in arms, I dedicate this work with equal portions of respect and appreciation.

Tim Wolter
October 2001
Chippewa Falls, WI

1

Kriegies

The German word for prisoner of war is a formidable mouthful: *Kriegsgefangener.* Almost universally the 90,000 or so Americans who found themselves captives of the Third Reich shortened it to "Kriegie," a title they bore with some pride.

Germany had already been at war for over two years by the time of Pearl Harbor, so American captives found themselves entering a well-established and, as with all things German, well-organized prison system.

Each of the German armed forces, Army, Navy, and Air Force, had custody of prisoners of war from equivalent enemy services. Each maintained its own interrogation centers and hospitals, and each had a system of permanent camps, or *lagers.* In general, there were separate camps for officers, noncommissioned officers (sergeants and corporals), and enlisted personnel (privates). The permanent camps where these prisoners were held were called *Stamm Lagers,* shortened to *Stalag.* In the case of officers the designation *Offizer Lager* was used, again trimmed to the more manageable *Oflag.* The German Air Force, or Luftwaffe, added the designation *Luft* to its camps but did not use the designation Oflag, even in camps where officers predominated.

Camps in general were designated by a combination of roman numerals and letters. The series did not always follow a logical pattern, and camps would sometimes change names, go out of service entirely, or be moved. For the convenience of the reader I will use the more authentic roman numerals only for camps with designations under 10.*

To complicate matters further there was a general effort to segregate prisoners not only by rank and service, but also by nationality. This could

The Germans also used Arabic numerals for the higher-numbered camps, such as Stalag 353.

9

either be by camp or by compound within a camp. So for instance American and British prisoners were not commonly housed together, and mixing Western POWs with the unfortunate mass of Russian prisoners was unheard of except on the occasional work detail. One effect of this policy was that the vast majority of American POWs taken before the final stages of the war were housed in only nine camps. To a greater or lesser extent ball was played in all of them.

The story of Canadian POWs is quite a bit more complex. Although fewer in numbers the Canadians fought and were captured over a longer period of time and in a wider variety of places. Since they were generally housed with the British, Australians, and New Zealanders, they appear in a confusing number of camps. The topic of Canadian prisoners merits a separate chapter.

Germany was signatory to the Geneva Convention, and in general attempted to follow its provisions within the constraints of a pressured and ultimately collapsing economy, but there were some notable exceptions. As the bombing campaign against Germany began to take a heavy toll of lives the attitude of German civilians hardened. With the encouragement of propaganda denouncing bomber crews as "Terror Fliegers" or "Luft Gangsters" there were numerous instances of downed air crews being beaten or even executed by enraged civilians. The German military, especially the S.S., was also guilty of atrocities toward prisoners on occasion. But once the POW was within the stalag system the treatment was generally "correct" and in keeping with accepted military traditions.

Russia had not signed the Geneva Convention and Germany made no effort to treat captured Russian prisoners with the same degree of humanity. Russia reciprocated, and these nations contend with Japan for the dubious distinction of the worst treatment of captives.

The picture most Americans have of life in the stalag system is probably formed in some part by the television series "Hogan's Heroes." This modestly successful comedy was based loosely on the movie Stalag 17, which was in turn modeled on a play by the same title. The original play was written in large part by former prisoners of war from Stalag 17B.

"Hogan's Heroes" produces mixed responses from former Kriegies, although most seem to appreciate it on some level. At the time it originally aired it was felt to contain a large amount of ludicrous fabrication as it portrayed crafty Allied prisoners collecting valuable intelligence data, communicating frequently with London, and generally bamboozling the clueless Germans guarding them.

As time has passed and classified records have been opened, it has become apparent that the series was actually more of an exaggeration than

An informal ball game at Stalag IIIB, 1943 or 1944. (Photographer unknown. Courtesy Stephen Napier, Jr.)

a work of pure fiction. There really were secret tunnels, hidden radios, and methods of two-way communication between the camps and Allied forces. There were certainly some guards akin to Sergeant Schultz who were willing to look the other way on occasion for a variety of reasons. The tale of how baseball played a small role in this secret war is covered in the chapter "Stealing Home."

There were many paths to captivity, but most Americans were captured in one of three groups. The first were the ground forces in North Africa, some 5,000 of whom were captured during German counterattacks around Kasserine Pass in the first few months of 1943. Perhaps to have them as negotiating chips the Germans went to some lengths to evacuate these prisoners just a few months before their own forces in North Africa were surrendered and "went into the bag." These prisoners had the best opportunity to play ball, entering the stalags when they were functioning efficiently and spending the bulk of two baseball seasons behind barbed wire.

The second group of American prisoners began falling from the sky in large numbers in the second half of 1943. It was a time when British and American heavy bombers were attempting to bring Germany to its knees by constant day and night bombing raids. German defenses were quite potent at that time, and casualties were high. It was not until after the Normandy invasion and the extension of the range of American fighter cover that the skies over Europe were survivable by bomber crews, and even then there were continued losses to the very end of the war. A high percentage of these prisoners were officers. Since under the Geneva Convention officers could not be required to work, they had ample opportunities for recreation such as athletics.

The final large group of captives were ground troops taken during the German last-ditch offensive through the Ardennes in December 1944. These Battle of the Bulge prisoners had a short but miserable captivity in improvised, poorly supplied camps. Conditions did not permit any recreation to speak of, and they were liberated in the spring of 1945. These men have no part in the story of POW baseball.

There were several factors that had an effect on the degree of athletic activity within a camp. Some camp commandants seemed more concerned than others about the possibility of a mass escape attempt arising from a large athletic gathering. Some camps had ample amounts of open space while others were cramped. And since enlisted men could be forced to perform nonwar-related work under the Geneva Convention, there were some camps where a sizable number of the prisoners were out on work details most of the time.

The playing surface in most stalags was the parade ground. This was a large open space within the camp where the Germans required the prisoners to gather twice a day for a head count, known as *appell*. Some semipermanent athletic improvements were allowed, such as football goal posts. There were also specific areas set aside for ball diamonds, but permanent installations such as bleachers and backstops were unusual. Contemporary photographs suggest that the playing surface was all dirt and was usually rough to a degree that would challenge the most skillful fielders. Despite the lack of seating (no corporate luxury boxes in this league!) the games were often well attended, with spectators standing or sitting along both base lines, beyond the edge of the outfield, and sometimes even watching from the roofs of nearby barracks.

In the early days of captivity POWs were quite creative in their improvisation of bats and balls. But the majority of the athletic equipment was of commercial quality. The YMCA was active in collecting baseball and softball equipment, which was then transported, stored, and distributed to the camps by the International Red Cross, which had a protective role for prisoners of war of most nations during the Second World War. The amount of athletic gear sent cannot be determined with precision, but a figure quoted by the YMCA in a letter distributed to returning POWs in 1945 claims that 1,754,254 sports articles were shipped from the United States to Europe in the previous two years. This tally of almost 2 million items staggers the imagination, even if every ping-pong ball was somehow accurately counted. The system seems to have been efficient. In some cases sporting goods arrived in camps only a few weeks after the first American prisoners got there, suggesting that these items had been stockpiled in Red Cross warehouses in Switzerland in anticipation of such needs. The Red Cross also supplied many prisoners with blank books called wartime logs in which to record details of their captivity. These logs are personalized documents, with poetry, sketches, and essays that add much human detail to the picture of stalag life.

Within a camp there was generally a command structure that preserved a degree of military hierarchy. By custom the most senior officer present would be in charge. In camps with only NCOs or enlisted men a spokesperson was usually democratically elected by the prisoners and designated as the "man of confidence." His primary duty was representing the interests of the men in dealings with the German administration. Various subordinate duties were parceled out in areas such as security, escape committee, food distribution, and so forth. Often there would be a recreation officer, and in the larger camps there would be an entire organization with different men in charge of different sports and even commissioners of the various ball leagues along with official statisticians, umpiring crews, and so forth.

Most sports programs had to make do with whatever space could be spared, but one unspecified camp in Germany had a separate hut used as a sports center. Over the entrance to the building, which also served three times a week as the camp laundry, was a crest of arms bearing crossed golf clubs, a boxing glove, and a ping-pong racket.

Nearly all of the problems that exist in the world of baseball were duplicated within the stalag leagues. There were complaints about the quality and objectivity of the umpires. There were allegations of recruiting irregularities, with some barracks seeming to pad their rosters by offering inducements to better ballplayers to come and live there. There was betting on the games, with the action running to large numbers of the standard camp currencies, cigarettes and chocolate bars. No allegations of game fixing were voiced openly, but the potential was certainly there.

Most of the camps had one or more newspapers that took an active interest in sporting events. Stalag Luft III had at least seven. These were generally handwritten or typed, and a few copies would be posted on bulletin boards around the camp so that all could read them. They first had to be approved by the German censors, a fact of life that caused one paper to have in its masthead the motto "All the News That's Been Gepruft [approved]." The content of these papers varied somewhat, but arrivals of new prisoners, news from back home, girlie pictures, and reviews of camp theatrical productions took their places alongside the box scores, sports columns, and player profiles.

There were a couple of camp publications that merit special mention. Oflag 64 had a paper that was commercially printed in sufficient quantities to provide a copy for each man. On one occasion they even sent copies to President Franklin D. Roosevelt and to the Library of Congress. There was a publication called *POW-WOW*, which was headquartered at Stalag Luft I but somehow managed to have branch editions come out at no fewer than seven different camps and in three foreign languages. In most of its incarnations it seems to have been an underground paper, circulating secretly among the prisoners to pass along war news that had been received by clandestine radios. It is said to have published a special edition announcing the Normandy invasion several hours before the news was made public on American radio!

In contemporary documents such as the camp newspapers and individual diaries the terms *baseball* and *softball* appear with about the same frequency. But it is certain that the game generally played in the stalags most closely resembled softball, with a larger ball and with the pitcher delivering in an underhand motion. Just why this is has never been explained completely. The Red Cross delivered both hardball and softball equipment. The most common explanation given is that the limited space of the parade grounds did not permit baseball play, as too many of the balls would go over the fence and could be retrieved only with difficulty. But this seems simplistic. There are reliable accounts of a hardball league in one of the most cramped stalags, while other camps with unusually large athletic fields, such as North Compound at Stalag Luft III, uniformly played softball.

My guess is that the predominance of softball over baseball was dictated by several considerations. Space was a factor, but so was the poor quality of the fields. They were uneven, with many soft and hard patches. It may have simply been unsafe to play hardball, especially when the more specialized equipment such as catcher's gear and even gloves and athletic shoes must have been in short supply. Softball is a more forgiving sport, but close enough to the game the soldiers had grown up on to satisfy them.

Of course in the case of homemade balls concocted out of boot heels and socks the distinction of hardball versus softball loses all significance.

The German attitude toward the ballgames is seldom recorded. A guard at Stalag Luft IV took enough interest to snap a few photos of games from his watchtower. The commandant of Stalag Luft III seems to have become something of a fan. There are a few sketchy reports that the guards at Stalag 17B once stacked their rifles and tried to play an inning or two, but the usual German attitude, while sympathetic to sports in general, was indifference toward this curious American game.

It was German policy to locate prison camps in the eastern part of Germany. Supposedly Adolf Hitler himself had dictated that they all be at least 1,000 miles from the English Channel to deter potential escapes. This caused considerable worry to Allied leaders late in the war, as there was concern that the prisoners might be massacred to keep them out of the hands of the advancing Russian Army. Some of the more farsighted may also have already begun to mistrust their Eastern ally. There was at one point a serious plan to stage a rescue mission to one camp deep in Poland by having prisoners stage an uprising, commandeer a nearby airfield, and have stripped-down B-17 bombers land to evacuate them.

In the end there were no massacres, but the majority of the POWs did have to endure their harshest ordeal of the war, a forced march in the depths of winter. Most were evacuated by their German guards in January 1945; the shivering columns of hungry Kriegies, with their guards perhaps equally miserable, marched back and forth for hundreds of miles across the collapsing Reich. Along the way they were sometimes strafed by their own aircraft, which could not tell the difference between columns of prisoners and columns of German troops.

Upon their ultimate liberation the American prisoners blended quickly back into civilian life. A few went on to play professional baseball, but the majority just joined the great postwar economic expansion of the nation. Only many years later, when the now-old men began to reflect on the past, to write their memoirs, and to pass along their stories to the next generation has the story of Kriegie ball begun to emerge in bits and pieces. Gathered together it is a remarkable tale, a story of how grown men trained to fight and kill instead found themselves back on the sandlots of their childhood, playing the games of their younger days.

2

Stalag Luft I

As its designation suggests, Stalag Luft I, located near Barth, Germany, on the Baltic Sea, was the first camp established to house captured enemy air crews. It appears to have been opened in July 1940, with the first inhabitants being French. When officers of the British Royal Air Force (RAF) started showing up a few months later they did not take kindly to their French brothers in arms, some of whom were said to have packed their suitcases and quietly waited on their runways to be captured. In short order the French were moved elsewhere and Luft I became an all-British camp. For some reason the camp was abandoned in April 1942, and the inmates were sent to the newer Stalag Luft III. But by October of that year Luft I was reopened and many of the same prisoners were returned to it. By February 1943 a few Americans had already "dropped in." Throughout its existence the camp was reserved for prisoners of officer rank with a scattering of noncommissioned officers.

The history of this camp was in part determined by its geography. It was located on a bay of the Baltic Sea, and the climate that far north in Germany, on the same latitude as Hudson Bay, was colder and wetter than in other permanent German camps. This had an adverse effect on several POW activities, including baseball. And tunnel digging.

Stalag Luft I was divided into several compounds. By early 1944 there were South and West compounds. In February 1944 a new compound called North 1 was opened to house the increasing numbers of American prisoners. Compounds designated North 2 and North 3 were opened in September and December, respectively. Because of the cramped nature of the camp the only compounds with recreational open space were West and North 1. These compounds had "full-sized football and baseball fields."[1]

Prisoners in less spacious compounds could go to West and North 1 compounds under an arrangement that allowed travel between compounds, something of a rarity in the stalag system. Until the spring of 1944 the gates between compounds were open at all times, presumably the policy only being tightened up in the wake of the Great Escape at Stalag Luft III. After that only the teams were allowed to go for these "away games"; their fans had to stay home. Sports equipment was widely available, and it sounds as if even prisoners in South, North 2, and North 3 managed to improvise opportunities to at least practice ball in available spaces. North Compound 2 for instance had a patch of hard-packed ground some 80 by 50 yards, just barely big enough for softball games.[2]

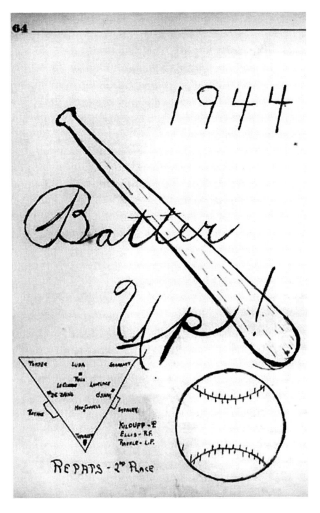

A page from Art Starratt's wartime log, stalag Luft I, 1944.

To a much greater extent than any other camp the guards at Luft I seem to have worried about the possibility of ballgames being used as a staging area for a mass escape. It was not entirely an unreasonable notion since at some of the bigger athletic events there might be a thousand spectators surrounding the field. To prevent an escape attempt the Germans added an extra fence where the outfield approached the main fence. It was three feet high and 10 to 20 feet in from the main fence. No prisoner was supposed to cross this fence in pursuit of a ball, on penalty of being shot. Several former Luft I POWs recall narrow escapes under just these circumstances, although actual shots were seldom fired and nobody seems to have ever been hit. Concern over ballplayers approaching the fence created some unusual ground rules for Luft I. Several versions are remembered by former Kriegies. Colonel C. Ross Greening recalled: "Over the fence was really out in our camp! We had arrangements with the guards whereby a man carrying a special flag could go out and retrieve balls knocked over the fence. As long as he was carrying the flag the guards wouldn't shoot him."[3]

Other versions had special white flags issued to spectators who would wave them if an outfielder was running after a ball without keeping an eye on the location of the warning wire. Still another version had a POW wearing a special multicolored "parole jacket" to retrieve errant balls.

Sometimes the game would simply be over when the ball crossed the "shoot line." It lay there until the guards felt like allowing its retrieval; perhaps if the guards were feeling mean it might be the next day.

An interruption of play of this sort could be a major disappointment. Because of the disparity between interested players and available playing fields teams might wait weeks for a chance to play a league game.

It is difficult to track the history of ball playing at Luft I, and in several places gaps must be filled in with educated guesswork.

In 1940 the camp was just getting started, and athletic equipment was not likely on hand. With a mixed French-British population soccer would seem to be the only plausible team sport. By 1941 it was more or less an all-British camp, with cricket being played. The 1942 season was canceled by the temporary abandonment of the camp. By 1943 there were enough Americans and Canadians on hand that softball took its place alongside cricket and soccer. But Americans were few in numbers at that point. Even by January 1944 there were only 507 Americans among the inmates.

Equipment too was short in the early days. Colonel Greening recalls improvising bats out of bedposts and balls from the uppers of old shoes. Play was likely on a pick-up basis. Softball was only one of several sports in active play: basketball, football, soccer, and boxing all had notable popularity.

The year 1944 was the big one for ball at Luft I. By September the camp was crowded with 6,000 prisoners, perhaps 5,000 of them American. Red Cross equipment was reaching the camp in good amounts, and until late in the year there was even an ample supply of food to keep morale and energy levels up. Camp administration was a bit harsher than in earlier years, but not to the point of prohibiting athletic activity.

An account of sports at Barth written soon after the war relates that North I had two leagues organized in the spring of 1944, with the Terror

Fliegers taking the American League pennant and the Kriegie Kats prevailing in the National League. Betting on the games was said to be quite prevalent. With the wrap-up of the first round of league play enough new players were on hand to organize two additional leagues, the Big Ten and the Ivy League. From the four leagues, players were selected for an all-star team to compete with teams from South Compound. (This would appear to be at odds with the report that only West and North I had space for ball fields.)

There were also hardball teams organized for intercompound play, but the constraints of space resulted in only limited play.

A former Luft I prisoner, Art Starratt, made some notes and sketches in his wartime log that give a few details of the 1944 league. He was from North I compound, so his records listing teams in five leagues* seem to correspond to the second half of the 1944 season. The status of the Twilight League is uncertain.

Starratt recorded that in addition to the enigmatic Twilight League there were two "groups" with two leagues each. Group I was from Barracks 1 through 6 and had American and National leagues of eight teams each. Some of the team names are straightforward, such as Homeless Ten, All Sergeants, Stalag Pee Wees, Ramblers, Camp Cats (perhaps the previously mentioned Kriegie Kats?), and Timid Ten. Others had a specifically military theme. The Flying Forts no doubt were a tribute to the B-17 bombers so many of the men had flown, and the Blockbusters would seem to be a reference to the special bombs used for targets such as dams. Some of the team names were more whimsical. The Baltic Bums may have been lonesome for the Dodgers. The Rockettes were more likely to have been thinking about leggy showgirls than any form of military ordnance. One might expect teams named Meat Balls and Cellar Dwellers to perform poorly, but the record shows that they took first and second in the National League that summer. A couple of the team names would be meaningless to those outside the world of the POW. The D Bars referred to a chocolate bar that came as a ration item in the crucial Red Cross packages. It was in addition a form of camp currency, although it never rivaled the cigarette as the standard medium of exchange. The Oleo Kids also named their team after a Red Cross item; in an effort to maximize the calories in a parcel, oleomargarine was a staple.

The second group of ballplayers was listed as Group IV. It included

---

Starratt lists the top teams in two of the leagues as Big Ten and Ivy League, rather than having two of the leagues so designated. Perhaps the names reflect the presence of former collegiate athletes.

teams from Barracks 7 through 10, along with 11A and 11B. In this group-ing there were two eleven-team leagues, apparently also designated Amer-ican and National. Some accounts indicate that this was considered a minor league.

Second place in the National League in 1944 went to Starratt's team, the Repats. This was a shortened version of Repatriated, the status given seriously wounded prisoners. Stalag Luft I was especially fortunate in this regard; it was right on the Baltic Sea and but a short boat trip to Sweden. Transportation home for repatriated soldiers was swift and direct; one vet-eran with whom I spoke even claimed that they could see the liner *Grip-sholm* in the bay when it came for a prisoner exchange.

Team names in Group IV also ranged across the spectrum of the pris-oners' experience. The Typhoons might have been former pilots of that particular aircraft. The Hitless Wonders must have had pretty good pitch-ing to finish the 1944 campaign in third place. Homer's Hopheads and the Barley Bashers were obviously missing some of the creature comforts of their previous lives. The Klim Kats might have had a special fondness for Klim, a sort of condensed milk that came in Red Cross parcels. The lead foil from these cans was extensively reused by the POWs to make all man-ner of crafts, something for which Luft I was particularly well known among the camps.

Some of the team names from Group IV hint at the lives of the play-ers but can do no more than that. Were the Junior Birdmen all officers of lower rank? Were the Young Yankees all New Yorkers or the Elgineers all from that Illinois town? Did the Miracle Men pull out more come-from-behind victories and were the Dark Horses really just that? It seems like something of a slur to military men to compare them to Shoe Clerks, but there was a team by that name. They were tenth in an eleven-team field, so one hopes they were better soldiers than ballplayers. There also was a team named Nemos. Since there were no significant numbers of naval aviators in the camp it seems unlikely to be a reference to the submariner of the Jules Verne story. At about this time there was in circulation a surreal comic strip called "Little Nemo in Dreamland." Perhaps for these young men so far from their familiar homes life in the camp did have a dreamlike quality.

One thinks of MIA, a designation for missing in action, as being a modern term. But it was recognizable in 1944 to the point of one team naming themselves that. Other teams dubbed themselves Bow-Wows, Sackers, Crusaders, and Liberandos, the latter perhaps a reference to the B-24 Liberator, which was the other standard heavy bomber of the Army Air Corps at that time. Finally there were a few teams identifying specific individuals or barracks designations. These seemed to occupy the lower notches in the league. The Zimmer Six (translated from the German as "Room Six") could only manage a ninth-place finish, while Schultz's Foul Balls and Bromley's Follies really were cellar dwellers.

The Twilight League had only six teams, divided into two groups of three. The name suggests that they had the field at the end of the playing day. Something about the team names hints at a lesser degree of competitiveness. Wheels does not sound too bad, and the evening circuit entry of Big Ten might have some of the luster of its Group IV champions. But Night Hawks sounds questionable, Ring Dang Docs was probably a team of medical personnel, Luft Waffles as a team name inspires little dread, and the bottom finisher, Ersatz, probably deserved the name, which technically translates from the German as "replacement," but has the strong connotation in everyday usage of a dismally inadequate substitute. Several sources do mention a hardball league at Stalag Luft I, and it is possible that the Twilight League was it.

Not all of these teams covered themselves with glory and laurels. A wartime log kept by another Luft I prisoner has the following to say about his team, the Bow-Wows: "BASEBALL— Under the cognomen 'Bow-Wow' the following aggregation struggled mightily for victories in a not-too-good league but could be proud at the end of the season only in this: that they had not finished last."[4]

On some occasions there were inter-Allied sports jamborees. According to American Colonel John Vietor: "One of the unexpected reversals of the war occurred when we beat the British at rugby and they promptly turned around and beat us at baseball."[5] This event may have been the Great International Athletic Meet, which was staged at Barth on July 10, 1943. For the occasion the prisoners were allowed to use the camp printing press to turn out a 17-page program describing the various track-and-field events, cricket, rugby, and so forth. Baseball was not mentioned in the admittedly very British source of this information.

Speaking of the British, there were some in Stalag Luft I even later in the war when it became predominantly an American camp. In a poem preserved in a wartime log, a RAF officer named A .E. Bullock wrote, describing his American campmates:

> Strange games they play with sticks and balls
> Sometimes they utter curious calls
> Of "Huba-Huba, let's get two"
> We don't know what they mean, do you?

With a high degree of softball activity going on, it is surprising that a fair number of Luft I prisoners have no memory of seeing any of it. This is a remarkable phenomenon. At most other camps former prisoners uniformly at least remember the games being played, even if they themselves were not involved. Some of course may have arrived late in the war, when league play might have been over. Even during its peak during the summer of 1944 it is possible that prisoners in compounds that lacked playing fields may have never have seen a game once the free passage between compounds was halted. Still, for the prisoners who arrived in 1943 it is hard to imagine they would not have seen play, and for all POWs one would imagine that at least some of the many empty hours would have been occupied with talk of the camp ball league. But memory is a tricky thing, and it is certainly understandable that the stronger memories of hunger or the uncertainty of one's future would crowd out lesser matters.

There seem to have been some players with extensive experience playing at Luft I, including a few former semi-pro players. One former Oklahoma Oilers pitcher is recalled by ex–POW Earl Rathke to have thrown "so fast that you had to start your swing when his arm started down."

At other camps it seems that lower-ranked prisoners such as sergeants did most of the officiating of games. Perhaps the inherent challenge to authority that comes with being an umpire was offensive to more senior officers. But at Luft I there was a Colonel Spicer who was an exception. Quite a forceful individual, he spent the last six months of his imprisonment in solitary confinement, by some accounts under a death sentence for advocating defiance of German regulations. When he umpired he wore his eagle insignia on his shoulders as a notice that there would be no disputing his calls. He remained in the service after liberation and went on to attain the rank of general.

The latter days of Luft I became chaotic as the Allied armies approached. By the fall of 1944 food supplies had dwindled due to the strain on the German transportation system caused by the invasion of France and the westward surge of the Red Army. But remarkably there was something of a 1945 season. The same early thaw that slowed down the Russian advance provided weather warm enough to play ball by April. It sounds as if there was an attempt to resume league play. A former sports officer for Block 4, North Compound 2, recalls that his team started playing on April 5, competing against various other blocks. After a week or so the teams were divided into leagues, with his rating the A League. Alas, despite having two of the best pitchers in the camp they could only manage one win against two losses in league play.[6]

There also seems to have been some intercompound all-star play. A bombardier named Norman Quast kept a diary, which had the following brief entries:

April 6th. Took shower. Played softball. Clark Recd. parcel.

April 17th Warmest day of year so far. All-Star softball game North 2 and West compound. 1–1 tie. Identity roll call. Water on and off during day.[7]

The reason that the Kriegies of Luft I were still able to play ball is simple. Of all the camps where Americans were held in any numbers this was essentially the only one where the prisoners were neither evacuated in a forced march nor living in hopelessly overcrowded conditions due to the consolidation of several other camps. At Barth with the Russians approaching the German commander received his orders to evacuate the prisoners. But instead, after conferring with the senior American officer, the prisoners were allowed to remain in their barracks as the guards instead marched away alone. A quickly organized detail of American prisoners took their places on guard duty, armed with the most formidable weapons on hand: baseball bats. The Russians showed up a few days later, on May 2 or 3, to an enthusiastic welcome.

The countryside surrounding the camp proved to be too hazardous for excursions, so the liberated Kriegies mostly stayed in the camp. Occasional ballgames continued to be played under the new camp management into early May. Problems soon arose, foreshadowing the era of Cold War tension. Some of the healthier POWs had offered to sign on informally with the Red Army in its ongoing march. After a few days of witnessing Russian atrocities on civilians the Americans turned around and went back to the camp. Then too, there was the Russian proposal that the Americans be evacuated eastward through war-ravaged Eastern Europe for eventual repatriation through Russian Black Sea ports. With American and British troops only a few hundred miles away and with some misgivings about the true depth of Russian friendship, the prisoners declined with as much diplomatic grace as could be mustered. Arrangements were made instead to put a nearby airstrip back into working condition so that Allied planes could begin an evacuation of Luft I.

Luft I was unusual among permanent prison camps in that the prisoners finished the war there. As a result artifacts from this camp survived in somewhat greater numbers. Among the many photographs there are a few that show ballplayers, so if the photographic record is a fair indicator, the national pastime was a small, symbolically important part of camp life.

3

Stalag Luft III

The task of chronicling the history of ball playing at Stalag Luft III is a daunting one. The size of the undertaking alone is a challenge, for this camp represents the absolute pinnacle of POW baseball. Nowhere else before or since have so many POWs participated. During the peak summer of 1944 there were probably upwards of 200 teams active in the six compounds of Stalag Luft III. A precise number would be hard to establish, but with the assumption of ten players per team one can document that Center Compound had 40 teams, East Compound around 35, South around 40. West Compound had several very active leagues, and was actually the largest compound with 16 barracks each holding around 100 men. It is reasonable to assume that as in other compounds each had more than one team per barracks. North Compound was a mixed British and American area and had the largest sports field. Roughly twice the size of the all-British East Compound, it probably had a significant number of participants; one undated source suggests 24 organized teams.[1] Belaria was an outlying compound that was mostly British, and although softball was played there it was more of a hotbed of cricket fanaticism. With a population that steadily rose throughout the history of the war, Stalag Luft III ultimately held 10,000 prisoners, and it appears that at least 2,000 were ballplayers on an organized basis.

Another difficulty in describing Stalag Luft III is that it is one of the few POW camps for which at least some people have a mental image, thanks to *The Great Escape*, a popular film that depicted events leading up to the mass escape in the spring of 1944. Although the filmmakers employed numerous former Kriegies as technical advisors and therefore did depict many details of camp life faithfully, the overall tone of the movie is a bit deceptive. Americans play a prominent role in the film, whereas they had

24

a minor role in the escape, which was largely a British affair. As a practical matter the escape did cause most subsequent escape activity to be suspended altogether. This freed up energies that were enthusiastically invested in the various sports programs.

Luft III was opened in April 1942. It was a new camp, carved out of a pine forest near the city of Sagan some 100 miles southeast of Berlin. The site was well chosen and the complex laid out with German efficiency.

The first prisoners were RAF, both officers and noncommissioned officers. There were initially only two compounds, but the steady flow of new prisoners necessitated the construction of four additional compounds. Eventually it evolved into an all-officers camp, although there did remain a small cadre of sergeants who acted as orderlies for the officers. The shortage of such labor was a persistent concern to the officers, who had little enthusiasm for doing their own laundry and housekeeping. At one point a group of ground forces privates were in the camp for this duty. When the Germans decided to forward them for agricultural labor there was actually a serious attempt on the part of the American officers to give all the GIs battlefield promotions to sergeant, so that they could not be removed from the camp. For the genuine sergeants at Stalag Luft III there were some compensations: they seem to have had a fairly firm hand on the black market trade and consistently fielded the most proficient sports teams.

Luft III was intended to be a model camp, and to a certain extent it was. Hermann Goering, the head of the German Luftwaffe, was said to have a special concern for POWs as many of his men had been captured by the British during the battle of Britain. To ensure that they were treated well the treatment accorded Allied POWs under Luftwaffe jurisdiction was almost always better than that given prisoners of the German Army. It is also true that the Germans had a certain appreciation of class distinctions and showed it in their better treatment of captured officers as opposed to enlisted prisoners.

From the beginning the population at Sagan was a cosmopolitan bunch. Poles, Czechs, Norwegians, and of course Canadians were all serving with the RAF and were imprisoned among the British; the uniform they were captured in was somehow more significant than the country of their origin. Within a month or so of its opening the first Americans turned up. Lieutenant John E. Dunn, who was shot down in April 1942, is given official credit for being the first American inmate of Luft III, although there were almost certainly a few American volunteers from the RAF American Eagle squadron who got there before him.

Other than a contingent of special guards referred to as ferrets, who patrolled the grounds looking for evidence of tunnel construction, there was little daily contact between the prisoners and the Germans. To a significant extent the Kriegies were allowed to build their own little world, a world in which many hometown institutions were imitated in barbed-wire versions.

There was a University of Sagan, which offered a wide variety of courses. It was actually possible to get credit for these courses from American and British universities. There was a library that eventually accumulated 2,000 volumes. There was a swing band called the Luftbandsters that was on a par with any similar group stateside. Theatrical entertainments of a professional quality were constantly in production, with shows having multiple performances to accommodate the large audience in the smallish theaters. Officers from many backgrounds gave lectures on topics ranging from sex to the future of the Army Air Corps. The former was better attended. Movies were a fairly regular feature; once there was even a Three Stooges short.

In addition to all of the above activities there were ongoing efforts to escape the camp. Some of the attempts were clumsy and earned their participants a stern lecture and a stay in the cooler. Others enjoyed more success, such as the British escapees who used a wooden vaulting horse set up near the wire to conceal a tunneler hiding inside its base. But Sagan will always be associated with the Great Escape of March 1944, a mass break by British prisoners in which nearly 90 men made it through a 340-foot-long tunnel dug out of North Compound. Tragically, most of the escapees were rounded up quickly, and the Gestapo on the direct orders of Hitler executed 50. It put an immediate damper on all subsequent escape activity. With the harsh reprisals that could now be expected and the overall improvement in Allied fortunes, the prisoners were instructed by their commanders to cease all further escape attempts.

According to Red Cross observers Stalag Luft III had "the best organized recreational program of the American camps in Germany. Each compound has an athletic field and volleyball courts. The men participate in basketball, softball, boxing, touch football, volleyball, table tennis, fencing. Leagues have been formed in most of these sports."[2]

The daily activities of the camp, sporting and otherwise, were dutifully reported in several prisoner-run newspapers, which were produced by hand and posted where they could be read by the men. These were not underground papers such as the Luft I POW-WOW, but openly produced publications. As such they bore the official *gepruft* mark of the German censors and tended to deal more with events inside the camp, making only passing references to the progress of the war. South Compound had the

Circuit. West Compound had the competing *Kriegie Clarion* and the *Stump*, while in Center the loyalties of the men were divided between the *Kriegie Times* and the *Gefangenen Gazette*. It is the good fortune of any researcher on the Stalag III story that the editors of the *Gazette* labored hard to cover all aspects of camp life in their improvised pages and then thought so highly of their work that they carried out copies of their entire run when they made their midwinter forced march in January 1945. One can only wonder how tempted they must have been at times to use these invaluable documents to start a fire and warm themselves.

Since the *Gefangenen Gazette* is the only Sagan paper that survived the war in its entirety, the picture of camp life that emerges is necessarily tilted toward the doings of Center Compound. It covers the era from November 1943 to January 1945. Generally one can assume that life in the other compounds went on along more or less similar lines.

Without a reliable contemporary source it is impossible to say just when softball arrived at Luft III, but it appears to have come early, taking its place alongside cricket sometime in the summer of 1942. One of the few comments in a near-contemporary source comes from a 1946 publication called "Wirebound World," apparently a memento book published by former inmates of North Compound. It relates: "After the Rugger and Soccer the most popular sport was American Soft Ball. Introduced to the camp by Canadians in 1942, it started out with a home made ball and bat."[3]

One Canadian prisoner serving in the RAF remembers that the difference was felt immediately. It just sounded different. The British cricket players and spectators were a quiet lot, perhaps offering just a bit of polite clapping for a good play. But on the softball diamond there was loud cheering and infield chatter. The Germans did not know what to make of it but seem to have feared that it was some sort of riot. Later some of them did learn to appreciate the game, and the commandant, a Colonel von Lindeiner, was said to have often attended and to have applauded vigorously by beating his cane on his leather boot.

Another faint trace of the 1942 season at Sagan can be found in a letter from a Canadian sergeant writing home in March 1943. He appears to be reacting to a public perception that Stalag Luft III was some sort of country club, an idea that was in circulation after German propaganda reports on the place became known in Allied nations:

> We must be careful not to create any misunderstanding with the folks at home.— Recently, letter from ENGLAND reveal that people there think this place is a "REST HOME" with swimming baths, beergardens, radio, and that we have oodles of RED CROSS food. And in

CANADA, people there heard a short-wave broadcast of a soft-ball game from the camp!! and our own "RED" GORDON was playing first-base!!! (As a matter of fact, RED is a catcher.) That takes the cake, I think. Well, people *will* misconstrue reports of our life here.[4]

It is not entirely clear from the above if there actually was a game broadcast from Luft III in 1942. If it did happen it must have been a unique event in the history of baseball.

By the spring of 1943 softball leagues were established in the various compounds, with both American and Canadian participants. Out of the American teams, then concentrated in North Compound, an all-star team was organized. The members seem to have been mostly sergeants. A Canadian officer named Harold Garland, who was imprisoned in East Compound, recalled a rare intercompound game with the American all stars:

> After they'd been there for a while, the Americans got permission to come over and have a softball game with the Canadians. All these Americans had baseball uniforms, all these lovely, white, fitting baseball uniforms. And the Canadians, we were in clothes we'd slept in for two or three years. And there were some professional American baseball players in there, too.
> The Canadian pitcher was Bill Paton, and he had pitched in the Beaches League in Toronto. And the umpire was Larry Wray, our Senior British Officer. And Larry Wray had to go to Bill about inning number five or six and say "Please let them hit, Bill." They hadn't touched the ball all that game![5]

In a comment from the summer of 1944 the *Gazette* remembers the defeat of 1943, commenting on the East Compound: "Best team over there is the one composed almost entirely of Canadians, the same one that took the American sergeants over last year in an inter-compound game. ... Being prisoners for such a long period has made them tops thru long practice in softball."

Since the *Gazette* did not begin publication until late in the year details of the 1943 ball league are fragmentary. One GI's letter home that year mentions: "I'm on the 'Sad Sacks' ball team which is tied for first in the league. We take our ball playing as serious as a major league game."[6]

In 1943 the majority of Americans were held in North Compound. But early in 1944 most were moved into Center Compound, previously occupied by British NCOs. The American exodus probably had a negative impact on softball in North Compound, but it did remain a major sport.

In an interesting view of North Compound softball through the eyes of a soldier unfamiliar with it, a British or possibly Australian writer noted:

> Softball after a very short time captured the hearts of sport fans, who searched for a faster game than cricket and this was no doubt due to the well organized schedules. The Major league exhibition matches pulled in large crowds and the peculiar jargon that is more than half of the game soon came from as many novices' lips as veterans. Clare's Cardinals pulled off the league championship, a series of hard fought matches between the "Tigers," "Giants," and "Noble's Indians." The intermediate and minor leagues were equally well attended, and the promotion from the minors to the intermediate and major leagues — no mean effort — occurred several times by players who never saw a softball until Sagan.[7]

The off season of 1943–44 was disrupted by the Great Escape, with the descent of the Gestapo on the camp for top-to-bottom inspections, and with the dismissal of Colonel von Lindeiner for supposed lax discipline. But the 1944 ball season still started on schedule.

On April 15 the first game was played in Center Compound, with the American senior officer, Colonel Delmar T. Spivey, getting the first hit of the year on a pitch one might assume was lobbed in ready to hit.

Soon Center Compound had active play going in three leagues, the Majors, the A, and the AA. These were grouped by the quality and seriousness of the players, with the Majors contesting every game vigorously and the lesser leagues being more easygoing. It is unfortunate that the organizers of the leagues decided to give the teams designations based on their barracks of origin rather than anything more creative. Thus the top three teams in the Majors were 55, 43 and 41 South. The one exception to this rule was a team in the AA league designated Colonels. This squad was made up of the senior officers in the compound. Colonel Spivey maintained that they were not very skilled, but it is worth noting that while they were a second-division team, they did not finish last.

Although it is mentioned seldom in the *Gazette*, several of these numbered teams did have nicknames, such as the Racketeers of 39 and Thompson's Troublemakers of 44. Other compounds were more creative in their designation of teams. In South Compound teams were formed on the basis of their military vocations with names such as Crack Pilots, Bombardiers, and Fighter Pilots. In most other respects the arrangements in South paralleled those of Center, with a Major, a Minor, and a beginners' Sandlot League. The British Commonwealth's North Compound also had Fighters and Bombers teams, as well as East Canada and West Canada squads.

The parade ground of Center Compound had enough room for two ball diamonds. The backstops must have been removable, as photographs of roll call being held do not show them. As to the quality of the fields and the effects on play, a long essay on the subject that appeared in the *Gefangenen Gazette* on August 13, 1944, deserves to be quoted verbatim, as perhaps the single best description of the challenges facing POW ballplayers:

> Baseball and its offspring, softball, have always been the instigators of many arguments and controversies—Here, at Stalag it serves to pass the time both at the games and the numerous bull sessions afterwards.
>
> The stomp meeting at the southeast end of Block 52 late one midweek afternoon gave rise to an interesting discussion on softball—said discussion wandered to the proverbial four corners—re: the Center camp—subject matter "The pitcher has had the advantage in Stalag long enough."
>
> Since pitchers happened to be in the Bull Ring, the debate was off to a flying start—as all bull flies—
>
> It seems that the pitcher is aided and abetted by these advantages—high left field which enables fielder to capture line drives that ordinarily would be softies—dead ground past infield that reduces chances of extra bases—batters box becomes a sand pit after one game, thereby giving runner a poor start—and as a final point, batters are using inferior bats.
>
> Turning the other cheek, we find the following detriments to the pitchers and help to the batters—Rough infield makes ground ball scoring erratic—sloping outfield coupled with sand and holes makes ball hogging hazardous—pitcher delivers the pill from a hole upwards to batter and not down from a mound—finis—the proximity of Block 52 enables some sluggers to garner extra bases from blows that otherwise would be outs.

Edging away from the partisans of both points the correspondent concluded that the pitcher was at a disadvantage.

The league set up at Stalag Luft III was similar to that at other camps: there were scheduled league games in which men played in their fatigues. One former Kriegie recalls these being called "inner combat" games. But on Sundays there were special games, called "uniform games." For these events two top performing teams from the previous week would be matched in a game designed to provide entertainment for the entire compound. The teams would don the baseball uniforms supplied by the Red Cross, consisting of shirts, pants, and cap. One set was gray with red trim, the other gray with blue trim.

Other camps may have had to make to with improvised equipment, but Stalag Luft III was the administrative and postal headquarters for the luft stalags, and supplies usually arrived on schedule. Some of it came from unusual sources. For Red Cross Week in 1944 the students of Clifton High School in Omaha, Nebraska, donated all of the school's baseball equipment to the camp. But most of the gear was rounded up in the usual fashion by the YMCA and forwarded by the Red Cross. A typical shipment received in August 1944 had as Center Compound's share: "83 each sports shoes, shirts, shorts. 1 dozen bats, 50 new softballs." The quality of the equipment and its durability proved to be problematic. The travails of the sports officer of Center Compound, a Lieutenant Van Able, were graphically described in *Gefangenen Gazette* on July 26, 1944:

> Nothing like the Truth. The thinning pate of the local sports czar, Van Able, is losing another handful of hair each time he hears the familiar crack of a bat. The bludgeons, while not of the finest calibre, should last much longer than they do. Their short life is essentially due to improper use by bats men.
>
> All swatting should be done so that the ball meets a bat at right angles with the grain.
>
> Any efforts on the part of participants will go a long way in saving Van's hair.

Actually Van Able was one of a number of officers charged with the organization of sporting events. In overall charge of the camp sports program was a Lieutenant Colonel Saltzmann, with Van Able being his subordinate for softball. There were also presidents for each of the three leagues and even an official statistician for the Majors.

Some of the problems encountered in stalag ball did not have equivalents in the free world. One game report mentions that the game was suspended due to an air raid. Another extra-inning game was called on account of hunger. On still another occasion a campwide round of typhoid shots left many of the athletes out of commission. In trying to explain another temporary lessening in interest in the ballgames, the Gazette mentioned that Kriegie ball had a hard time competing with Lynn Bari, who seems to have been a pinup girl who enjoyed a brief but intense popularity.

Other aspects of Kriegie ball had obvious counterparts. Recruiting of new talent was an ongoing concern for the better teams. In the middle of league play a Colonel Purinton was said (*Gefangenen Gazette*, July 2, 1944) to be "busy as the proverbial bee in the theater last Friday, trying to pick up a pitcher for 46 from newly arrived Kriegies. His only mistake was in choosing the wrong theater of operations— 55 had a delegation at the gate!! Sam Magee set his standards up high — he wanted nothing but men with professional baseball experience!!! Confidentially, Block 56 is in the market for a couple of .400 hitters. There's chocolate in it boys!!!!" This was not a farfetched commentary. The competition for good players was intense, and inducements did change hands. A cartoon from the *Gazette* of this time period shows a group of jug-eared Sad Sack types hustling a large wrapped bundle through the door of their barracks. The caption reads, "There goes those fellows from 39 smuggling another ballplayer into their block." Other forms of skullduggery were not unknown. A stern lecture in a sports column mentioned that one fellow had been seen playing in league games on teams representing two different barracks.

Umpires never have an easy time of things, and the prison camp leagues were no exception to this rule. The *Gefangenen Gazette*'s leading sports columnist was J. O. Hall, who complained on June 14, 1944:

> Much has been said lately concerning the umpiring of league ball-games, and unfortunately, a great majority of the comments have been of a derogatory nature, if not downright insulting. It's high time something is said in way of appreciation of the men, who fully recognizing their own limitations, are willing to do the best job they can in handling a difficult situation, and should be given a vote of thanks for their efforts instead of constantly being made to feel like the proverbial illegitimate child at a family reunion.

Sportsmanship was a persistent problem at the camp, and a special committee was proposed late in the 1944 season for the purpose of addressing the "incessant wrangling and insulting jibes which have made recent sports contests a parody of the words." Other than an appeal to the participants as officers and gentlemen little seems to have come of this idea.

Perhaps barbed-wire fences tend to focus one's attention inward, for the *Gefangenen Gazette* offers only rare glimpses of life in other compounds and at other camps. There seems to have been some exchange of information through the Red Cross observers, as Stalag Luft I is discussed a few times. The shortage of adequate field space and athletic equipment is mentioned specifically. But there does appear to have been a closer link with East Compound than with other areas of the camp. It was probably just a matter of proximity. East lay just across a double barbed-wire fence from Center. The barracks in East were positioned in such a fashion that prisoners sitting on the roofs had a great view of the ballgames in Center. This arrangement, reminiscent of rooftop fans across the street from Wrigley Field, did have the occasional drawback. One Canadian spectator was said to have gotten so excited that he forgot the precarious nature of his perch and slid off the roof entirely, breaking his leg.

Most spectators kept both feet firmly on the ground, but beyond that they seemed to have been a diverse bunch. The *Gazette* on August 13, 1944, ran an essay on the topic entitled "Stalag Types":

> Some of the softball contests played here in the past week had as much lift as a war model bra and even less interest, and so the *Gazette* began looking around and found that the crowds watching the stellar players could almost be classified into types.
>
> For example, one Kriegie, along the first base line, makin' with the "hubba-hubba," when asked what he did as a civvie, the *Gazette* discovered that he was a tobacco auctioneer and stated that he was just keeping in practice.
>
> Another, classified as the "mourner" or "It shouldn't happen to a dog" type was sitting behind home plate just shaking his head from side to side. His story was that he had been spotted some points plus by the manager of the Block 55 team for five "D" bars. Since he was a little superstitious he believed with all of those "D"s he couldn't lose … but the team didn't know it and double-crossed him!
>
> One onlooker, known as the "Do it this way" type, was busy telling one fellow how the losing team should be run, particularly now with two men on. He was quieted when his listener turned round and said "Shut up! I'm the manager of that team!" This chap was last seen heading for the nearest abort [latrine].
>
> To top everything, one of the fellow[s] watching sat thru two games. When asked if he liked softball games he piped up, "Not on your life! I'm just proving to myself that I'm all right. I've always maintained that this game is the dullest watch and basketball is the —wow! Look at that triple!"
>
> This stumped us so we quit. What position do I play? I don't even know the rules of the game!

Keeping the league play interesting was an ongoing challenge. After all, there was no goal to the contests for either players or spectators other than diversion, something to take their minds off the monotony of prison camp life. For the players there were no salary concessions to play for, no shoe contracts to land. And the spectators lacked the traditional solace of a hot dog and beer when the action on the field flagged.

To keep the leagues fresh, play was organized into rounds of about six weeks each. Teams would play each other in a round robin fashion and then the top teams would play for a championship of the round. In some compounds there seems to have been an overall championship decided. For instance in West Compound in the summer of 1944 Barracks 163 claimed the title, with the victors perhaps compromising their amateur status by claiming 62 D bars, 61 packs of cigarettes, and two cigars.

Since the majority of the inmates of Stalag Luft III were officers, who under the rules of the Geneva Convention could not be made to work, there was plenty of leisure time to play and watch the games. Other than twice-daily appells and of course meals, there was not much else for them to do. During the peak baseball season the playing fields were in use for five games a day, six days a week. They probably could have squeezed in a few more if not for the need to break for roll calls and meals.

Most of the league games were routine but occasionally an epic contest would develop. An enthused *Gazette* columnist described one such contest in an article called "56 and 43 Stage Thriller" on June 2, 1944:

> At 1030 a few fans were out to watch the softball game between 43 and 56. At 1300 every able bodied man in camp, and some on crutches, was out witnessing the thrilling finish of the best game ever played here.
>
> 56 had drawn first blood in the 4th when Niemeyer tripled, scoring Hull, and scoring himself on the poor throw home. 43 forged ahead in their half of the 4th on 3 errors and two singles for 3 runs. 56 tied it up again in the 5th on a single and 3 walks.
>
> From the 5th inning on, the teams settled down to some fine ball holding each other scoreless 'til the 13th.
>
> The unlucky 13th opened as Morris walked, Connelly singled, and a play was made at third on Norton's bunt. But all hands were safe, filling the bases. Hull flew out to the shortfielder and then Niedemeyer came through again with a single and two runs scored. After the 56 team took the field for the last half of the 13th the fans were ready to go home and eat. But they wanted to watch the last 3 outs. Their wish was never granted for 43 opened up when Gatewood walked, Jones singled, Bullock flew out to short field, Redding walked to fill the sacks. Then Merriam singled two men home and Wolfram singled the winning run in.

The writing style would not have been out of place in any stateside daily.

Most of the league games were a bit more routine, although a home run clear over Barracks 52 was dutifully reported as was a fiercely contested 27-inning marathon between 56 and 42. But there was a natural tendency for the regular season to become a bit tedious, especially in rounds where one team dominated the play from the start.

To help counter this phenomenon there were several special event days. On the Fourth of July a special sports day was held, which featured a ballgame between the winners of the first round in each league against an all-opponents game of all stars from the rest of their league. It was not a success, as ad hoc collections of players proved no match for a practiced, well-functioning championship team. All three of the all-star squads lost.

Later in the summer the camp sports committee tried again. This time it was for Labor Day, or Arbeit Day, as it was called. This time competition was scheduled in softball, basketball, track, and soccer. All were organized on an East-West basis, with teams of players hailing from either side of the Mississippi squared off. The *Gazette* played up this competition to no end, analyzing the strengths and weaknesses of each squad and proclaiming them even, giving the betting line among the "D bar bookies," and referring to the teams as cowboys versus dudes or city slickers versus boys from the wide open spaces. The Arbeit Day celebration was an event of such magnitude that the second appell of the day was canceled by Major Simoleit, the camp's adjutant officer, who was also invited to be in attendance.

Although the East prevailed in the other three events the baseball game was again a disappointment with a less-than-thrilling 10–0 victory for the Westerners.

By September the interest in the ball leagues was waning. There was a chill in the air, and athletic energies were diverted to touch football and to soccer, a sport whose popularity required the creation of a second league. The news from the fronts, East and West, suggested that an early end to the war might be on hand.

Finally, on October 1, a meeting of the athletic organizers was held regarding the diminished interest in sports in general. Most of the softball program was suspended, with the Majors stopping play altogether and the Minor leagues playing on as weather permitted. Somewhat pointlessly, baseball equipment continued to be delivered.

The high hopes of the Kriegies for an end to the war in 1944 were dashed by the German Ardennes offensive, but by January 1945 it was clear that the war was nearly over. Rumors of a possible evacuation had been circulating for some time, and the prisoners had been preparing. All able-bodied men were ordered to start daily walks around the perimeter wire to get in shape for marching. Some astute Canadian prisoners got the idea of making sleds to carry food and supplies, supposedly using hockey sticks as runners in some cases.

Finally in late January the order came to evacuate the camp. The prisoners were given 30 minutes to gather their belongings, but most were already packed. Different groups had different start times and marches of varying length, but that of Ralph Kling was typical:

> Then on January 29, 1945, they marched us out of camp at 10:30 at night, and we marched for four days. We made 60 kilometers, about 30 miles. A foot of snow on the ground and below zero weather. Then 3 days in trains to Moosberg. ... In my knapsack, which I had made out of a second shirt[,] I had a baseball glove and a softball. As I remember I threw those two as far as I could after a few hours on the road.[8]

The tired, shivering columns of Luft III Kriegies eventually outpaced the Russian advance, which had been slowed by an early thaw. There were few places to which they could march in the contracting Third Reich, so most ended up at Stalag VIIA near Moosberg, where General George Patton showed up in April to offer them a ride home.

4

Stalag Luft VI and Stalag Luft IV

These two camps are a study in contrasts. Superficially they should have had many similarities: both were for Air Corps NCOs, and many of the same men did time in both places. But one camp was on the good end of the spectrum for care of prisoners and the other among the worst of camps.

Stalag Luft VI was located near the Prussian-Lithuanian border at Hydekrug, by far the most distant of the camps where Americans were held in any numbers. One questions the wisdom of building a camp way over in Lithuania in the summer of 1943, at a time when the Eastern Front was starting to unravel for the Germans.

The first prisoners at Luft VI were British NCOs, who began arriving in June 1943. Americans did not begin to arrive until February 1944.

Physically the camp was laid out well, on a grassy plain in a forest near the Baltic coast. Three compounds were established: one was to be American, one British, and one mixed. The usual barracks were present, as well as a kitchen called the Fodder House, two latrines called Hangars No. 1 and No. 2, and smaller buildings that served as theater, library, camp office, and barbershop.

In the early days of the camp, recreation space was quite limited. The British man of confidence was Sergeant A. G. "Dixie" Deans, who wrote in August 1943:

> We are badly off for sport here as space is limited. We have been able to play a fair amount of cricket and softball, however, although I am afraid the windows of our billets have suffered.

The first Test Match between England and Australia provided a grand day's sport. England lost in an exciting finish by only three runs. We were able to bring some sports gear from Luft III but with so many new people coming in we are short of sports kits. We have had a visit from the Secretary of the World Alliance of the Y.M.C.A. and submitted an overwhelming list of requirements to him. He has promised to do all he can and we are hopeful as the YMCA has done great things for us in the past.[1]

Over time the camp was expanded and a sports field was assigned, laid out, and leveled. Located on the backside of the compound this facility was sometimes referred to as Kriegie Stadium. In addition to the larger barracks there were small structures known as huts, each holding 25 to 30 men. The total population of the camp by the summer of 1944 was about 10,000 men.

As a camp for NCOs there were no senior officers, and the interests of the Americans were represented in an official context by a man of confidence, in this case a capable tech sergeant named Paules. He was able to win a fair number of concessions from the German commandant, Colonel Von Hoerbach. Hoerbach was considered one of the most lenient camp commanders, either from some innate sense of humanity or perhaps because the proximity of the Eastern Front gave him a more realistic opinion of the long-term prospects of being called to account for his actions.

The sports program at Stalag Luft VI was highly developed with football, basketball, and softball all being popular. The ball teams were set up in the usual fashion with each barracks fielding a team and the teams being organized into American and National leagues with a World Series at the end of the season. The best of the American players formed an all-star team and hiked over to the British compound, known as the Canadian Compound due to the high percentage of that nationality there. The ensuing contest was well played, enjoyed by spectators and guards alike, and resulted in an American victory.

There were several talented players in attendance at Luft VI, including Augie Donatelli, a minor league shortstop who would go on to be a major league umpire, and Don Kirby, who would later play a few seasons with a minor league team in Muncie, Indiana.

But the best athlete at Stalag Luft VI was without a doubt Cliff Barker. Barker was such a phenomenon to watch that one Kriegie devoted an entire page in his wartime log to a series of sketches of Barker playing football, baseball, and basketball. Under the heading "Top Athlete of Hydekrug" are such accolades as: "No one could stop him from catching passes in the touch football games. ... At baseball he looked good any place. One of the best hitters and pitchers in camp!!! ... Don't be surprised to see him in the major leagues." And in a more astute observation: "He stood by far as the outstanding basketball player in camp!!! A great ball-handler and passer." Barker survived the war and went on to play on the University of Kentucky's NCAA national championship basketball teams of the late 1940s, and on the American team at the London Olympics, which captured the gold medal.

Another interesting character to pass through Stalag Luft VI was Brice Robison. An engaging conversationalist, Robison claims to have been through more different prison camps than any other American, including the interrogation center of Dulag Luft, Stalags VIIA and 17B, and Stalag Lufts I, III, IV, and VI. In addition to the usual wanderings through various transit camps Robison says that he was part of a small detachment of men thought to be escape risks, who were moved from camp to camp to prevent them from gaining enough familiarity with any one site to pull off an escape. Of his time at Luft VI Robison has pleasant memories of a well-run camp in a picturesque rustic setting.

Robison and his fellow travelers had some interest in playing ball when they were at Stalag Luft VI, but could not muster enough players to do so. So they joined forces with some of the medical personnel and formed a team called the Ward Healers, a nice pun on the medical members of the team and on ward heeler, an obsolete term for a shifty minor political functionary. He says that they were leading the National Luft League when they had to ship out again.[2]

The entire camp had to ship out in the summer of 1944. The Eastern Front was caving in along its entire length, and the Germans were pulling out. The Kriegies were moved by rail to the Baltic coast, then transported in the holds of cramped, dirty steamers for a three-day cruise. They disembarked at the port of Swinemunde and were packed into boxcars for another couple of days of uncomfortable rail travel. Finally they were dropped off at a little train station called Kiefheide. They were greeted with an impassioned speech by a German captain, in which they were accused of being *Luftgangsters*, who murdered women and children. The guards became agitated, and as the Kriegies staggered along the road burdened with their personal belongings and Red Cross parcels they were subjected to beatings and jabbed with bayonets. This was their welcome to Stalag Luft IV.

Stalag Luft IV was opened in May 1944. (There does not appear to be any explanation for it having a lower number than the earlier Stalag Luft VI.) The camp was located in Pomerania, some 28 miles from the Baltic

Sea and near a hamlet called Grosstychow. In layout it was similar to other stalags, with barracks formed into compounds and surrounded by barbed wire and guard towers. But the prisoners just arrived from Stalag Luft VI found little else familiar.

The German officials in charge of Stalag Luft IV were openly antagonistic to their charges and seem to have done little to make their lives easier. The majority of the early occupants of the camp were the refugees from Luft VI, many of whom had left behind most of their belongings. Still, available Red Cross parcels and clothing allotments were withheld for no reason. A steady influx of new prisoners eventually more than doubled the original group of 3,000 who came over from Luft VI, and crowding contributed to the problems of this camp. (The British inmates of Luft VI mostly went to Stalag 357.)

Red Cross field reports and the postwar provost marshal report suggest that outdoor recreation at Luft IV was minimal, due to the hostile regime and the abandonment of most of the athletic gear during the evacuation of Luft VI. But several former Luft IV prisoners describe it differently and tell a tale of ball playing on a moderate scale.

The first attempts were not total successes. A sports committee was set up early in the summer of 1944 and charged with improvising the equipment that they lacked. Word was passed around that all the Kriegies were to save the small rubber seals found beneath the lids of instant coffee cans, as well as any scraps of thread or string. The rubber seals were rolled into a hard ball about two inches in diameter, which was wrapped with thread and string to the appropriate diameter. Finally a worn-out flying boot was sacrificed to make a cover, although the material was cheap imitation leather of dubious durability.

The next need was for a bat. The German commandant was petitioned by several Kriegies who asked that they be allowed to go out under guard and cut an appropriate tree limb near the camp. This was not allowed, but as a compromise he said he would send his men out to fetch a piece of wood for this project. That afternoon the prisoners were presented with a green pine log five feet long and four inches in diameter. It turns out that the commandant had never seen a baseball bat before and had no concept of its true dimensions. It took two weeks to whittle the ponderous timber down into what was still perhaps one of the heaviest bats ever constructed.

As it turned out, a great deal of labor was wasted on this project. The first time the mighty bat made contact with the ersatz ball the latter exploded into fragments, putting a temporary hold on ball playing at Stalag Luft IV.[3] Before too much more time elapsed the ever-efficient Red

Prisoners of war playing ball, Stalag Luft IV, Grosstychow, Germany, 1944. Photograph was taken by a German officer from a guard tower. Courtesy United States National Archives.

Cross came through with a bit of equipment, which served alongside improvised gear.

Play at Luft IV appears to have been a bit looser than at some camps. Kriegies speak of the field being akin to a cow pasture, with no formal foul lines and scraps of wood serving as bases. Surviving photographs of games in progress on the parade ground show no backstops or bleachers, with spectators standing around. Sometimes games were said to go far beyond nine innings, with the usual rules being ignored and the game being over only when everybody was tired. In addition to the usual prohibition on running after balls hit near the fences, it apparently was necessary to ask the permission of the guards to retrieve any ball that rolled under the barracks buildings. Guards seemed to have taken some interest in the games; the photos of baseball at Stalag Luft IV were taken by an officer of the guard from one of the watchtowers. They especially enjoyed the occasional fights that broke out.

After a while things got a bit more organized. In one of the compounds, designated Lager B, each of the ten barracks formed an A and a B softball team. Five barracks were located on each side of the parade ground. Each group of five formed its own A and B leagues, with the top teams from each league meeting in a World Series. The A series went the full seven games before Barracks 4 prevailed.

Interest in stateside baseball was also notable at Stalag Luft IV, and it is said that new batches of prisoners were met at the gate by long-timers whose first question was usually who was leading the American and National leagues.

Perhaps because they got a late start playing the Kriegies at Luft IV extended the season quite a bit. Some games were played in snow nearly a foot deep. Eventually the weather got too cold for even the most determined ballplayers. Not long afterward a rumor began to circulate that the Red Cross was about to deliver ice skates. Encouraged, some 50 prisoners removed shutters from barracks windows and put them to use as crude snow shovels to clear space on the parade ground. A bucket brigade was started using water from two wells. After several days of labor a fine skating rink was completed. Impatient, the prisoners tried maneuvering on the ice in their boots and shoes, with uncomfortable results. The skates never showed up, being just another of the many rumors that pervade all prisons.

Soon the prisoners got another dose of snow and ice, as the camp was evacuated by forced march in early 1945.

5

Stalag IIIB

Stalag IIIB was located near Furstenberg, Germany, some 60 miles southeast of Berlin. Not so much a camp as a teeming city of captives, the stalag at times had more citizens than Furstenberg itself. Among this motley congregation of the enemies of the Third Reich could be found Russians, French, Serbians, Croatians, and, beginning in early 1943, Americans.

Physically the camp was 800 meters square, divided into an assortment of compounds. Two of the compounds were reserved for Americans, who were present in about equal numbers of enlisted men and noncommissioned officers. Quarters were large brick buildings, each housing 300 to 450 men. Typically each barracks, or block, was divided into an A and a B side, a common arrangement in the stalag system.[1]

Stalag IIIB had a large parade ground where the daily head counts were held. It also served as an athletic field. It had a loose, powdery surface, resembling a giant sandbox more than a proper infield. Perhaps because of this soil consistency there does not seem to have been any significant tunneling activity at this camp.

The administration of the camp was a curious mixture of harshness and leniency. The guards were constantly harassing the prisoners in small ways: withholding Red Cross parcels for minor infractions, puncturing all canned goods to prevent hoarding for escapes, and tossing offenders into the cooler with liberality. But in other ways the prisoners got away with a lot. There was an active trade in all commodities across the fences with the Russians and French, and the Americans were given little or no punishment when caught. On the other hand, several Russians were shot on the spot for their end of the transaction.

Perhaps the most remarkable example of *(continued on page 52)*

Ballgame at Stalag IIIB, 1944. Pitched ball can be seen on its way to the plate. Andersonville National Historic Site/Photograph by Angello Spinelli.

Ballgame at Stalag IIIB, 1943 or 1944. Seems to be cold weather. Note basketball backboard. Andersonville National Historic Site/Photograph by Angello Spinelli.

Ballgame at Stalag IIIB, summer of 1944. Playing field was next to fence and guard tower. Andersonville National Historic Site/Photograph by Angello Spinelli.

Ballgame at Stalag IIIB, summer of 1944. Appears to be all-star play from varied uniforms of players on "bench." Andersonville National Historic Site/Photograph by Angello Spinelli.

Pitcher delivering underhand. Stalag IIIB, summer of 1944. Andersonville National Historic Site/Photograph by Angello Spinelli.

Preparations for all-star game, Stalag IIIB, 1944. Grounds crew chalking lines, players warming up, umpires conferring. Men with backs turned to the field in left field corner are probably band marching off after playing national anthem. Andersonville National Historic Site/Photograph by Angello Spinelli.

Ballgame at Stalag IIIB, probably 1944. Field appears to have been moved, as barracks are now seen along first base line. Andersonville National Historic Site/Photograph by Angello Spinelli.

Probably a ceremonial first pitch, Stalag IIIB, summer of 1944. Soldier with the ball is in dress uniform and is not wearing a glove. Possibly American man of confidence or medical officer. Note St. Louis Cardinals uniforms. Andersonville National Historic Site/Photograph by Angello Spinelli.

Ballgame at Stalag IIIB. Much smaller crowd than previous all-star game pictures, but still a few spectators on roof of barracks. Andersonville National Historic Site/Photograph by Angello Spinelli.

Mickey Grasso batting at Stalag IIIB, summer of 1944. Andersonville National Historic Site/Photograph by Angello Spinelli.

A play at the plate, Stalag IIIB, summer of 1944. Most spectators appear to be watching something more interesting out near second base. Andersonville National Historic Site/Photograph by Angello Spinelli.

Band playing before all-star game, Stalag IIIB, summer of 1944. Presumably they are not playing the national anthem, as the players are wearing their hats Note scoreboard on lefthand barracks. Andersonville National Historic Site/ Photograph by Angello Spinelli.

Combined all-star teams, Stalag IIIB, summer of 1944. Mickey Grasso, *far right, top row.* Note Chicago White Sox and Pittsburgh Pirates uniforms. Andersonville National Historic Site/Photograph by Angello Spinelli.

Ballplayers at Stalag IIIB, summer of 1944. Dirt on uniforms suggests that a game has just ended. Mickey Grasso, *far left, front row*. The three Chicago players do not seem to fit into this team photograph. Andersonville National Historic Site/Photograph by Angello Spinelli.

laxness on the part of the camp staff was the amazing degree to which various photographers were able to practice their art. Using cameras obtained from the guards and even getting them to send the film in for processing, GI shutterbugs were able to compile an unparalleled photographic record of life in a stalag.

Foremost among the photographers was the intrepid Angello Spinelli. Spinelli was an Army Signal Corps sergeant whose duty was as a combat photographer. Captured in North Africa, Spinelli found himself in Stalag IIIB, and promptly set about to continue his career. He obtained a serviceable camera from a guard and concealed it in the front of a pair of paratrooper coveralls. So attired he was able to take photos of all aspects of camp life, naturally including a fine series of images of ballgames and ball teams. At no small degree of risk to himself Sergeant Spinelli regularly had the film developed and, almost unique among Kriegies, saved the negatives. His photos have a remarkable degree of clarity, which coupled with his professional's eye for composition puts his work in the premier place among POW photographers.

There also seem to have been at least two other photographers at work among the prisoners. Images that Spinelli does not recall taking have turned up in two different film formats. A diary entry of a IIIB inmate mentions that a certain "GC" had taken a photo of his ball team. But the identities of these other courageous lensmen remain unknown.[2]

To a greater extent than most camps Stalag IIIB seems to have endured numerous visits by the brass from Berlin. Perhaps the relative proximity of the camp made it an easy one to visit. Various generals on inspection tours were harmless enough, but on one occasion in November1944 a detachment from Berlin tried to get the prisoners to part with certain uniform items, such as field jackets, shirts, and pants, "for new prisoners" who did not have sufficient clothing. Of course the real motive was to outfit German Special Forces troops who were going to be infiltrating American lines during the upcoming battle of the Bulge. Ever suspicious, the POWs of IIIB chose instead to tear large rips in the requested clothing to make it useless for such treachery.

The proximity to Berlin may have also been helpful. This camp seemed to always have an ample supply of Red Cross packages, and the Red Cross representatives visited frequently to ensure that all complaints and requests were addressed. So much food was around that the prisoners did not rely overly on the German rations, and they were often able to spare a few morsels for the long-suffering Russians in the adjacent compounds.

There was a wide range of recreational activities available to the American prisoners in IIIB: basketball, soccer, football, boxing, and, of course, softball.

Most of the Americans captured in North Africa were taken between December 1942 and March 1943. It took them a month or so to work their way through the German and Italian prison systems before arriving at Stalag IIIB in the spring of 1943. By late May informal softball tournaments had started but things got much more organized by June. On the 25th of that month the IIIB edition of the *POW-WOW* had the following entry:

ON THE BALL

By Joe Bush

June 21st, first day of summer and also the opening day of the new HAUDEGAN and MACHORKOW LEAGUES. The first game got under way at 1:30 P.M. The INDIANS of BKS. 20A defeated the SHARPS of 20-B by a 7 to 1 count. Bennett pitched beautiful ball for the winners. He was robbed of a shut-out by a home run in the last of the seventh inning. A big hand for the winning team. We'll have to watch them from now on.[3]

A listing of teams followed, with the Haudegan League containing the Indians, Rangers, Puddin' Heads, Zoot Suiters, Little Bears, and Sharps. The Machorkow League had only four teams: the Tigers, Nestle's Ten, Angel Faces, and Yanks. The naming of these first two organized leagues at IIIB is something of a mystery. Haudegan seems to be a bit of German military slang. Machorkow is a colloquial Russian term for a homemade cigarette. It is possible that the GIs picked up this phrase in the course of the active intercompound trade in tobacco and other commodities.

The *POW-WOW* expounded a bit more on the early play in a section entitled "Smoke Rings":

Watch Grasso of the Zoot Suiters for 3rd base honors. It looks like the League from the Quarantine Compound has folded. Reason: Lack of Red Cross boxes. Bouquets to: Bennett, Indians—Grasso, Zoot Suiters. Rotten Onions to: Whidby, Champs and Swaitman, Lions, for quitting losing team in middle of a game. Because we must have the *POW-WOW*, we cannot offer you much on sports this week. We do promise you a much bigger and better column next week.

It is most unfortunate that this inaugural edition of the IIIB *POW-WOW* appears to be the only one that survived. The copy I found was in the archives of the Historical Society of Wisconsin. There was a personal greeting to the German censor on the front page, and he seems to have saved the paper for that reason. He is said to have presented it to a small gathering of former IIIB Kriegies at a postwar dinner in a New Jersey restaurant.

Some of the references in the "Smoke Rings" column are obscure. No team by the name of Lions is listed in the rosters of the two active leagues, so that might be a reference to earlier play. And none of the IIIB veterans I have located have any recollection of a Quarantine Compound. It is possible that mention of a ball league there was in some fashion a joke, understood by the readers of the *POW-WOW* but meaningless in the current day.

Mickey Grasso deserved the tribute given to him, as he later went on to a career in the major leagues. Bennett may have been the former professional softball pitcher from Iowa who is recalled by several IIIB veterans.

Athletic equipment arrived regularly courtesy of the Red Cross. One shipment that came in June 1943 contained 12 each of hardballs and softballs, 24 boxing gloves, and two "ball protectors," perhaps an item eagerly sought by those playing catcher. Basketballs, volleyballs, and various musical instruments came in the same shipment.

Softball, or as some named it, kitten ball, was played actively throughout the summer of 1943. There seem to have been two or three rounds of play, with a team from Barracks 18B taking the top honors when play wound down at the end of August.

Meanwhile, the war went on. Italy changed sides, and an estimated 10,000 Italian POWs were sent to Stalag IIIB, mostly being housed in tents and other makeshift quarters. More Americans also turned up, prisoners taken in the Italian campaign.

With increased numbers of players, ball made a vigorous comeback in the spring of 1944. By late March the weather was warm enough for up to three games per morning to be played. Again the early play was mostly pick-up games, with the goals being to get into shape and to try out new players.

In early May league play started again. This time there were Major and Minor leagues, with the majors divided into American and National divisions. The team names mostly conform to the Major League teams of the day, with St. Louis Cardinals, Philadelphia Phillies, Washington Senators, Brooklyn Dodgers, Boston Red Sox, New York Yankees, Cleveland Indians, Cincinnati Reds, Detroit Tigers (or possibly, and inappropriately, Browns), Pittsburgh Pirates, and New York Giants being represented. There also seem to have been Boston Braves and Newark Bears squads, but the record is vague on this point.

Informal ballgame at Stalag IIIB, 1943 or 1944. Photographer unknown. Courtesy Stephen Napier, Jr.

Games were well attended, and the quality of play seems to have been high. Photographs from this era show some games being played in GI fatigues, perhaps for practice games. But some teams appear to have gone to great lengths to modify Red Cross-supplied uniforms to resemble those of their parent clubs. The Pirates stood out in this respect, appearing in uniforms that are authentic down to the buccaneer's face that appears on each shirt. They were not just well attired; they seem to have been one of the more successful teams.

During the height of the season there would be up to five games per day played on the athletic field. Since this area was also used for twice-daily roll call, and since time off had to be taken for meals, this must have made for some tight scheduling.

If the regular games were a prominent feature of camp life, the special games truly held center stage. There were several of these in 1944. Memorial Day was recognized with a band concert on the diamond prior to a game. This musical group was pretty proficient, as it was a regimental band captured intact during the fighting in North Africa.

The Pittsburgh Pirates club, Stalag IIIB, summer of 1944. Photographer unknown. Courtesy Mrs. Eileen Cahoon.

July 4 saw all-star games for both Minor and Major leagues. In a rare comment on the junior circuit of the camp one source notes that the International League won over the Pacific League 6–2, while the Majors action found the National League all stars prevailing over their American counterparts by 5–4. Numerous photos taken by Sergeant Spinelli appear to be from this date, including images showing the band playing before the game, the grounds crews chalking the lines, the umpires conferring, and both all-star squads. Of course there are also numerous action shots of the game, some of which show the home plate area to be directly under a guard tower.

There was also a World Series played in August 1944, but by that point interest in ballplaying seems to have waned a bit. Perhaps the excitement of the Normandy invasion and subsequent expectations of an end to the war played a role. New teams start to appear, and old ones fade out. A team of Medics took the field, and several pick-up teams with names like Jigg's All-Stars, Caparnie team, Capp's team, and Pete Foster's team appear. Eventually they seem to have condensed play down to a six-team league, but other transient entries show up, including Dallas, Capos, Cannon, and Martins. Some of the previously existing league teams seem to have also continued play or to have reconstituted themselves from time to time. Play seems to have ceased in the third week of September.

The attitude of the Germans toward ballplaying seems to have been cooperative; by one account they even moved a fence back to improve the playing area.[4] Overall, and notwithstanding the sometimes obstinate camp administration, Stalag IIIB seems to have been a fairly decent place to be a captive. There was a library with over 10,000 books, a superb theater with many near–professional quality productions, and a canteen where one could even purchase beer on special occasions.

One sporting figure of some prominence made a cameo appearance at Stalag IIIB late in the war. Arriving in a huge automobile Max Schmeling, the former heavyweight boxing champion, spent a few hours chatting with his "American friends." He even signed autographs and handed out photos of himself. (He also turned up at Stalag Luft I for a visit along the same lines.)

When the order to evacuate the camp came in late January 1945 the prisoners were given almost no advance warning. A chilly seven-day hike followed, with minimal rations being issued on the march. By this point there were not many places where the marching columns of prisoners could be directed away from the advancing Russians. Most of the IIIB prisoners ended up at Stalag IIIA, near Luckenwald.

Stalag IIIA was yet another overcrowded, polyglot encampment. Men of different ranks and all sorts of nationalities were packed in together. Accounts of life there are remarkable for how well things actually functioned. Red Cross parcels turned up, typhoid shots were given, and rations, after a fashion, were issued. The chief pastime seems to have been watching the numerous air raids and cheering the advancing Red Army, but there was athletic activity on a limited scale.

Most of the restrictions on communication between the various compounds appear to have been relaxed by the Germans, who clearly knew that their time was limited. Basketball and volleyball were played between the Americans and teams of French and British. Rugby was played on what open space was to be found. And there were at least a few ballgames, possibly between Americans and British, if certain cryptic references to playing "the Irish" are correct.

Still early for ballplaying, the liberating Russians showed up on April 22, and the process of repatriation put and end to the brief 1945 season at Stalag IIIA.

6

Oflag 64

Oflag 64, near the Polish city of Schubin, was a unique environment for American prisoners of war. It was the only camp exclusively for ground forces officers, and due to the unpredictable fortunes of war some of these officers spent an unusually long time in captivity.

The camp was converted from a school of some sort. Various accounts describe it as a "Polish college," a "girls' school," or "an academy of some sort for teen-aged youths."[1] The facility included a large main building known as the Big House, or more commonly as the White House, along with an assortment of dormitories, a greenhouse, a hospital, and a sports field, which naturally included a ball diamond.

During 1940–43 the facility was known as Oflag 21B and held French officers and later RAF officers. A few British enlisted men stayed on when the Americans arrived. Presumably they had served as orderlies, or "batmen" in the British vernacular, and continued in the same role until American enlisted men could be found for this function.

The first batch of Americans arrived at the newly renamed camp in June 1943. These were largely officers captured in the Axis counterattacks in Tunisia earlier in the year, and they came to Oflag 64 after short stints in various British officers' camps.

Oflag 64 had a very active sports program, with softball being the most popular game. The chief source of information on ballplaying at Oflag 64 is the camp newspaper, the *Oflag Item*. It devoted about one quarter of its space to sports news and was in many ways a remarkable publication, worthy of a few comments off the topic of POW baseball.

The *Item* billed itself as the "World's Greatest POW Newspaper," and it was no idle claim. Its editor was a former newspaperman, Second Lieutenant Frank Diggs. He had a talented staff to assist him, including Second Lieutenant Robert Cheatham as sports editor. The paper came out monthly, with daily bulletin board updates put out by the same basic staff.[2]

The really remarkable feature of the *Oflag Item* was that it was professionally printed. Under an agreement with camp authorities and a cooperative guard who was boarding in a local print shop, the editors of the *Item* were each month allowed to go out on parole. They set the paper in type and ran off enough copies for each prisoner, a number that started at 250 copies but grew to nearly 1,400 by the time the camp was evacuated. The professional quality of the production allowed headlines, cartoons, sketches, and even photographs. A major feature was entitled "The Gals We'd Like to Go Home To," which showcased photographs of the wives and girlfriends of Oflag prisoners in some rather alluring poses, which may or may not have eased the rigors of captivity. Prisoners carried out all 15 editions of the *Item* when the camp was evacuated during the winter of 1945.

The original contingent that opened Oflag 64 had some experience of POW ball in the various camps in which they spent time in the spring of 1943. But on arriving at Schubin there was no equipment on hand to start play. In a column entitled "Sandlot to Big League" the sports editor of the *Oflag Item* related the development of athletics in the camp:

> Oflag 64's first year of sports is a story of rags to riches.
>
> From the first pick-up softball game, played with a home-hewn bat and intermittently stopped for re-sewing the ball, Athletic Director Herb Johnson has developed a well-rounded calendar including softball, basketball, volley-ball, hand ball and other minor sports.
>
> Organized athletics started early last summer with the forming of a 10-team softball league. The most popular sport in camp, 360 games had been played when the season ended in October.
>
> Basketball and volleyball got underway in August when the necessary athletic equipment arrived from the YMCA.
>
> By the end of August, sports were in full swing. The turn out of officers was large. Many had previously played for colleges and high schools and formed the backbone for the various teams. Others with less experience but plenty of pep gradually developed into adept players.
>
> Other athletics during the summer season were badminton, horseshoe pitching, tenniquoits and ping pong.
>
> Touch football attracted a large following before falling temperature forced players indoors.
>
> A mild winter played havoc with the winter sports program.

Efforts to maintain a skating rink failed. Brief periods of skating
for small groups were, however, held outside the camp.

Indoor winter sports were handball, ping pong and weight lift-
ing.

Sports and sunshine ushered in a late spring on April 17. Winter
weary Kriegies were high spirited in those initial games. The flesh,
however, was lacking. A lot of pet charley horses resulted. But the
stiffness soon wore off.

Many new names have been added to the team line-ups this
year. Numbers of teams and officers playing in the leading sports
are:

	No. of teams	No. of players
Softball	20	220
Basketball	10	90
Volleyball	20	160[3]

The play in 1943 was not quite as improvised as the above article might
suggest. The inaugural edition of the *Oflag Item* in November of that year
mentions that the third series of games in the softball tournament had just
concluded. Teams seem to have been unimaginatively numbered rather
than being named.

The same issue mentions that the baseball diamond was to be flooded
for a skating rink, but because of the mild winter, this did not work out
as well as when the British POWs had done the same thing in the previous
winter.

One cannot really speak of a "hot stove league" at Oflag 64 during
the 1943–44 off season. The only heat provided to the barracks came from
bricks of peat burned in inefficient European-style porcelain stoves. Some
prisoners felt that the only reason that the stoves were even a little warm
was from the body heat of the Kriegies huddled closely about them.

But finally spring came, and a new ball season was off and running.
There were many new recruits thanks to a stream of officers captured in
the Italian campaign. Several of the Kriegies old and new had some high-
level experience. Herb Johnson had played first base for New Hampshire
University from 1937 to 1940. Ted Pawloski had played shortstop for a
couple of years for East Stroudsburg Teachers College. Frank Aten had
played in the East Texas League and had caught Dizzy Dean when they
were both on GI service teams. Lloyd Taylor was a former shortstop from
the Class C Kitty League. And several other prisoners had at least tried
out for professional ball.

Softball came back strong in April 1944, and the next month the *Item*

Playing ball on Johnson Field, Oflag 64, July 1944. Courtesy American Red Cross Archives.

was able to announce the results of the initial round of play. In the American League there were teams designated Tigers, Yanks, White Sox, St. Paul Saints, Athletics, Browns, Red Sox, Indians, and Kansas City Blues. The National League was a similar mix of major and minor league team names: Phillies, Reds, Cubs, Pirates, Braves, Orioles, Cards, Newark Bears, Dodgers, and Giants. An official statistician tallied results, and after five games the Phillies and Tigers led their respective leagues with perfect 5-0 records.

As seems to be the usual pattern in POW ball there were multiple, relatively short seasons, each lasting only a month or so. Since the games were intended as a distraction from captivity, there would be a downside to a single, long season. Interest would die down as some teams fell significantly out of contention. Instead, every once in a while the competitors would start over again with even records, perhaps after some jostling of rosters to ensure competitiveness.

Another ploy to keep play interesting were special games. There seem to have been several at Oflag 64. In the later stages of the 1944 season there was a special Captains versus Field Officers game and a separate Orderlies League for the enlisted men. There was also a game in early September that was announced under the following headline: "Bachelors to Battle Benedicts in Ball Game this Sunday." The outcome of this battle between the married men and the "lone wolves" is not recorded.

There were also special games organized for significant occasions. On the Fourth of July 1944 there was a full slate of entertainment. The first activity of the day was an all-star ballgame between the Conquerors and the Invaders. The latter team had the services of yet another former minor leaguer, an enlisted man named Tom Lawson, who supposedly had played for the Kansas City Blues. Other activities of the day included all-star basketball, a fair, and a carnival featuring "beer, games of chance and an Honest-to-Gawd race meet with horses drawn from each room." A special holiday meal was served at dinner, with music by the camp orchestra, and the finale of the day was a theatrical production of *Boy Meets Girl*.

About one month previously there had been another special day of activities scheduled. It commemorated one year of captivity for the pioneers of Oflag 64. An all-day celebration was planned with a ballgame between the stars of the Big House and the all stars of the Out Houses. No doubt reflecting one of the main interests of the men the two teams were designated Lucky Strike and Old Gold. Later in the day there was a burlesque show featuring a strip tease by "Queenie," a six-foot, 210-pound former University of Dayton quarterback.[4] The evening concluded with a revue at the end of which each actor held up a letter that put together spelled out LET'S GO IKE. It was June 6, the day of the D-Day invasion. The Germans were quite nervous all day, fearing that the mass activities were a cover for an escape attempt in concert with the invasion.

Much of the softball news in the *Oflag Item* comes in small snippets, isolated bits of information that made perfect sense to the prisoners living day after day in the compound. But not all of it is clear in retrospect. When the YMCA representative visited the camp in November 1943 he was given a list of requests that included "baseball-bats, balls, mitts, shin guards, chest protectors and masks. Softball-bats, basketballs." Since the correspondent clearly understood the difference between baseball and softball equipment one wonders if the hardball gear was never delivered, or if it was never used for some other reason, such as space constraints. The written record and the memories of surviving Oflag veterans offer no clues.

In July there was a listing of "Sports Sidelights" which gave the following information:

> Tooth carpenter Hugo Fieldschmidt is the spectator's new favorite right fielder, replacing twinkletoes Joe Friedman. ... Bob Bonner's softball team played 16 innings before beating Bill Bingham's squad, 2–1, in the longest game on record. ... George Muehlbauer fanned 22 batters in this marathon. ... Local weather has caused postponement of an estimated 25% of softball games scheduled. ... Barracks 6 leads the inter-barracks exhibition league."

This reference to an interbarracks league is explained a bit more in the next issue (August 1944). The headline reads: "Three Major Sports Regroup for Big Mid-Summer Offensive at Oflag Sportsplatz Sector This Week. New Schedules to Go into Effect":

> Re-shuffled leagues in the three major sports will begin play this week as Oflag's sports leaders Leo Farber [who, by the way, was "Queenie" from the anniversary celebration!], Bob Bonner and Ed Spicher regroup their forces for the mid-season drive.
> The new softball set-up includes two leagues, one composed of barracks teams and the other made up of a dozen diamond combinations selected from the camp as a whole.
> Bill Luttrell, White House; Eddie Berlinsky, Barracks 3; Lynn Hunsaker, Barracks 6; and James Jordan, Barracks 7 and 8, captain the barracks teams.

This realignment may have been necessary to accommodate the new arrivals as the ground campaign in France heated up. Or it may have simply been a way to revive interest, which may have lagged after several months of play.

"Sports Sidelights" in August include:

> Cheers to the enlisted men for presenting the classiest sports event to date, their July 4 softball game. ... Johnny Kamps made an unassisted double play while playing left field. ... Lawson and J. Cox lead the orderlies league in hitting. ... Faster base running and smoother fielding are the results of more than a dozen loads of top soil on Johnson Field. ... By administering a 22–0 shellacking in five innings, the Lucky Strike All-Stars sent Pop Noonan's ersatz all-stars back to the bushes to stay."

The later days of the 1944 season did see some unusual plays, as shown by this entry in the September *Oflag Item*:

OFLAG SOFTBALL FREAK PUTS FOUR OUT

A one-in-a-million softball freak with four put-outs on one play, confused and amused both spectators and players last month in a Barracks 3–White House league game.

Barracks 3's John Shirk, with the bases FULL and no outs, rapped a sharp liner to short stop Herb Johnson who snagged the ball inches from the ground. Assuming that the ball had been trapped, Lou DiBella and Birly Grimes advanced and were doubled off first and second and Ed Ward was tagged crossing the plate for the fourth out of the quadruple play.

Doc Salerno administered first-aid to stop Berlinsky's bleeding and he led his 3 team to a 5–3 victory.

Another late season event of note was the pitching of the camp's first perfect game, with Major Jerry Sage retiring 21 straight batters in a 9–0 win.

Along with the other outdoor sports, softball play was suspended on November 1. By this time the weather was turning cold, and life in general at Oflag 64 was taking a turn for the worse. With the German transportation system collapsing and the Russians on the march, it became more and more difficult to get sufficient supplies for the nearly 1,500 prisoners. Finally in January 1945 the order came to evacuate the camp.

Up to this point life at Oflag, while far from pleasant, had been more a matter of inconvenience than of serious hardship. The march that followed was another matter. On minimal rations the Kriegies trudged 45 days in bitter cold, finally ending up on the other side of Germany, where they were liberated by American forces.

7

Stalag Bush Leagues

Although ball was played on a grand scale at places like Stalag Luft III and widely played at a half dozen camps, it would be a mistake to assume that it thrived everywhere in the stalag system. There were camps where some crucial ingredient to successful ball leagues was for one reason or another lacking. Still, the Red Cross delivered sporting equipment and some makeshift play did occur almost everywhere that Americans or Canadians were held. The information that follows could be considered a tour of the low minors of stalag ball, a sort of POW bush league.

Stalag VIIA

This large camp was located near Moosburg, a suburb of Munich. It was a multipurpose camp, serving as an early home for Air Corps non-commissioned officers, as a transit camp for ground forces officers and enlisted men captured in North Africa, and as a work camp for ground forces privates. The numbers of Americans varied greatly, there were over 2,000 present in October 1943, but the number dropped to almost zero in the fall of that year as prisoners were transferred to permanent camps elsewhere. With the increased pace of the ground war in 1944 the number of privates held there rose again to over 1,000 in July 1944. Finally, as a collecting point for the columns of prisoners from all over eastern Germany, the camp grew to enormous size in the spring of 1945, with around 15,000 Americans crowded alongside prisoners from many nations into a huge captive mass of perhaps 100,000 men.

There were several impediments to ballplaying at Stalag VIIA. First, it was a transit camp, a place where prisoners came and went, leaving little time or inclination to develop the institutions of prolonged captivity such as organized athletics. Second, the majority of the inmates of the camp were enlisted men, who under the rules of the Geneva Convention could be forced to work in non–war related industries. Quite a few of the privates were pressed into service in acceptable roles such as agricultural labor, questionable roles such as clearing debris from bombing raids, and just plain improper jobs such as loading ammunition. With no shortage of useful labors at hand the Germans did not permit much free time for the privates of VIIA. Finally, by 1944 the camp was just too crowded to play ball. Although there was a decent athletic field on which ball was played in 1943, by the next summer it was covered with tents in which Italian prisoners were lodged in uncomfortable squalor.

The attitude of the German authorities did not help either. This camp was run by fanatical Nazis, who attempted such measures as segregation of Jewish POWs from the other Americans. Treatment both in the camp and on work details was harsh, ranging from prodding with bayonets to increasing roll call from the traditional twice daily up to four times a day regardless of weather conditions. It is said that three days after American forces liberated the camp in 1945 several German officers in charge of the camp were shot. It is sadly true that American compliance with the Geneva Convention with regard to the treatment of prisoners fell short on a few occasions.

Most of the ball playing at VIIA happened in 1943 and was done by the Air Corps NCOs prior to their transfer to Stalag 17B. The provost marshal's report lists the main diversions of these men as baseball and bridge, with basketball suffering after the backboards were torn down and used for fuel. There was a camp baseball league with teams such as the POWs, Wildcats, Bomber Aces, and Luftgangsters. The games were played on an area designated as a soccer field behind their compound. Little or no sporting activity happened at VIIA after the transfer of the Air Corps NCOs in October 1943.[1]

STALAG 17B

The American presence at Stalag 17B began in October 1943, when some 1,350 noncommissioned Air Corps personnel were transferred from Stalag VIIA. Americans eventually occupied 5 of the 12 compounds of this camp, which at its peak held around 30,000 American, Russian, French, Italian, and other prisoners.

Since the Air Corps men were only a small contingent in the camp the establishment never was designated a "luft" stalag. The Americans resented the slight, and felt that if they were in a luft camp that the treatment would have been better.

Treatment at this camp was indeed poor, with numerous instances of prisoners being beaten or even shot. Oddly, morale was quite high, with credit being shared by effective American leadership, a steady stream of good news from the battlefields, and good recreational and educational activities.

Stalag 17B had a large recreation area, to which the men had access during most of the daylight hours. Basketball, volleyball, baseball, boxing, and track meets were among the favorite outdoor activities.[2] The delivery system for Red Cross athletic supplies is said to have been quite efficient. It might have helped that the camp was located near Krems, Austria, with Switzerland a conveniently short distance away.

Softball in the camp was organized in the usual fashion with teams raised by individual barracks and organized into leagues. A rare surviving copy of the camp newspaper, the *Gremlin*, from June 1944 gives the following revealing information on ball at the camp. (It also has a very revealing cartoon of a Daisy Mae–like hillbilly gal on its front page.)

SPORTS

The A teams completed the first seven game series in the softball season with "The Sad Sacks" and 16B winners in compounds one and three. The three-cornered tie between 39A, 39B and 37B in compound two, will necessitate a play-off. The inter-compound series will follow at a later date depending on what is termed "Circumstances beyond our control."[3]

Circumstances must not have been too much out of control, because only a few weeks later there was an all-star game played on the Fourth of July. North and South teams were organized, with the designations seemingly based on the geographic origins of the players as there were not North and South compounds at this camp. There certainly was an effort to get the maximum number of players in the game: North had a 20-man squad and South fielded 18. Somebody preserved an official scorecard, which must have been posted for general study as it bears a censor's *gepruft* mark approving it for camp bulletin boards. It records that on this patriotic holiday the North prevailed by a 3–2 margin, presumably once again preserving the Union intact despite a southern rebellion.[4]

There are a few other interesting tidbits that have come down through the years. One former Kriegie, now deceased, recalled that one day the

German guards stacked their rifles and took the field for an inning or two. He did not comment on their proficiency. Another former soldier recalled that the quality of bats provided to the camp was less than adequate, with frequent breakage. Finally they discovered that an English cricket bat could be pressed into service and that it had a much longer life expectancy.

STALAG IIB

This was a camp for enlisted men, located near Hammerstein in eastern Germany. It was said to be the worst camp in the system, barring the hastily organized establishments set up to handle prisoners from the Battle of the Bulge.

Physically the camp occupied 25 acres divided into four compounds. There were about 1,000 Americans at the base camp, with the remaining 3,800 out on 141 work detachments, some as far as 350 kilometers away. These work detachments varied quite a bit. Some were agricultural labor assignments, with generally humane treatment and the opportunity to lay hands on stray foodstuffs with some regularity. Others were tougher duty such as railroad work and coal mining. On some work *kommandos*, the German authorities were quite indifferent to the fate of their prisoners, and at least eight Americans were killed under suspicious circumstances.[5]

The combination of difficult administration, a prisoner population of privates who were expected to work, and the dispersion of the POWs to so many sites did not make for a promising environment for baseball. Indeed, in the summer of 1943 and spring of 1944 the prisoners were allowed no outdoor recreation at all except for walks in a 50-yard-square space behind their barracks. Finally in the summer of 1944 permission was granted for use of the athletic field. This area was large enough that football, softball, basketball, and volleyball could be played simultaneously. But the softball field was off limits until 1700 hours, and the other recreational areas had to be shared with the prisoners of other nationalities.

Although the environment at Stalag IIB itself was not hospitable to ball playing there was at least one work detail where it improbably did take place. Jack Dower was captured at Anzio during the Italian campaign of 1943. In the usual fashion he made his way through a couple of Italian camps, now under new Teutonic management since Italy's capitulation. Eventually he arrived at the great transit camp for ground troops, Stalag VIIA. His garments being unsuited to a winter of captivity he was costumed in a truly outrageous outfit consisting of a blue overcoat with brass buttons, black velvet collar and cuffs, red piping on the cuffs and lapels, four gold bars, and the insignia 57 on each sleeve. It came with a matching blue hat with a dangling tassel. Knowledgeable British and French prisoners were eventually able to identify it as a French artillery officer's coat circa 1880. By this point in the war the necessity of providing even a token amount of supplies for their millions of captives was forcing the Third Reich to scavenge the supply depots of the entire continent. Thus decked out Dower was forwarded to Stalag IIB.

After researching the issue with veteran Kriegies and cooperative guards, Dower and a group of friends volunteered for a work detail. Moving by train, by horse cart, and on foot they made their way to a small village called Benzin near the Polish border. The group of 20 GIs were put to work alongside eight Frenchmen, a half dozen sturdy teenaged Ukrainian girls, and such local German peasants as had been excluded from military service by their extreme youth or old age. They were quartered in a brick building formerly used to house pigs, which had for the occasion been cleaned, equipped with bunks, and surrounded by barbed wire. There were a few guards, mostly elderly reservists or men invalided by battle wounds. The "guarding" was pretty loose, and breaks to visit the local *gasthaus* were not unknown.

Dower had been voted man of confidence, the official spokesman for the prisoner detail. Among his duties was liaison with the Red Cross. One fine day he climbed into a horse-drawn wagon with a single guard and a farm lad named Hans. Reclining comfortably among sacks of grain he sat back and enjoyed the ride. As they approached the city of Stolp, remnants of peacetime Germany could be seen, including a sign that encouraged "Trink Coca-Cola." But their destination in Stolp was a more martial site. Stolp had been a military town for centuries and had been the headquarters for the elite Uhlan Cavalry regiments in the days before mechanized warfare. The military headquarters, or *Kasserne*, was a huge complex covering six city blocks, with a half mile of stables and massive stone buildings surrounding a parade field. Entering the central headquarters building Dower walked past display cases of weapons and regimental colors, and endless ranks of file cabinets. Down he went into the lower levels of the place, until his guard stopped in front of an oak-paneled door deep in the second subbasement. A small, neatly lettered sign announced "American Red Cross." His guard said he would return in an hour and left him.

Inside the office was a single occupant, a man named Jack Schick from Omaha, Nebraska. His duty was to supervise the affairs of all American POWs within a 15-mile radius of Stolp, some 1,000 in all. After an exchange of local gossip and carefully worded war news Schick offered his treasures: Red Cross food parcels, shirts, shoes, pants, razor blades, underwear, socks, overcoats, books, and in one of the most far-flung reachings of the national pastime, a bat and a ball.

On the way home their guard surprised Hans and Dower by suggesting a stop at a still-functioning beer hall, where a barmaid alongside whom "Jane Russell was an anemic stripling" poured the appreciative men a cold beer.

Back at Benzin the food parcels and books were well received, and Dower was happy to exchange his comic opera uniform for something more fitting. But the bat and ball were the most prized items.[6]

The prisoners worked hard at Benzin, spending six days a week cutting lumber or tending potato fields. But every Sunday they had a rest day, a time to take a bath and clean their quarters. Then they would put on their least-ragged uniforms and march down to the local sportsplatz about a half mile away. Here they would have a weekly softball game. German civilians would often watch the proceedings, with little understanding but some degree of enjoyment.

It was a good life, as life in captivity goes. Their main guard by this point was a kindly gent in his sixties nicknamed "Uncle Ben." At one point the prisoners removed the firing pin from his rifle, to prevent any accidental discharge, but "Ben" never seemed to notice. There was sufficient food, little harassment beyond some verbal bluster, and at least some possibility of romance with the Ukrainian peasant girls.

But as 1944 wound down, the roads began to be busier, as frightened Germans packed their belongings and headed west in a scene reminiscent of the great folk migrations of ancient times. The Russians were coming. Soon the men of the work kommando were packed up and taken back to Stalag IIB, from which they were later to join the westward march.[6]

Marlag und Milag

Under the German system each military service maintained its own prisoner-of-war camps. Since the German naval effort was relatively small the *Kriegsmarine* made do with a single camp, which was opened for business in August 1942. Prior to that time naval captives had been held in a separate compound at the Army-run Stalag 10B near Sandbostel.

Marlag und Milag held both Navy and Merchant Marine captives, a rather eclectic lot as is the case with nautical men everywhere. The camp, with some 4,500 captives, was said at one point to have had representatives from 41 nations and races.

By most accounts life at Marlag und Milag was Spartan but not oppressive. The majority of the prisoners were captured in the early years of the war, so there was not the unrelenting pressure of new captives, which hampered the logistics of other stalags. There did appear to be some element of camaraderie among the prisoners and their captors, perhaps a residue of the fellowship that all seagoing men share. The prisoners were more or less allowed to run the camp as they saw fit, with the camp commanders rarely interfering. As for the guards, they were mostly elderly naval reservists with whom a measure of understanding was soon established. Even the guard dogs were quickly befriended with the judicious distribution of foodstuffs.

Toward the end of the war when the inhabitants of other camps were marched into Marlag und Milag they expressed wonder at the place. There were flowerbeds and ornamental shrubbery planted around the barracks, and senior officers were only one or two to a room. With a high percentage of technically skilled mariners there were numerous clandestine radios, and a highly efficient secret newspaper transmitted world news within hours. Some of the men had during their long captivity developed a well-attended barbed-wire college, with courses in 25 subject areas. One less scholarly fellow had spent much of his spare time writing letters to various Hollywood starlets and had by war's end acquired an impressive gallery of autographed pinup photos.

Toward the end of the war some civilian internees were also moved to Marlag, including the famous British novelist P. G. Wodehouse, who presumably accorded himself with the cool, unflappable demeanor of his most famous character, Jeeves the butler. (The remarkably clueless Wodehouse was surprised to find the German Army at the doorstep of his French villa one day in 1940. While spending time in several *ilags*, or civilian internment camps, Wodehouse made a series of humorous but controversial radio broadcasts describing life there. He mentions improvised cricket, but not baseball.)

Marlag und Milag would seem to have been an ideal environment for ballplaying. Indeed, sketches of the camp do show at least one diamond, and substantial quantities of sporting equipment were supplied by the Red Cross and, curiously, by various shipping companies. But there was one significant hindrance to the development of the American national pastime: few Americans.

The German naval effort in the Second World War was mostly a submarine campaign, in which few prisoners were taken. Such raids by surface ships that did occur were mostly in the first two years of the war, long before Pearl Harbor. By the time Americans were officially belligerents the German surface fleet was mostly rusting somewhere, either at anchor or on the bottom of the ocean. Various surveys of Marlag by the Red Cross never show more than 71 Americans among the prisoners, and these reached the camp by unusual routes. A few were picked up by U-boats and taken to Germany for interrogation; others survived the sinking of American ships in the Arctic Ocean during the Murmansk convoys; and a handful of Air Corps officers ended up there by some bureaucratic error.

The population of the camp, however, was of such a cosmopolitan nature that this handicap was easily overcome. There were numerous Canadians captured on naval or merchant ships early in the war, and of course many British, who at least had a background in cricket. And for many of the Merchant Marine sailors the designation of a home country may have been somewhat arbitrary. Doubtless there were quite a few who were born in America or had lived here long enough to learn the basics of the game.

Baseball appears to have been played from the early days of the camp. An Australian seaman who was repatriated in early 1943 recalls American prisoners being brought into the camp after being captured in Arctic waters. They were quickly relieved of their warm leather jackets, which supposedly were needed on the Eastern Front. Soon the Americans and Canadians were playing ball on a rough, sandy field. The Americans, despite their small numbers, dominated play.[7]

A letter in the January 1944 edition of the Red Cross *Prisoner of War Bulletin* gives this information on ballplaying at Marlag und Milag, presumably a wrap-up of the 1943 season:

> Our athletic director, Mr. Ashworth, has whipped nine baseball [softball] teams into shape and at present the Yanks are shading the Detroit Tigers, and the Phillies are up there too. Baseball this year is one of the big three sports and ranks equal with the English soccer teams in fans among our 29 nationalities of seamen, some 3,000 in all. We hope to put an American football league in the camp, and shall, when the gear arrives.

It was signed, "Vernon L. Frank, American Spokesman."

Ball was also played in 1944, with the Red Sox taking the title. In memoirs of his time at Marlag, a British officer who was repatriated near the end of the war recalls the sounds of the camp, including: "The cheering from the football pitch was for the Dodgers hitting a home run against the Cardinals."[8]

It is unfortunate that accounts of life at Marlag are rare in this country. It was an unusual place with a fascinating cast of characters.

STALAG 383

A camp populated entirely by British and Commonwealth soldiers would not seem to be the most likely place for the American national pastime to flourish. But Stalag 383 was an unlikely sort of place. It was located in Bavaria, between Munich and Innsbruck. Originally it had been an officers' camp designated Oflag IIIC, but in September 1942 it was transformed into a camp for NCOs and renamed.

Some accounts describe 383 as a "punishment camp," but the regimen there does not seem to have been any worse than in other similar establishments. There were two theaters and a highly developed recreation program. One explanation for the apparently good treatment of the prisoners was that both the British man of confidence and the German commandant were Masons, and they got along famously because of this common bond.

Stalag 383 had a population that eventually reached 7,000, and it had a high percentage of Australian and New Zealand troops. They even had their own section of the camp, with the road running between their huts being designated Anzac Avenue. The Australians tended to stick together, forming their own athletic teams and sponsoring events such as Old Diggers Night banquets.

There were several special athletic events at Stalag 383. In the summer of 1943 there was an Empire Games held, which was in effect a miniature Olympics with a heavy track-and-field emphasis. There was even at least one former Olympic athlete among the competitors. The games began with a parade around the camp with each contingent marching behind its national flag. The Australian team wore singlets with a kangaroo and an emu on the front. Alas, no athletic shorts were to be found, so they had to march and compete in their boxer shorts.

In the first Empire Games the British trounced the Australians and rubbed it in a bit. This set the boys from down under to hard training for an entire year, at which point the drubbing was inflicted on the British teams in the 1944 version.

There was also an aquatic Empire Games, featuring water polo in the large cement-lined pool of stagnant water that the Germans kept in the center of the camp for fire-fighting purposes.

Many of these men were captured in 1941 and 1942. It seems that the inmates of Stalag 383 adapted to their lengthy imprisonment by a remarkable devotion to athletics of all sorts. So it is not surprising that they got around to playing softball after a while. In a booklet produced on the one-year anniversary of their arrival at Stalag 383 an Australian recorded the following:

SOFT BALL

By L. D. RYAN

The 1943 Softball season at Stalag 383 was unfortunately curtailed owing to lack of material. Sgt. Ken Laing, R.C.A.F., was the
owner of one of the only two bats in the camp. Our catcher's mit
[sic] was homemade; and as fast as our few balls were re-sewed, we
knocked the stuffing out of them again. These drawbacks, however,
served rather to stimulate the keenness of players and to put it in
old fashioned phrasing—"A good time was had by all."

After a few scratch games early in May, it was decided to form
an Australian League. A General Meeting was called and remarkably well attended and the following officials were appointed: President, W. O. (I), R. Stacey; Secretary, Sgt. A. Le Vier; Committee,
W. O. (I) R. Stacey, Sgt. A. Le Vier and Cpl. L. D. Ryan; Selectors,
Sgt. S. Browne, Cpl. A. King, and Sgt. A. Le Vier. Eight Australian
sides, each comprising a judicious mixture of experienced and
inexperienced players were selected, and it was decided to enter
two of them (Red Sox and Cardinals) in the Camp International
Competition.

The Australian League Games were noted more for their exuber-
ance and enthusiasm than for skilful play, and after an amusing
and enjoyable series of games the season ended with the teams in
the following order: Brumbies, 24 pts: Kookaburras, 22 pts: Kanga-
roos, 20 pts: Magpies, 12 pts: Wallabies, 12 pts: Swans, 12 pts: and
Cockatoos, 8 pts. We would like to take this opportunity of thank-
ing Sgts. Laing and Hewitt, of the R.C.A.F., for the generous and
unselfish manner in which they placed both their time and gear at
our disposal. It was mainly due to the hard work and organizing
abilities of these two Canadians that the International League ran
so smoothly.

The International League at times produced some really first
class Soft Ball. Our boys showed remarkable aptitude in picking up
the finer points of the game, the Cardinals in particular moulding
into an even and well balanced side. This side suffered their only
defeat in their final game against the Red Sox and ran out easy
winners of the League. The Red Sox were defeated on two occasions but they derived considerable solace for their fine win over
their hitherto undefeated colleagues.

The Canadian side is deserving of a special meed of praise for
the splendid showing they made under such adverse conditions.
There are only about ten Canadians in the Stalag against 500 of our
chaps and the advantages derived by them in superior knowledge
of their National Game was more than offset by their paucity of
numbers. It is greatly to their credit that they never once forfeited

a game; and it is our opinion that without the "Canucks" the season would have been a dismal flop.

Naturally enough, we are all keen to be exploring "fresh fields and pastures new," next summer, but should our genial hosts decide to extend their unprecedented hospitality, we shall all enjoy further clashes at Softball with the Kiwis, English, Welsh and Canadians![9]

This chatty but insightful essay was written in September 1943. It suggests that there were teams from the other Commonwealth nations competing in the International League, but sadly there is little information given on teams other than the Canadians and the two Australian entries.

By 1944 the Red Cross had reached the peak of its efficiency in providing sports equipment to the camps, so it is reasonable to assume that there was indeed a 1944 season.

Stalag 383 was one of the unusual camps that did not have to evacuate at the end of the war. It was liberated by American forces on April 22, 1945. As a result, there are numerous photographs of life at this camp, many of which portray the various sporting events.

8

Bad Nauheim Internment

The average Kriegie, struggling from day to day just to obtain the necessities of life probably would not have believed it if he saw a posted set of camp instructions that began: "Members of the group are requested to behave in public rooms and corridors of the hotel as they would behave themselves in normal times in any first-class hotel with a high-class clientele." And further continued: "no slackness from ordinary standards of dress. ... Men are requested not to frequent the lounge or dining room without coats or neckties."

But those were the rules at the Grand Hotel in the resort town of Bad Nauheim.

The internees at Bad Nauheim were a mixed bag, essentially all the Americans who happened to be in Berlin at the time of Pearl Harbor, joined later by contingents from Vienna, Paris, and Copenhagen. In anticipation of hostilities the American embassy had been operating with a reduced staff, but diplomatic personnel still were the largest group. There was also a batch of journalists and assorted others like Charlie Smith, a full-blooded Yakima Indian stranded in Europe with a failed entertainment troupe.

In the usual course of events these are the sort of folks that a belligerent nation wants to unload as quickly as possible. Some of the diplomats were military attaches, a job that is essentially officially sanctioned spying. Journalists in general cannot be counted on to write positive stories about the nation that has them locked up. But there were some unexpected snags involved in repatriating the German diplomats and journalists stuck in America, so a temporary place of residence was required.

The site selected was the Grand Hotel. This six-story, 400-room palace had been closed since the onset of hostilities, and had suffered some from the neglect. For one thing the heating did not work particularly well. At

76

one point when some essential repairs were necessary the Gestapo took the remarkably direct approach of simply having a substantial number of plumbers and electricians arrested, then put them to work and released them on completion of the job!

The internees were not restricted as to their baggage, so when their train left Berlin it was laden with some 1,250 items of luggage, weighing around 40 tons. Five dogs, one cat, and three birds joined the internees, who numbered some 132 U.S. citizens once the outlying groups were brought in. It was to say the least an odd confinement.

While the Gestapo was always watching, there were no real rules beyond restriction to the building and grounds. One could order from the wine cellar, and over the first seven weeks of their confinement the internees supposedly went through 3,000 bottles of wine and 400 liters of beer per week. This seems like a generous allotment of spirits, but one does have to remember that there were quite a few newspapermen in the group.

The diary of Alvin Steinkopf, a reporter interned at Bad Nauheim, contains entries such as: "Jan. 5. Champagne party. Speck, Steinkopf, Fischer" and "Jan. 11 Dinner, fried roebuck, red cabbage."[1]

With a contingent of young embassy secretaries on hand there were music recitals and weekly dances. This is surely the only group of captives during the Second World War who were ever photographed dancing in formals and suit coats. An impromptu university was organized with courses on a wide range of topics. Preserved in Steinkopf's papers is the text of a satirical commencement address extolling the myriad virtues of the university's mythical founder, Ichabod Badheim.

Relations with the Germans were generally good. Of course there were complaints about the quantity and quality of the food, especially a nasty sort of dessert called Nauheim pudding, which some claimed to be a coal tar derivative. This concoction gave its name to the internees' inhouse newspaper, the *Bad Nauheim Pudding*. It was published with an all-star cast of 19 foreign correspondents and was mimeographed in quantities sufficient for each internee to have a copy. (Although a few other prison camp newspapers, such as the *Oflag Item*, may have had a more polished appearance, the *Bad Nauheim Pudding* was, in my opinion, the most literate and humorous example of the genre.) Ultimately it was closed down by the heavy hand of censorship — not by the Germans, but by the head of the American embassy contingent, who feared it might offend their captors.

Volume 1, number 1 of the *Pudding* came out on February 7, 1942. It hopefully looked forward to baseball. Under the headline "Baseball Season in Offing," it related: "Arrival of a bat, indoor and regulation baseballs,

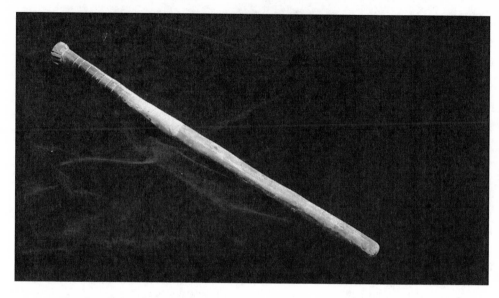

Handmade bat from the Bad Nauheim internment. National Baseball Hall of
Fame Library, Cooperstown, NY.

and two gloves obtained by Major Lovell makes it possible to look forward to a Bad Nauheim baseball season if playing space can be found. The
Pudding staff repeated a long standing challenge to take on the combined
Army and Navy units stationed here."[2] The diplomats were able to nego-
tiate use of the municipal athletic field about a mile away from the hotel,
and the internees were allowed to walk over and play under the eyes of
their bemused Gestapo guards.[3]

The regulation equipment acquired by the farsighted Major Lovell
was reserved for game play. For practice equipment the internees had to
improvise. When the guards were not looking a branch was broken off a
tree and fashioned into a bat. A ball was made "of a champagne cork, Glen
Stadler's pajamas, cut into strips—courtesy of United Press—a lot of sticky
tape from the health unit, somebody's sock, and the stitching is courtesy
of the U.S. Health Service physicians."[4]

Four teams were organized: Journalists, Army-Navy, and Embassy
Blue and Red teams. Steinkopf's journal contains frequent updates on
the league: "March 26 First practice for soft ball baseball," "March 27
Journalists directed Stadler and Fisher to organize a baseball team," and
"April 9 Chalker unveils cup, fashioned of purest tin, which is to be trophy
in group baseball league play. Baseball results: Journalists 1, Army-Navy-
Airforce 3."

As an aside it might be worth mentioning that at this point there was no such thing as the U.S. Air Force. They were still known as the Army Air Corps. The cup mentioned was known as the Wurlitzer Cup and was made from an old cracker can engraved with a metal punch. It was to be awarded to the winner of the Bad Nauheim Wurlitzer Cup Baseball Series.

Continuing Steinkopf's journal entries:

> April 13 Air raid on Frankfort. Baseball: Embassy Reds 21, Journalists 12.
>
> April 16 Air raid. Baseball Embassy Blues 7, Journalists 6. Gossip about departure now says May 6 to 10.
>
> April 22 Notice of departure 28 April with penciled note. Baseball Reds 21 Blues 6.
>
> April 24 Baseball Journalists 12, Army-Navy-Airforce 9.
>
> April 25 Shanke borrows all our paste because he and Graubart are making a kite. No great engineering feat because one doesn't need a mitre box. Steinkopf made a boomerang out of an official baseball scoring card.
>
> April 27 Baseball, Embassy Reds 26, Journalists 9. Shanke pitching walked first five men, which is a world's record, and a commentary on correspondents who make kites.
>
> April 28 Shanke and Graubart scolded by Gestapo for flying kite on Usa bank.* There's a German law against kite flying. Formal protest to embassy. Baseball: Embassy Reds 16, Army-Navy-Airforce 4.

By the time the group was repatriated in May the Embassy Reds had been crowned the champions. The whereabouts of the Wurlitzer Cup are unknown, but the handmade practice bat was lugged home by an internee and eventually presented to the National Baseball Hall of Fame in Cooperstown, New York.

The Bad Nauheim Baseball League was given credit by some internees for a significant improvement in morale. All were crabby after a long winter in the drafty, if picturesque hotel. A fine outing was generally had not only by the players, some 50 men in all participating, but also by the numerous spectators, who enjoyed the stroll beyond the hotel's grounds out to the park, which was said to be in a "marvelous natural setting. Surrounded on three sides by forest and set on a high knoll, the field enjoyed a wide-sweeping view from its open side. Even for those not concerned with athletics, the park-like area provided a pleasant stroll. The Ameri-

---

*The river Usa was a sluggish creek that ran through the hotel grounds. The Germans liked to joke about how close to the U.S.A. the internees were.

cans could use the field four times a week which provided a consistent physical outlet."

Bases were made from diplomatic mail pouches, and home plate was fashioned from wooden commissary boxes.

Arguments arose over rules interpretations, eligibility, umpire's decisions, and talent distribution. Since nobody had a rule book a Lieutenant Colonel Smith became the league president and arbiter of disputes.

The victory of the diplomats over the military is difficult to understand, as the latter had several athletes of note among their ranks. Major Lovell, for instance, boxed at West Point and coached the 1936 U.S. Olympic Boxing team.

When the internees were shipped by train to neutral Portugal for repatriation there was a mad dash by the journalists to get their stories into print. When things had settled down a bit Alvin Steinkopf wrote a curious letter entitled the "Burning Deck Bugle" to a friend. In it he mentions, "I can lift my dislocated baseball shoulder now, but I don't like to." Since his diary makes no mention of his playing during the brief existence of the Bad Nauheim League it is hard to know if Steinkopf, who had a wry sense of humor, is being serious.

The Bad Nauheim internees went easily back into civilian life. Those with diplomatic and military backgrounds were mostly called into immediate service. The journalists also went right to work, and several of them attained a degree of prominence in their trade. Many years later a reunion was organized in New York City. The announcement for that event reported: "Believe it or not, the baseball and bat we used for our softball games have survived and we hope to have them on display." A photo of the event shows a couple of former internees reminiscing over these artifacts.

9

Stealing Home:
Baseball and Escape

In general American and British prisoners of war felt that they were under a military duty to attempt to escape. Actual successful escapes from established camps, however, were quite unusual, and the majority of escapes in the Second World War were either evasion before actual capture or slipping away from the increasingly disorganized marching columns as the camps were evacuated. But for a significant part of the war, preparations for escape along with preparations for self-defense in the event of attempts to liquidate prisoners went along at a steady pace. And baseball played a cameo role.

In some camps where active tunneling was going on, ballgames were scheduled as diversionary activities, and there seem to have been persistent efforts to dispose of telltale tunnel dirt on athletic fields in a creative bit of groundskeeping. Soccer and football had some advantages over baseball in this regard, as larger, less-organized groups of players could be milling about while dumping dirt from special leg bags.

Actual baseball equipment was seldom used for escape activities with the remarkable exception of the Japanese mass escape attempt at Cowra, Australia (discussed in "Axis Prisoners of War"). But there is a brief mention of a bat being modified for use as a pick handle for digging at Stalag Luft III.

There was another level of escape activity, however, in which baseball equipment played a larger role. Emulating a successful British model, the United States maintained an active program to smuggle escape equipment into prisoner-of-war camps. It was called MIS-X and was a program so secret that even the meaning of the acronym is a matter of some dispute. Basically the system worked like this. Military personnel heading overseas were lectured by MIS-X officers on the basics of escape and evasion. Promising individuals were identified for additional training as code users. These men were mostly unknown to their comrades. They learned a simple but elegant code that allowed ordinary letters to and from the camps to convey messages that would slip past the censors. In part this allowed POWs to pass along information on military targets they might have seen on work details or while being transported into captivity. But it had a larger purpose.

Hidden messages were sent into the camps announcing the arrival of special parcels, which contained hidden escape and evasion equipment. These were in general not regular Red Cross packages as the work of that organization was recognized as being too valuable to compromise. But the rules also allowed other charitable organizations to send parcels to POWs, and an array of dummy organizations was created for just this purpose. Families were permitted to send parcels directly to loved ones, and this was also felt to be fair game for MIS-X.

At a workshop on the grounds of George Washington's Mount Vernon estate a small organization assembled the packages and their clandestine contents. Playing cards were made that could be peeled apart revealing sections of a map of Europe. All 52 cards made up the entire map. Compasses and flexible wire saws were hidden inside buttons. And there was doctored baseball equipment. It was a natural selection. Baseball equipment was unfamiliar to German guards, but obviously delicate material that could not easily be investigated without actual destruction. The problem was finding a way to conceal it.

A MIS-X operative named Lloyd Shoemaker was sent to Cincinnati to speak with the president of the Goldsmith Baseball Company. Shoemaker had already been given the specifications for miniaturized radio components manufactured by a company in Massachusetts. The problem was persuading Goldsmith to manufacture baseballs containing these aluminum capsules—without actually saying why it was necessary. It proved to be a delicate task.

Goldsmith had been told only that he was being asked to work on a government project of some importance. Now Shoemaker was telling him he had to make 48 baseballs, one dozen with each of four different components wrapped inside their cores. Puzzled, Goldsmith observed that the balls would never fly properly without their usual contents. A long and awkward silence ensued. Finally the ballmaker said resignedly, "I don't understand, but I'll do it." The balls were duly built around their hidden contents and dispatched to a Ben Franklin store in Baltimore, Maryland, which served as a drop for MIS-X.

The arrival of one of these balls at Stalag Luft III is recounted in Shoemaker's memoir, *The Escape Factory*. Alerted to the arrival of a special item a Captain Oliver was dispatched to the parcel sorting room outside the camp to retrieve it. Working alongside the Americans were German guards, who displayed highly variable degrees of interest in the contents of the parcels. Often a friendly invitation to share some coffee or chocolate from the packages made them much less inquisitive.

After retrieving the ball, Oliver

> immediately began a conversation with the bored English-speaking guard standing next to him, inviting him to feel the soft skin of the ball. The guard did what Oliver hoped he would do and not only felt the ball but picked it up. Smiling as he felt it, the guard then passed it over to Oliver. Stepping back, Oliver gently tossed the ball back to the guard, who in turn took a step back and tossed it back to Oliver. Soon their game carried the guard to the door of the office, so he stepped outside where they could continue increasing the skill and distance of the game. When the guard's back was to the camp's fence, Oliver wound up and let fly a fastball that passed over the guard's head, over the fence, and into the compound. Some POWs who were standing by, idly watching Oliver and the guard, picked up the ball and began a game among themselves. An escape committee officer then came and took the ball away, and Center Compound had the fourth and final part of its much sought-after radio.[1]

Interestingly the *Gefangenen Gazette* at roughly the same time as the above incident announced the arrival of a "shipment of Goldsmith baseball gloves." This was one of only two occasions when mention was made of a specific brand of equipment, Goldsmith in each instance. One wonders if this were some sort of code announcing the arrival of clandestine material, or merely a coincidence.

Because of the sporadic mail delivery, and the fact that there was no time to train code users before the war, MIS-X never enjoyed much success in the Pacific. Certainly no doctored baseballs ever reached the POWs. The only traces of MIS-X activity can be found in the peculiar letters some men received from imaginary relatives, which contained veiled references to various successes of their "uncle."

With the winding down of hostilities in Europe, the staff of MIS-X was ordered in late 1945 to destroy all their equipment and records. Into the fires went all the doctored athletic gear. But Shoemaker claims to have acquired by devious means a single surviving example of a "loaded"

Goldsmith ball. A photo and X-ray, showing the capsule within, appear in his book. Unfortunately the credibility of his tale is marred by a discovery when the ball was later donated to the Stalag Luft III collection at the U.S. Air Force Academy. An X-ray showed that the donated ball contained nothing but the usual cork center. Somewhere along the line a switch must have been made. Shoemaker died with this secret and probably many others besides.

There are a precious few clues about MIS-X to be found here and there. An account from Stalag Luft VI claims without specific attribution that one POW had the job of retrieving radio parts from softballs before they were "hit out of the park." Colonel C. Ross Greening, writing about his experiences in an Italian POW camp, relates that the guards, in a rare display of Italian military efficiency, "ruined all the YMCA athletic equipment by sawing it up in searching for hidden messages or escape tools. They never found any, but dutifully turned the wreckage over to us."[2] Presumably some serviceable bats were dispatched in this manner.

A British operative who worked in the program that inspired MIS-X writes of cricket balls being used in a fashion similar to what Shoemaker describes. In his memoirs the former commandant of Stalag Luft III makes reference to the extensive concealment of escape equipment in various aid parcels. Indeed, at Colditz Castle, where the prisoners with the highest escape potential were held, the Germans had a museum of escape material that had been intercepted over the years.

The story of MIS-X and its efforts to smuggle compasses, maps, currency, and even small firearms into the POW camps remain in the shadows, but there can be little doubt that at least some balls and bats were pressed into service in this secret war.

10

Mickey Grasso

An edition of the *POW-WOW* camp newsletter dated Friday, June 25, 1943, gives a nice biographical sketch of Mickey Grasso, a Kriegie who went on to have a career of some duration in the major leagues. The newspaper is hand lettered, and there are unfortunately a few areas of text that have not survived the rough handling to which the newsletter was subjected in the perilous trip from Stalag IIIB into the twenty-first century.

INTRODUCING

Mickey Grasso

In delving into the personalities of some of our better known "Stalag Stars" perhaps it would be best to start with Mickey Grasso, one of the more pleasant members of Stalag IIIB. Mickey is a very likable fellow, and an excellent ballplayer having begun with the Trenton Senators and later a member of the Boston Red Sox.

To begin with Mickey was born May 10, 1919 of Irish-Italian parents and almost within the shadows of Ruppert Stadium, home of the Newark Bears of International League fame.

Mickey's earlier ball playing was confined to grade school and later sand lot ball, not being allowed to play in high school because the coach decided he was too small being only 5 ft. 1½" tall and weighing 125 pounds. His first chance to play on a real team came when only a 5th grader when the catcher of the 8th grade team broke his arm and Mickey was asked to catch. He finished the season with the team and was voted All City grade school catcher.

As an amateur ballplayer Mickey played on neighborhood teams until 1935 when he joined the Newark Dukes. After one year this team broke up and he then joined the Temox of the Newark D[illegible] League. This was a good ballclub, and after two seasons he gave up baseball playing occasionally.

85

Mickey Grasso. National Baseball Hall of Fame Library, Cooperstown, NY.

During 1940 while working as assistant Mgr. at Chief's Restaurant he was one of [illegible] who tried out for the N.Y. Giants. After [illegible] days of trying he was one of the 80 left. [illegible] he went back to work. This may have been a costly mistake, and one he still regrets.

Bob Ciascia, an uncle of Mick's, and an ardent fan of the Trenton Senators was responsible for Mickey breaking into pro-baseball. While watching him catch in a game they were playing he suggested trying out for the Senators. Mickey went back to Trenton with his Uncle, and was introduced to "Goose" Goslin, hero of the 1935 World Series and then mgr. of the Trenton Senators.

The next morning, April 7, 1941 he was one of the 200 hopefuls trying for a spot on the team. Twenty two of these were catchers and only one could be chosen. After a month of hard work and living in velvet at the club's expense, Mickey was chosen second string catcher.

After three weeks of International League competition he was advanced to first string catcher, replacing the regular who was a former Washington Senator player.

Mickey played ball to his best advantage in an exhibition game with the Washington Senators when he caught George Case off second by 15 ft. when trying to steal.

Herb Pennock, formerly of the N.Y. Yankees and now scout for Boston Red Sox was in the stands and after watching this game stayed around for a couple of days. Two days before the closing of the International League season Mickey was told to report to Boston for the next seasons tryouts. After two week's trying, he was given a contract by Joe Cronin and placed for the remainder of the Major League season on the club as bullpen and batting practice catcher.

With the promise of a 1942 Major League berth with the Boston club, Uncle Sam stepped in and gave Mickey a contract for the All-American Club, the U.S. Army.

Mickey's Christian name is Newton Mickey Grasso. He is 5' 11" tall and weighs 185 pounds, has a perpetual grin on his face and is always ready for a joke. He is well liked by the comrades he associates with and in civilian life is a very snappy dresser. His ambition is to return to America and the Boston Red Sox. In Barracks 18B, Mickey is known as a regular guy.

The identity of the sports columnist is unknown, but there is a nice little hand-scrawled note at the bottom of the column: "Best Wishes to Herr von Fricken, from the Staff." This salutation was presumably aimed at the German censor who reviewed all camp papers before they could be posted on bulletin boards for general reading. Von Fricken was an interesting fellow who spoke fluent English and claimed to have lived in America for many years prior to being drafted against his will into the Wehrmacht. Opinions varied as to whether he was an American spy or a Gestapo agent.

Grasso is said to have gotten in some experience as a pitcher before switching over to catcher on the advice of Hans Lobert prior to his Giants tryout. Mickey never really hit for much power or average, but it is recorded that in his first at-bat in professional ball, with Trenton, he hit a home run. It was to be his last one that year and his last for quite a few years, as he was drafted following the 1941 season.

Grasso's military career was fairly brief. He appears to have made the transition from ballplayer to soldier fairly well, as we find him in early 1943 serving in North Africa with the rank of sergeant. During one of the German counterattacks following the American invasion Grasso's small unit found itself surrounded by a superior force. The second lieutenant in charge is said to have asked Grasso, "Mickey, shall we fight or go along with 'em?" With commendable prudence Grasso is said to have replied, "Hell, let's not be so brave."[1] So began his two years, three months, and ten days as a prisoner of war.

Grasso never seems to have commented publicly on his experiences as a POW. When he was presented with a lifetime membership to the American Ex–POW Association in a special pregame ceremony at the home plate of Griffith Stadium he supposedly "shuffled up to home plate with a deep blush tinting his face."[2]

Of Grasso's ball career in Stalag IIIB there is little detail available. Various campmates recall him playing on teams named after the Boston Red Sox and the Newark Bears in addition to the Zoot Suiters team mentioned in the 1943 edition of the *POW-WOW*. He was a standout player, one of the few who could hit off another player in the camp, a former professional fast-pitch softballer from a league in Iowa. In surviving photographs taken by campmate Angello Spinelli, Grasso is seen posing as part of an all-star squad, then batting in what was for Stalag IIIB the equivalent of the 1944 World Series. Probably none of the numerous spectators would have guessed that a decade later Grasso would play in the real thing.

At the time of his liberation in 1945 Grasso was some 60 pounds underweight and several years behind with respect to any real baseball experience. But he remained determined to play and seems to have renewed some of his prewar baseball contacts. The 1946 season saw him returning to where his professional career started: Trenton, New Jersey. As the season progressed he moved through several minor league teams in places like Jersey City and Jacksonville, Florida. Finally he made it to the major leagues, called up to the New York Giants in August 1946. Incidentally, his registration card with the Heilbroner Baseball Bureau lists his year of birth as 1922, a fairly transparent attempt to make up for the "lost years" in the stalag.

His first tour of the big leagues was brief, only seven games. It may be that he was moved along too soon, a common problem as ballclubs long starved for talent during the war years tried to quickly bring popular ex–service men onto their rosters. Other than brief early season tours of duty with the Giants, presumably during spring training, he would be down on the farm until 1950.

Grasso had a creditable year with Jersey City in 1947, batting .268, then spent 1948 and 1949 with Seattle in the Pacific Coast League. When Grasso was called up to the Washington Senators in 1950 his manager became Bucky Harris, who had seen him play when he managed the San Diego club and had predicted great things for Mickey in the major leagues: "Grasso was the top catcher in the Coast League, and he's bringing a great arm to the American League. ... They won't try to steal many bases against him."

While playing in the Coast League Mickey acquired a reputation as a baiter of umpires. In the spring of 1950 the *Washington Post* greeted him with an article titled "Grasso May Give Umps Headaches." It claimed that the "rookie Senator catcher" was "allergic to arbiters." Indeed, he was ejected from 23 games during the 1949 season, said to be a Pacific Coast League record.[3]

Grasso's public comments (*Post*, March 27, 1950) on the topic were philosophical: "I'm not saying it was all the fault of the umpires. ... But it certainly was half and half. Why one day an umpire [Hal Gordon] chased me because I wouldn't throw a new ball back to the pitcher after a foul tip. 'You throw it back. It's your job,' I told him. Out of the game I went."

Apparently in the minor leagues it was common practice for the club to pay players' fines. And a good thing it was for Grasso, who tallied up no less than $1,100 in penalties in 1949.[4] In the Big Show the fines came out of the players' paychecks, perhaps exerting a moderating influence on Mickey's behavior. While he still "got the hook" three times in the 1950 season with Washington he was only penalized $50. Before spring training was completed in 1951, however, he had already been fined and suspended for five days for "roughing the umpire, refusal to leave the bench and for abusive and obscene language."[5]

Already 30 years old when he broke into the majors Mickey Grasso had a workmanlike career, being prized mainly for his defensive skills. He was with Washington from 1950 through 1953; his best year of playing was 1952, when he made it into 114 games. During one memorable game that year he picked men off second and third on consecutive pitches with Ted Williams at bat.

In January 1954 he signed with a contending club, the Cleveland Indians. He was slated to be their backup catcher, but disaster struck on March 24. The Indians were playing an exhibition game with the Chicago Cubs in spring training at Mesa, Arizona. Grasso was running hard toward second base, trying to avoid being forced out. The field was wet from heavy rains, and Grasso's spikes caught in the dirt as he slid toward the bag. Bob Rush, who was pitching for the Cubs was quoted as saying: "He knew what happened right away. I heard him holler, 'It's broke. I heard it snap.'"[6] Ironically, there was not even a throw coming.

Grasso's left fibula was broken in no fewer than six places. It was almost a season-ending injury. Although Grasso sat out nearly the entire 1954 season, he was later quoted as saying that playing for the pennant-winning Tribe was the highlight of his career. Official statistics show him playing in only four games late in the season.

The year 1954 was a World Series year for Cleveland, and Grasso, the ex–Kriegie, did get his chance to play in baseball's premier event. If the world was a fair place he would have had a chance to come to bat there, completing the journey that was started ten years earlier in the Stalag IIIB World Series. But it was not to be. He appeared in but a single game, as a defensive replacement. He never came to the plate.

His age and perhaps his injury telling, Grasso attempted to catch on with his old club, the New York Giants, in 1955. But after appearing in only eight games Mickey Grasso retired from baseball.

After his retirement Mickey worked as a supervisor at the mutual windows at Gulfstream, Hialeah, and Tropical racetracks and at Miami Beach, Biscayne, and Flagler dog tracks. He began collecting his major league pension in 1972. Mickey Grasso died in Miami in 1975 at the young age of 55.

Grasso's career major league statistics show him appearing in 322 games, all as catcher. His batting average was .268 with 87 RBIs.

11

Augie Donatelli

If there is a common thread among the handful of former POWs who made their mark in the major leagues it is a gritty tenacity, just the sort of quality that a stay in a prisoner-of-war camp might be expected to enhance. None of them had this quality to a greater extent than Augustine Donatelli, ex–Kriegie and National League umpire.

Universally known as Augie, Donatelli was one of eight children of Italian immigrant parents. He was born and raised in the coal country near Heilwood, Pennsylvania, working alongside his father and brothers in the mines for eight years after high school. He played multiple sports, including football and boxing. He also played baseball, spending three years in the minor leagues. Some sources have him playing shortstop in the Penn State League until it went bankrupt in the late 1930s.

At the age of 26 he enlisted in the military soon after Pearl Harbor and was trained as a B-17 tail gunner in the Army Air Corps. Augie successfully completed 17 missions before being shot down in March 1944 on a daylight raid on Berlin.

Augie spent 15 months in captivity, first at Stalag Luft VI and later at Luft IV. By some accounts he fractured his ankle when parachuting from his plane, but if true it must have been a fairly minor injury. Campmates recall Augie was already umpiring at Stalag Luft VI in early 1944, and he was fit enough to play shortstop for a team that competed in the Luft IV World Series in the later part of the summer of 1944.

Donatelli is said to have attempted escape twice. Sportswriters sometimes tend to embellish the facts, but the column by Jerome Holtzman has the ring of truth: "Twice he was recaptured. 'He always laughed when he talked about his second attempt,' recalled veteran ump Doug Harvey, who also served his apprenticeship under Donatelli. 'He was hiding in a haystack, but he didn't get all the way in. His rear end was showing. One of the German guards got him out with a pitchfork.'"[1] If there is any truth to the escape stories then they probably occurred not during Augie's time in the camps, but on the chaotic midwinter march away from the camp in early 1945. It was not uncommon for Kriegies on these marches to slip away from the columns for a while. A few stayed on the loose until the Allies showed up, but more were recaptured or simply rejoined the prisoners once it became obvious that there was really no safer place to be during the collapse of the Third Reich.

Returning home after being liberated by Russian troops in 1945, the 29-year-old Donatelli declined to go back to mining coal and decided that his best bet for a career in baseball was not among the ranks of the players, but as an umpire. In 1946 he attended Bill McGowan's School for Umpires in Cocoa, Florida, on the GI Bill. A letter from McGowan, an American League umpire, to Elmer Daily, president of the Mid-Atlantic League, in November 1946 mentions that Donatelli had umpired that season in the Pioneer League, where he was felt to be "head and shoulders above the field," and makes the amazing claim that he had heard "not one complaint about Donatelli, from manager or club owner during the entire season." During his long career in the majors, Donatelli would make up for lost time in this regard.

Donatelli served as an instructor at the umpire school while serving the traditional hitch in the minor leagues: first the Pioneer League, then the Sally League, and finally the high minors with the International League. In 1950 he came up to the National League, beginning a colorful 24-year career.

There is no shortage of Donatelli stories circulating in baseball lore. By all accounts he was a tough, expressive umpire. His ball and strike calls and especially his famous "to the showers" ejection signals were said to be unmistakably demonstrative. He had a reputation as a "quick thumb," and he got to use it often. Exact statistics are not kept for ejections, but Augie claimed to lead the National League in this regard, giving scofflaws the toss an average of ten times each season. Perhaps his most famous call was the infamous "shoe polish" call in the 1957 World Series. In the tenth inning of game four Nippy Jones was pinch-hitting for Warren Spahn. On a pitch down in the dirt Jones claimed he had been hit. Donatelli examined the ball, and detecting a dab of shoe polish awarded first base to what ultimately proved to be the winning run for the Milwaukee Braves. Yogi Berra was catching and Casey Stengel managing for the Yankees. Neither of these gents, so seldom at a loss for words, tried to contest the call.

Once Donatelli suspected Don Drysdale of throwing a "spitter," doctored with some foreign substance. Stalking to the mound Augie closely examined Drysdale's hair for an illegal stash of grease. Finding none he started heading back to home plate. "Aren't you forgetting something, Augie?" Drysdale asked. "What's that?" the ump responded. "Well," Drysdale said, "usually when somebody runs their fingers through my hair, they also give me a kiss."

Augie appeared on the cover of the first issue of *Sports Illustrated* in 1954, calling a Milwaukee Braves game. At the time he did not think much of it, commenting, "Magazines come and go."

His time working the coal mines perhaps having given him an appreciation for the value of labor, Augie

Augie Donatelli. National Baseball Hall of Fame Library, Cooperstown, NY.

Donatelli was the driving force behind the organizing of the Major League Umpires Association, a controversial role that some feel might have resulted in his being demoted from crew chief despite his seniority.

Considered one of the best umpires in baseball, Augie was granted an exemption from the game's then-current mandatory retirement age of 55. Thus he extended his career to 24 Major League campaigns, including five World Series, four all-star games, and ten no-hitters.

Upon his retirement from baseball after the 1973 World Series Donatelli played golf, tried his hand at selling pitching machines to schools and Little Leagues, and remained a director of the Umpires Association. He died at his home in St. Petersburg, Florida, in 1990. A decade after his death, and a quarter century after he made his last call, Augie Donatelli was placed on the top ten list of modern-day umpires compiled by a survey of members of the Society for American Baseball Research.

"It is not an easy profession," Augie once said of umpiring. "It knocks the morale out of you. Mine stayed up because I was toughened loading coal."

The world of major league baseball being a rather small place, especially pre-expansion, there can be little doubt that Donatelli knew Mickey Grasso, although one was an American League man and the other a National Leaguer. At some point their paths must have crossed — perhaps in spring training, or maybe in the late 1940s when they were both coming up through the International League, or even during Grasso's brief comeback attempt in the National League in 1955. We can assume that the two former POWs chatted a bit before the game, recalling old times and games played behind barbed wire. We can also assume that once the game began, Augie Donatelli did not cut the catcher any slack whatsoever.

Phil Marchildon

Although Augie Donatelli had an exceptional career as an umpire, the other former POWs who made it to the major leagues had rather undistinguished stays—with the exception of Phil Marchildon, who for one shining year was among the dominant pitchers in the game.

Marchildon was born in 1913 in a place not known for producing baseball players, Penetanguishene, Ontario. Always a natural athlete in all sports, he never played any sort of organized ball before high school. He had the opportunity to go to school for a single year in Toronto on a football scholarship before returning to his hometown in 1932. There he played for the local town team, the Penetang Rangers. (Penetang was the trimmed-down version of Penetanguishene that served for everyday use.) They played, quite literally, in a cow pasture, and games sometimes had to be interrupted while bovine spectators were moved along.

Marchildon was a player of sufficient skill that a neighboring town desired his services, so it was arranged that he would get a job at a mine near the town of Creighton so that he could play for the local Cubs, who competed in what was known as the senior-level Nickel Belt League.

Marchildon attended a tryout for the Toronto Maple Leafs of the International League, landing a contract with them in 1939. Incidentally Marchildon describes himself as something of a rube at that stage of his career, saying that he was unaware of the *existence* of major league baseball at the time he went pro. He thought the Maple Leafs were the highest level of the game! His career moving right along, he was called up to the majors in September 1940 to play for the Philadelphia Athletics and their legendary owner/manager, Connie Mack.

By this time of course his native Canada was at war. Marchildon was able to defer military service for a while, as he was the sole financial support for his family. But there were awkward moments. When he tried to cross the U.S./Canadian border on his way to 1941 spring training, he was detained for several hours by customs officials who thought he was trying to dodge the draft. One wonders if any of these same flint-hearted bureaucrats were still at their posts 25 years later to see the flow of motivated tourists of military age reverse itself and go north.

Marchildon was also only allowed $25 per week spending money. The rest of his paycheck had to be deposited in a Canadian bank to help ensure his return. The ever-parsimonious Connie Mack probably approved.

By 1942 Marchildon had joined the ranks of the best pitchers in the game, posting a 17-14 record for a feeble Philadelphia club that finished 55-99, a full 48 games behind the perennial champion Yankees. But his baseball career was soon to be put on hold.

Drafted following the season's end Marchildon volunteered for overseas duty. At that time Canada was not sending anybody but volunteers into battle, and Phil probably could have opted for a nice safe berth as an athletic instructor on the home front. Instead he found himself in England training for the Royal Canadian Air Force. Although he had some hopes of being accepted as a pilot candidate he was a bit old for that assignment. Instead, by virtue of his excellent eyesight and coordination he was made an aerial gunner.

With their time-honored tradition of strict truthfulness the RCAF recruiters had promised Marchildon that he would have many opportunities to play ball while in uniform. But it did not work out that way. He did pitch in two games at Halifax but threw sloppily, actually losing one of the games 7–0. Later in England he did make several appearances as a ringer in an industrial league near London. The mostly American players were properly impressed when they found out that they had been struck out by a genuine major league pitcher.

Amid many close calls Marchildon flew 26 missions with the Porcupine Squadron before his luck ran out on August 16, 1944. Approaching Kiel by night on a mission to mine the harbor, his Halifax bomber was shot down by a German night fighter. Only Marchildon and one other crewman had time to bail out, and they landed in the North Sea off the Danish coast. They were picked up by a Danish fishing boat, whose crew assured them in halting English that they were among friends. Then they landed the boat and turned the two shivering airmen over to the Germans.

In later columns written by fanciful sports writers this incident was somewhat blown out of proportion. According to Bob Addie of the *Washington Times-Herald*: "Marchildon spent 18 months [probably a typo, since it was only eight months] in a prison camp, but perhaps that didn't break

Phil Marchildon. National Baseball Hall of Fame Library, Cooperstown, NY.

his spirit as much as the perfidy of that Danish fisherman. ... Somehow, that haunted Phil long after he came back. ... He couldn't believe that men were so treacherous."[1]

Actually, the fishermen were members of the Danish underground who fully expected to smuggle Marchildon into hiding, but with the soldiers showing up unexpectedly at the docks there was not much that they could do. Also in the category of "creative history" in the same account is a statement that claims that one of the Danish fishermen spoke perfect English — and was a rabid baseball fan to boot.

On his arrival at Stalag Luft III Marchildon posed for a photo identification card that listed his profession as "sportsmann." The card was filled out by a German guard who had lived in New York and spoke English with a thick Bronx accent. Although he did play ball while in captivity the big curve-ball pitcher appears cautious when writing about it in his autobiography, *Ace*. All he will admit to is being "a heavy hitting outfielder for the softball squad that won the camp championship 2–1."[2]

A fellow POW remembers another side of the story. Dwayne Linton, an American who enlisted in the RCAF, found himself imprisoned in East Compound, Stalag Luft III, a primarily British compound with a high percentage of Canadians.* Linton managed one team and played for another in the camp league. Upset when nobody from either squad was selected for the all-star team, he formed his own competing squad, with some of his own players and a ringer named Phil Marchildon. According to Linton: "I know damn well he was well enough to pitch. I was the catcher in the game he pitched when we played the all stars and won 18–1!"[3]

My guess is that the professional pitcher, with a mind to restarting his career in the majors, was none too eager to have it known that he had been spending his time tossing some oversized kitten ball underhand.

While a POW Marchildon generally was well treated, but he was witness to one chilling incident. As he tells it in *ACE*:

> There were also a few die-hard Nazis who delighted in making our lives miserable. The worst was a tall, middle-aged tower guard whose face was twisted in a permanent scowl. A group of us were playing softball one day when someone missed the ball and it bounced under the warning wire into no-man's land near his post.
>
> One of our players, a Canadian, walked to the wire and looked up at the guard. "Nict schiessen, Posten!" he called, which meant

---

*At the time the U.S. Army Air Corps was not accepting pilot candidates. The RCAF was, but only if they were single. Not easily deterred, Linton divorced his wife, fought his war, then returned from captivity and remarried her.

"Don't shoot, sentry." The German waved him in. When the Canadian had no more than a foot over the fence he shot him dead.

Although that is the story, no such incident appears anywhere in the well-documented history of the Stalag Luft III camp. The closest I can find is an episode where a Canadian was shot under similar circumstances at Oflag 79 while playing quoits. Since Marchildon gives some variation on this story in even his earliest postwar interviews, I assume that he had an awareness of the facts of the incident, but it looks to me to have been a secondhand story.

The men of Stalag Luft III were marched out of camp ahead of the advancing Russian army in January 1945. Tramping all over the northern part of the collapsing Reich they finally stopped at the end of April, having marched a futile circular route that brought them back to within 200 miles of where they had started. One of the first things the prisoners did when the British Army liberated them was to go to a British prison camp nearby, where the Stalag Luft III guards were now being held as prisoners themselves. Locating the scowling guard who had shot the Canadian softball player they had a few words with the British guards. The German was taken out to a nearby field and shot. Marchildon thought he had it coming.

At the time of his liberation Marchildon had dysentery and was some 30 pounds underweight. Although the pounds went back on easily during his days of rehabilitation the stress of captivity told upon him in other ways. He was haunted by the loss of his crewmates, jumpy at any sudden unexpected sound, and troubled by nightmares. Finally returning to his hometown he was granted a mere three weeks of peace before the telegrams started.

Connie Mack was not exactly deep in pitching for his lowly Athletics and wanted his former ace back in uniform as soon as possible. After persistent entreaties he got his way. Phil Marchildon rejoined the club on July 6, 1945, a ridiculously short nine weeks after being liberated from captivity. At first he just worked out with the team, stretching disused muscles and getting his strength back. But the lure of a big gate was potent, and on August 29 Shibe Park in Philadelphia was occupied by 19,267 fans who had come for Phil Marchildon Night. It was a tough outing for the pitcher. His nerves were on edge, and he did not have anything like his old stuff. But the fans, accustomed to minimal expectations, were lenient.

The 1946 Athletics were a bad squad, even by Philadelphia's low standards, finishing 49–105, 55 games behind the league leaders. Marchildon's effort that year, going 13–16, was fine work for a comeback season, and in 1947 he had his magic year.

Marchildon had learned a new pitch, the fork ball. He had tamed some of the wildness that plagued him throughout his career. There were even the makings of a decent club behind him on the field thanks to some astute player trades. Marchildon went 19–9 that season, once coming within a single bad umpiring call of throwing a perfect game. In anger and frustration the normally peaceable Marchildon heaved his glove at the umpire, who at least had the decency, while there was still a no-hitter on the line, to not give him the thumb that he certainly deserved. Soon, there was talk of a trade to a contending team, perhaps even the Yankees, but the dream was short-lived. The next year Connie Mack cut the payroll for the *entire* Athletics squad to $75,000. Marchildon began to suffer from a variety of aches, pains, and dizzy spells. He began chain smoking and lacked consistent pitching. Spending some time in a veterans hospital in the off season he was diagnosed as having psychosomatic illnesses, presumably because of his wartime experiences. On top of that he seems to have had some recurring arm stiffness, and he missed most of the 1949 season as a result. He was cut from the Athletics and, after an abortive comeback attempt at Buffalo and Boston in 1950, was out of baseball. He took it fairly hard, as those who have been at the top often do. But eventually he found peace back in Penetang among his family and friends. Living a long productive life and raising a family, he disproved the old adage that maintains that one can never really go back home.

Phil Marchildon, career mark of 68–75 and charter member of the Canadian Baseball Hall of Fame, died in Toronto in 1997.

13

Bert Shepard

All of the men who graduated from the stalags to the major leagues had a tough path to follow. But none of them had it tougher or stayed in the limelight for a shorter time than Bert Shepard.

Of Shepard's early years there has been little written. He was born in Dana, Indiana, and grew up in Clinton, playing baseball at every opportunity. In the prewar years he played in the minors, in the Wisconsin State League, the Evangeline League, and lastly for Bisbee in the Arizona-Texas League. The hype surrounding his later accomplishments makes it difficult to believe everything that was written about him. In one account he was said to have been offered a contract with the White Sox before he was drafted in 1942. But in a somewhat more plausible version the sore-armed Shepard was given his outright release from Bisbee, the fourth time in his short professional career that he had been cut loose in this fashion.[1] No one imagined that his best ball playing years were ahead of him — but only after he became an amputee.

With the coming of war to America, Shepard joined the colors and was trained as a fighter pilot. In addition to his flying duties Lieutenant Bert Shepard served as the manager of the baseball team for the 55th Fighter Group in one of the many service leagues then active in England. Some, but not all, accounts have him pitching as well.

On May 21, 1944, Shepard took off in his P-38 Lightning on a strafing mission as part of the lead-up to D-Day. It was to be his 34th and final mission, ironically on a day when he was not scheduled to fly. It was opening day for his ball team, and he was in something of a hurry to get back by game time.

Shepard's group was assigned to strafe a German airfield. It was a fairly heavily defended site, and Shepard's plane flew into anti-aircraft fire.

Bert Shepard suiting up before the game, 1945.

Only 20 feet off the ground there was no chance to bail out, and Shepard hit the ground at 380 miles per hour. Wounded in the leg and chin and lucky to be alive at all, Shepard lost consciousness.

At this point in the war the German civilians were being encouraged by propaganda to attack downed Allied pilots. P-38 pilots were especially hated, as they had a reputation — not entirely inaccurate according to

Shepard — for strafing civilians. But to Shepard's good fortune a German Army doctor dispatched to the scene was able to keep the mob at bay and remove Shepard from the wreckage.

Waking up two weeks later in a German hospital Shepard knew that his right foot was gone, the leg amputated below the knee. As the orderlies stood silently waiting for Shepard to react to his loss, he simply pulled back the covering sheet, took a look, and thanked them for saving his life.

Shepard spent eight months in captivity, ultimately ending up at Stalag IXC near Meiningen. His treatment was good there, perhaps in part because the commandant had a son in captivity across the Atlantic in Canada. While at Meiningen Shepard met an ingenious Canadian POW named Don Erry, who was able to fashion a prosthesis for Shepard out of scrap metal found around the camp. It worked well enough to start rehabilitation in the form of walking. As he gained strength Shepard and Erry located a glove and an old cricket ball and began playing catch. Later, to the amazement of the German medical staff, Shepard started practicing playing first base and even fielding bunts. Shepard was later to claim that as a left-handed pitcher, the right foot was the better one to lose as he did not have to push off with that foot during his windup. Shepard even got to play in a ballgame between patients and British Red Cross orderlies. In February 1945 he was repatriated via the Swedish liner *Gripsholm* on one of its many quiet missions of mercy.

Shepard's next assignment was a stay at Walter Reed Hospital in Washington, D.C., awaiting the fabrication of a new prosthetic leg. While there he was among four servicemen summoned for commendation by Robert Patterson, the undersecretary of war. Asked what he wanted to do with his life Shepard immediately responded that he wanted to play professional baseball. Once satisfied that Shepard was serious in this matter Patterson put through a friendly call to his friend Clark Griffith, owner of the Washington Senators. As Shepard recalls it, "Well, Mr. Griffith was not going to say no to the undersecretary of war."[2] A tryout was scheduled.

On March 14, 1945, a mere four days after receiving his new prosthesis, Shepard reported to the Senators' workout camp at College Park, Maryland. Reporters got wind of it and were present in numbers. At this point, by the way, Shepard had not even been reunited with his parents yet.

Shepard was the man of the hour, pitching and hitting with competence or, at least according to the unwritten subtext to the episode, with an amazing degree of courage and determination, which was a credit and inspiration to wounded servicemen everywhere. Movie footage of Shepard pitching and fielding was featured in newsreels around the country.

Undersecretary Patterson next flew Shepard down to the Yankee training camp in his private plane, setting off a brief spat between Griffith and Yankee President Larry MacPhail. Harsh words were spoken which included the term "kidnapping" until the Army announced that Lieutenant Shepard had made the trip to Atlantic City to work out with the Bombers under orders and for the morale of some 100 convalescent veterans among the spectators.

Of course Shepard had his photo taken alongside Pete Gray, the one-armed player who had a brief major league stint during the talent-starved war years. There are also photos of him receiving the Flying Cross and Air Medal from Undersecretary Patterson, who is shown pinning the decorations to Shepard, who is decked out in his Senators uniform.

The Senators signed Shepard to a contract as a coach and batting-practice pitcher, but they also dispatched him to play a series of exhibition games. On one occasion he played against Yogi Berra's New London, Connecticut, Navy team. Yogi claims to have not known until years later that Shepard was an amputee.

In the Pacific the war ground on, with American soldiers dying to capture miserable dots of otherwise worthless coral while preparing for the final costly assault on Japan. It was a time when morale on the home front needed to be kept up, and the Senators' call-up of Shepard to the Big Show in July had some element of this associated with it.

On August 4, two days before Hiroshima, Bert Shepard, the former POW, had his moment of major league glory. His only moment. It occurred in a game where Washington was on the very short end of a lopsided contest with Boston. To try to staunch the bleeding in a 12-run inning Shepard was called in to relieve an unfortunate fellow named Joe Cleary. It was to be Cleary's only major league game, and he departed with a career ERA of 189.0, the highest in baseball history. But Shepard threw well. Coming to the mound with the bases loaded, he struck out "Catfish" Metkovich to retire the side, then went five more innings, allowing only one run on three hits. He came to the plate three times and retired with a perfect career batting average of .000. The Senators were in the thick of a pennant race, finally coming up short by only a game and a half. For this reason Shepard never got the ball again.

After the 1945 season Shepard traveled with a winter barnstorming tour. While the competition was not serious by big league standards, Shepard does claim to have once retired Stan Musial four times in one game and to have gotten two hits off the premier fireballer of the day, Bob Feller.

Shepard would never appear in the majors again, but his baseball dream did not die easily. He pitched well in 1946 spring training, but the wave of recently discharged pro players denied him a spot on the Senators' roster. He voluntarily went down to their Chattanooga farm club, where he went 2–2 but surprised all concerned by hitting a double and running the bases with authority.

He barnstormed again after the 1946 season, mostly playing first base. At one point he actually hit two home runs.

Late in 1946 Shepard had to go in for further surgery on his leg. Things did not go smoothly. Complications set in and he had to have an additional section of his leg amputated. Five operations over two and a half years ultimately were needed. He was on crutches the whole time, and his shoulder muscles never really recovered from the ordeal. But he still did not give up.

In 1949 Bert Shepard signed on as player/manager of the Class B team in Waterbury, Connecticut. He went 5–6 as a pitcher, playing in nearly 50 games at first base. He hit four home runs and actually stole five bases. Not a bad season for an amputee.

For the next five years Shepard was in and out of baseball, managing or attempting a comeback as a player in such obscure places as Williston, North Dakota, and Modesto, California. Finally in 1955 he had had enough.

Shepard moved into civilian life, working for IBM and Hughes Aircraft. He played golf, once managing 52 holes in one day. He played semi-pro ball until he was 40. He was a two-time National Amputee Golf champion, taking the title in 1968 and 1971. He even got the chance late in life to return to Europe and meet the doctor who had pulled him from the wreckage and saved his life. Ladislaw Loidl, an Austrian by birth, admitted that he had taken Shepard's parachute, which his wife later made into a dress.

Shepard went through many prostheses over the years, of ever increasing sophistication. But he says that few have ever worked as well as the one fashioned out of scrap metal at Stalag IXC. Still in good health in the summer of 2001, Bert Shepard is the last ex–POW/ex–Major Leaguer.

14

O Canada

For all their native courage and determination it is unlikely that the British could have survived the initial years of the Second World War without the contributions of manpower from their Commonwealth allies. The record of the Indians is courageous but tarnished by the actions of some of the Sikh regiments, who changed sides and actually served as prison guards for their British officers after the fall of Hong Kong. But the South Africans, New Zealanders, and Canadians in the service of the Crown performed with great distinction. Without them England might have fallen. Indeed, at one point just after the Dunkirk evacuation the entire force of armed, trained soldiers on British soil consisted of a single newly arrived Canadian division.

In this history of POW baseball the story of the Canadians merits a separate chapter. Baseball served, after hockey, as a second national pastime for our northern neighbors. Because Canadians were at war for a longer period of time they had more chances to be captured and to play baseball behind barbed wire. Indeed, Canadians were generally the pioneers of baseball in the stalag system.

About 10,000 Canadians were taken prisoner during the war, not including Merchant Marine crews. Roughly 2,500 were air crews either serving in Canadian squadrons or as members of the RAF. Their story closely matches that of the Americans, with imprisonment in the luft stalag system being the general rule. The Germans did not specifically segregate the Canadians, so they turn up almost everywhere that British crews were held. On rare occasions the number of Canadians was high enough to merit special distinction. Thus there was a Canadian Compound at Stalag Luft VI, which of course fielded its own softball all-star team.

An entry from a wartime log kept by a Canadian named R. Watchorn gives a sense of the spirit of the Canadian ballplayers in a luft stalag. He spent time at Luft III and Luft VI. From later references to frequent broken windows the following probably is from his stay at Luft VI:

> A stampede.
> A lot of mad, roaring lunatics.
> An imbecilic pack of madmen.
> A bevy of prehistoric monsters.
> A crowd of bandylegged hill-billies.
> A contained mass of filthy humanity.
> A cursing, swearing yelling concourse.
> A knackneed, tintoed lot of bombastic hounds.
> A screaming, howling throat slashing throng.
> A pignosed, big chinned rabblelike mob.
> A line shooting dog eared mass of humanity.
>   "What's all this about pop?"
>   It's just a gang of Canadians playing their national game of soft ballll pronounced Baal as in the Bible.[1]

In late 1942 another large group of Canadians fell into enemy hands as a result of one of the great blunders of the war; the raid on Dieppe. The Allies were eager to try out the tactics of amphibious assault on a moderate scale. The plan was to seize Dieppe, a small French port, hold it for a few hours while destroying facilities useful to the Germans, then evacuate. The bulk of the raiding force was the Second Canadian Division.

Somehow security had been compromised, and as the troops hit the beaches they waded into an inferno. About 1,000 were killed and 2,000 taken prisoner. Many of the captives were told by the Germans that they had been expected; indeed, since the raid had been postponed for weather reasons, they were scolded for being four days late.

The Canadian prisoners were marched past cameras for propaganda photos, then off to the stalags. One of their early requests upon arrival was for athletic equipment. In a report from Stalag VIIIB near Lamsdorf, a Red Cross inspector made the following comment in September 1942: "Of the Dieppe prisoners 85% are Canadians; and they have specially asked for the variant of baseball which in Canada is called softball."

At first treatment in the stalags was fair; Canadians seem to have been for some reason popular with the Germans. But this changed. As the Germans picked through the rubble after the Dieppe raid they found numerous dead German soldiers with their hands tied. The Canadians contended that these were prisoners taken, bound, and put aboard landing craft for evacuation, with the boats being sunk by German fire. The Germans suspected that the men had been executed. Orders came down from head-quarters that the Canadian prisoners were to have their hands tied or chained. These orders were in effect from about October 1942 to November 1943. They applied mostly to prisoners taken at Dieppe and were enforced inconsistently with other ground forces prisoners and not at all with air crews. Initially the men had their hands tied with rope, which was quite uncomfortable. Later, handcuffs were provided, which was an improvement, especially once it was discovered that the opening key from the cans of sardines that came in Canadian Red Cross parcels could also be modified to open the handcuffs. After that point the cuffs came off any time the guards were not physically present. But it was still an indignity, and it deprived many of the Canadians of the chance to play ball in the summer of 1943. Some Dieppe prisoners commemorated the handcuffing incident by fashioning tiny pairs of handcuffs out of wood or tin and wearing them as a decoration during their prison camp days.

Compared to the huge volume of American POW memoirs, the body of firsthand information recorded by Canadian prisoners is rather small. They were fewer in number for one thing. But there also seems to be a certain reticence in the Canadian character. Having served with valor in both world wars our northern neighbors seemed content to turn to more pacific tasks, such as their commendable involvement with United Nations peacekeeping missions. As a result the picture of Canadians playing ball in the German camps is a fragmentary one.

We can catch a glimpse of the early days of stalag ball in this letter from a British prisoner of war at Oflag VIIB, quoted in the October 1943 edition of the Red Cross *Prisoner of War Bulletin*: "We have now 37 of your compatriots here from Tunis. They all seem fit and cheerful and are very popular. They and the Canadians are making us baseball minded." Given the understandable lag time in such communication it seems certain that this refers to play in the summer of 1943, perhaps indicating that not all Canadians were handcuffed at that time.

Another glimpse of the same camp (near Eichstatt) at about the same time comes from a brief log kept by an American officer held there prior to being sent to Oflag 64. His summary for April is: "From Tunis I fly the Med. to Naples + Capua — then by train to Germany. Innsbruck, Munich, Moosburg, Munich and at last to Eichstatt. Here life took up a semblance of reality and routine. We play, eat and sleep. John Moon, Shatz Warren, = Maj. White. — Chained men from Dieppe — the world is here." His entry for May begins: "We settle into the routine and grow to like it. Ball is the great game, soccer + hockey are played also."

Still another view of sports at Eichstatt can be found in this excerpt from a radio talk, "Repatriated from Oflag VIIB," recorded by the recently returned Major Charlie E. Page in November 1943:

> If you send prisoners a miscellaneous parcel, try sending running shoes, shorts, sweat shirts, and baseball caps—I suggest that because the sun is very strong there in the summer time and we play softball a lot, and the regular baseball cap shades you. In fact, we were making our own hats there, and very queer looking they were, too. We played a great many games in our camp. We had a three-quarter-size soccer "pitch"—as the English people call it—a softball diamond with forty-foot bases, a basketball field, and a field hockey pitch, two tennis courts and four badminton courts. The sports committee had quite a time figuring out a schedule so that everybody who wanted to play could. They made a very good job of it, and the fields were kept busy and the men happy. ... Canadian prisoners introduced softball in all the camps they were in in Germany, and it's now the most popular game in all the camps. In ours we started off with a league of six teams and by the end of the summer we had two leagues of twelve teams each. During two months in the summer, the football pitch is allotted to cricketers from 10 in the morning until 5 in the afternoon, because it takes all day to play cricket, and have tea. The English officers played softball too and were enthusiastic about it and played well.[2]

An interesting artifact of stalag ball is a photograph purportedly taken by Thomas McLean. It shows prisoners, presumably Canadian, playing baseball at Stalag IID near Starburg, Germany. The open area for sports is enormous, easily large enough for hardball play. Only the batter, catcher, umpire, and on-deck batter can be seen on one side of the picture, as a group of shirtless prisoners carrying a soccer ball stroll by on what looks like a running track. A half dozen spectators look on. The photo is undated, but McLean was known to be in this camp beginning in May 1944. The picture has a posed look to it and bears an official German censor's stamp, so presumably it had some propaganda purpose. Another photo from the same camp appears to have been taken at the same time, if the casual and minimal uniforms worn in both are any indication. It shows what appears to be a combination baseball backstop/soccer goal.

Another glimpse of this story can be found in a hand-lettered certificate carried home by a Canadian tanker captured in Italy in 1943. In fine script and in multiple colors it announces the Stalag 357 Major League Softball Tournament winners, and lists them complete with nicknames. Howard "Smokey" Seeley is listed first despite being a center fielder.

Canadian POWs playing ball at Stalag IID, Starburg, Germany, 1944. Note the improvised backstop. Courtesy Jonathan Vance.

Probably each hand-lettered copy listed the individual recipient first. It is signed, "Chairman, Camp Softball Committee."

A letter from Stalag 357 written on July 5, 1944, mentions: "At this time there are 235 Canadians here and naturally softball is the major sport, with volleyball a very close runner-up."[3]

Stalag 357 was the camp to which many of the British NCOs evacuated from Stalag Luft VI were sent, along with new drafts as the war went on. With some Americans who ended up there, they had a fairly active ball league. An RCAF airman named Charlie Hobbs wrote in his memoirs:

> The Yanks loved to play baseball and held a good game every evening. Cam and I enjoyed watching these games and got to know quite a few of the army boys, particularly the Essex Scottish, who were such a colourful lot. It was softball they played, because baseball mitts were at a premium, but it was a very good grade similar to the fastball they played at the Beaches in Toronto. The umpire, Charlie Surpliss, was a Sergeant with the Toronto Scottish who had been a few years ahead of me at Jarvis Collegiate. He had been

Canadian prisoners playing ball at Stalag IID, Starburg, Germany, summer of 1944. Courtesy National Archives of Canada, McLean Collection.

a Toronto policeman before the war for about a year and then joined up.[4]

Spotty references to ballgames are found in several other camps where Canadians were held. As early as July 1942 there is mention of baseball being played at Work Camp No. 737, which was a subsidiary camp of Stalag IXC, Obermassfeld. There is a passing reference to baseball being one of several sports played at Stalag 12A, Limburg. And several references from Stalag IVB at Muhlberg mention Canadians and Americans playing softball in 1944, with competitive leagues being organized and the games being played on the rugby pitch.

Despite the handcuffing episode the majority of the Canadians captured in the European theater were treated decently. The same cannot be said of the third large group of Canadian POWs. It is taking things a bit out of order to examine it, but the fate of the Canadians in the Pacific stands in stark contrast to the European experience.

In the latter part of 1941 Japanese intentions were known to the British and Americans. War was expected, but it was not clear where the first blow

Howard Seeley's championship certificate, Major League Softball Tournament, Stalag 357, summer of 1944. Courtesy Steve Martin.

would be struck. The British possession of Hong Kong was known to be effectively indefensible, and common sense would have dictated evacuation. But for some reason the call went out to Canada to supply two battalions of troops to reinforce the defenses of the colony. The two units selected were second-line troops, suitable only for garrison duty. One was pulled from the enviable duty of defending Bermuda, where the soldiers had had plenty of leisure time to play baseball. Arriving in Hong Kong shortly before the onset of war they had scant time for training before facing a Japanese invasion force. Of the 1,975 men in the Royal Rifles and the Winnipeg Grenadiers some 300 died in battle, and the rest were taken prisoner on Christmas Day 1941.

Many of the Canadians were held in the North Point Concentration Camp, a facility built previously by the British to house Chinese refugees. A rare photograph of the place shows closely packed primitive barracks huddled around a small exercise area. Small, but still big enough to play ball.

A diary kept by a Canadian named Georges "Blacky" Verreault has the following listing for May 18, 1942: "We had another concert the night before last. Between concerts and softball games we spend our time as interestingly as possible."

Other sources describe an active sports program in the first months of captivity. The original complement of equipment consisted of some softball bats, balls, and gloves; soccer balls; and some cricket bats and balls. No doubt the fact that the Canadians were captured and held in an urban area contributed to the availability of this gear. The playing field was about 100 by 150 feet, bounded on three sides by huts and on the fourth by an electrically charged fence with an inner barrier of concertina wire. One supposes that there were some unusual ground rules.

A softball tournament was organized in early 1942, but was largely abandoned by July as the effects of inadequate diet, sickness, and Japanese requirements for labor details took their tolls.

In addition to the Verreault diary there are at least two other extant diaries from North Point that mention softball and give a few details as to its play. Tom Forsyth with the Winnipeg Grenadiers recorded on January 25, 1942, "The [Royal] Rifles played the [Winnipeg] Grenadiers at softball." Another entry for July 23 of the same year mentions that "boys are beginning to play softball," presumably after some sort of lapse. A later entry for August 14 mentions, "no more soft ball games," with the apparent cause being a diphtheria outbreak at another camp in the Hong Kong area.[5]

Another diary was kept by Frank Ebdon of the Royal Rifles. Ebdon was a veteran of the First World War and a sergeant major with the Rifles at the time of his wounding and capture on Christmas Day 1941. His account of the camp gives a little more detail of the softball league and shows that play went on considerably later than other sources document. As Ebdon was transported to Japan in January 1943, his diary has no comments on North Point beyond that time. Ebdon's diary documents several games taking place over a short time period late in 1942. On "Sunday December 27 ... the W.G.'s [Winnipeg Grenadiers] beat us at Soft ball this morning. After dinner the H.K.V.D.C. [Hong Kong Volunteer Defense Company] beat a team from what is left of the Canadians." On December 28 the Hong Kong Volunteers again beat a Canadian squad, and the next day there is a nonspecific notation that Ebdon "played softball this afternoon."[6]

The overall picture that emerges of softball at North Point is that it occurred in two phases. First there was an organized league, which failed due to the poor health of the men. Later with cooler weather and perhaps some marginal improvement in the camp regimen another series of ballgames happened around the holiday season of 1942.

This is not to imply that life at North Point Camp was any sort of carefree resort experience. The food supply was inadequate, the medical care improvised, and the Japanese guards often actively hostile. There were many deaths among the Canadians, and the ultimate fate of most was to be shipped off to Japan, where conditions were even worse. But with commendable pluck the Canadians did the best that they could. An entry from the Verreault diary from July 26, 1942, could serve as an epitaph for all the prisoners of the Japanese who somehow found the spirit and energy to play ball: "In spite of the sickness and starvation we still play sports, especially softball and the games are so interesting that the whole camp attends and cheers. Just imagine, fifteen hundred skeletons cheering."[7]

As an odd postscript to the North Point story, brief mention should be made of what must be the only former prisoner of the Japanese to ever play organized ball after his captivity. Among the ranks of the Royal Rifles was Lieutenant Colin A. Blaver. Before the war he had played first base in the Ward's Island League at Toronto. This seems to have been a fairly low level of baseball, and the league struggled like all of its fellows to fill its ranks during the war years. But with the conclusion of hostilities things improved, and the 1946 season was one of the best in league history.

One of the top players in the league that year was Colin Blaver, former POW. Somehow he had recovered physically and mentally to the point that he not only played, but batted .400 for the season, second only to batting champion Jack Bradley's .471 mark.

Further details of Blaver's remarkable story are hard to come by. He was born in 1915 and played hockey as well as baseball. Articles written on his return from captivity mention that he was a former defenseman with the Quebec Aces hockey team. He is known to have been decorated with the Military Cross for his role in the defense of Hong Kong and can be presumed to be one of the players at North Point. After the war he found employment as a salesman for Benjamin Moore paint. But it appears that history has been impoverished by the failure of this remarkable man to write his memoirs.

15

Under the Rising Sun

The prisoner unfortunate enough to have been captured by the Japanese in the Second World War had a significantly worse lot in life than one captured by the Germans, or Italians. Mere statistics are inadequate to tell the whole tale of suffering endured by these captives, but the numbers are striking nonetheless. Of the roughly 94,000 American servicemen captured by the Germans only 1.1 percent died in captivity. For the 36,000 American soldiers and sailors taken by the Japanese, a variety of casualty statistics are put forward, with the death rate while a POW generally being accepted as about 40 percent.

For civilian internees the picture is only a little better. The Germans held some 4,700 American internees, with a 3.5 percent death rate. The Japanese rounded up nearly 14,000 American men, women, and children, with a death rate of about 11 percent.

The Japanese onslaught also captured significant numbers of British, Dutch, and Australian prisoners, with a smattering of Canadians. At places where there was a significant colonial population there were also large numbers of civilians from these nations who fell into Japanese hands. It is much easier to be taken prisoner when your army is in retreat. As a result almost all of the captives of the Japanese were taken in the roughly six months between Pearl Harbor and the battle of Midway. By far the largest group were the 22,000 captured with the fall of the Philippines.

The reasons for the harsh treatment of Western POWs by the Japanese are not easy to understand. That nation's treatment of prisoners taken in their two most recent conflicts, the Russo-Japanese war of 1905 and the First World War, had been decent and in some cases commendable. But in the interwar years there had occurred a shift in Japanese society, with an orientation toward an obstinate militancy based on a rigorous interpretation of the ancient code of Bushido.

Bushido is a body of belief that stipulates absolute obedience to the emperor. Under its provisions no surrender is allowed. Any soldier in World War II who did let himself be captured was considered a *horyo*, a dishonored captive who had surrendered not only himself but also all rights to humane treatment. The most junior buck private of the Japanese Army had absolute power to issue orders of any sort to prisoners of war, and to disobey could be death.

There was also an element of plain racism involved. The Japanese went forth and conquered with a slogan of "Asia for Asians" and were able in some instances to effectively tap into a reservoir of anti-imperialistic feeling among the long-colonized citizens of their conquered territories. Of course it did not take overly long for it to become apparent that the so-called Greater Asian Co-Prosperity Sphere was simply an exchange of a generally benevolent, well-functioning colonialism for one of brutality and inefficiency.

For most of the nations fighting in the Second World War, the Geneva Convention of 1927 outlined a set of rules for the treatment of prisoners. Even nations such as Germany, which had no shortage of brutal behavior and oppressive racial notions, usually adhered to the Geneva Convention's principles in dealing with Western POWs. Japan, while a signatory to the treaty, had never ratified it in its Diet, and at the onset of hostilities agreed to abide by its provisions only with modifications as the soldiers saw fit under the circumstances. In practice the convention was violated in almost all instances and in almost all possible ways. There can be no excuse for this brutality, but even had there been a general feeling for fair treatment of prisoners it is doubtful that the Japanese could have provided it. They severely underestimated the number of prisoners they would capture in places like the Philippines both because of shoddy intelligence work and by the folly of their own attitudes toward captivity. Since few if any Japanese soldiers would surrender, they assumed that American and British soldiers would also in most cases fight to the death. The sheer volume of prisoners that presented themselves to the Japanese overwhelmed their logistics.

Another factor in the care of Western prisoners was the relative isolation of their captivity. Thus in places like Burma and the Philippines, where there was essentially no contact with other Westerners, treatment of prisoners was atrocious. In places like Shanghai, where there was an active community of observers from Western nations that were either neutral or allied with Japan, the treatment was significantly better.

The Pacific war saw large numbers of American and British civilian internees. Hong Kong and Singapore were actual colonies, and other battle zones such as China and the Philippines had a sort of quasicolonial status. In many cases there were intact civilian communities of teachers, missionaries, businessmen, retired soldiers, and so forth. While the American military had sufficient sense to order the dependents of military personnel home late in 1941, no general evacuation of civilians was undertaken.

In Japanese eyes civilians were not bound by Bushido, so civilian prisoners under Japanese rule were not viewed with the same degree of disdain as military prisoners. As a result the conditions in civilian internment camps were generally quite a bit better. The guards were usually not military but detachments of a special police force associated with the diplomatic corps. Food was usually allowed to be brought in by outsiders, and a lively black market was often present. Among the sundry benefits enjoyed by the civilian internees was a general tolerance of recreational activities, and therefore baseball was played in most of the civilian internment camps.

In the West prisoners could generally look to the Red Cross to keep an eye on camp conditions in general and to provide both recreational equipment and much-needed supplemental food. Not so in the East. Without nearby neutral nations, such as Switzerland and Portugal, and without land routes to transport supplies, the ability of the Red Cross to deliver aid was severely impaired. It is remarkable indeed that any contact was made. But there was a shaky supply line that ran through officially neutral Russia, and repatriation ships such as the *Gripsholm* delivered a few precious loads. Unfortunately in many cases the Red Cross supplies were plundered by the Japanese or pointlessly stored in warehouses.

Unlike the German prison system, which displayed a high degree of organization, the Japanese system was chaotic. But a few general patterns can be seen. Most of the American prisoners were taken in the Philippines. This archipelago of thousands of islands had been under American control since the Spanish-American War of 1898. Technically granted independence in the late 1930s, there was still a major American presence, both military and civilian. The defense of the Philippines was entrusted to a mixed defense force, with American Army, Navy, and Air Corps units serving alongside units of the Philippine Army, which was mostly officered by Americans. American knowledge of Japanese intentions, aided considerably by some deft code breaking, prompted an attempt to reinforce the Philippines late in 1941. But many arriving units were dismayed by the general sluggishness of the Philippines' command; precious time and energy was expended on fancy dress balls, polo games, and even a baseball league.

It was the twilight of a magical era, as the sun set on the American raj. A new, brutal day was about to dawn.

Japanese attacks on the Philippines were synchronized with the attack on Pearl Harbor. Against all military common sense, planes were lined up in neat rows on airfields, ostensibly to help guard against sabotage. The majority were destroyed, as was any effective hope of holding the Philippines long enough for help to arrive from the United States. When the Japanese invasion forces arrived the American and Filipino troops put up a stout defense, but were driven back. Eventually the majority of Americans ended up in one of two places.

According to military planners the Bataan peninsula would be a retreat and refuge for Allied forces. But due to bungling of the highest order there were not sufficient supplies of food and medication there to sustain the retreating army. Finally after months of brutal jungle fighting, disease, and near-starvation the garrison was surrendered. The defenders of Bataan were then herded into a vast, straggling line and marched for days without significant amounts of food, water, or medical attention. Those who lagged behind were bayoneted on the spot. This was the infamous Bataan Death March, a lasting monument to human cruelty and stupidity.

Things did not improve much at all when they reached their destination, a former Philippine Army base known as Camp O'Donnell. The guards were indifferent or openly hostile, the sanitation system nonexistent. The prisoners, weakened by their long stay in the jungle and the death march, died by the thousands. Former prisoners of war, when asked about their stay at Camp O'Donnell, uniformly say that all they had time and energy for was the burying of their dead.

Camp O'Donnell seems somehow to have offended even the sensibilities of the Japanese, so after a few months it was closed and the prisoners transported to another former army base. This was the Cabanatuan complex. The Bataan-O'Donnell group generally ended up in Cabanatuan No. 1, which became the hub of the Japanese prison system in the Philippines. Conditions had nowhere to go but up after O'Donnell, but it was still a horrible place. Deaths from disease and beatings were common, and escape attempts were prevented by organizing the men into ten-man "shooting squads." If one man escaped, the other nine would be executed. Although inconsistently enforced, this did happen at Cabanatuan and elsewhere in the Philippines.

The other large group of Americans taken in the Philippines took a different route, one that was a little less brutal. The island of Corregidor, which had been heavily fortified, dominates the approaches to Manila harbor. To deny the Japanese use of the harbor, this stronghold hung on as long as possible, finally surrendering on May 6, 1942, some time after the Bataan garrison had given up. The Corregidor troops had been under continuous bombardment, but had not suffered the degree of hunger and disease that plagued the Bataan troops. There was to be no death march for them. Taken by boat to Manila they were paraded through the streets in an attempt to show Japanese domination, then taken to Cabanatuan.

The Corregidor troops mostly went to Cabanatuan Camp No. 3. Since they arrived in better condition and since the water supply was less contaminated, they did not suffer nearly the degree of disease and death as the Bataan troops. Perhaps because of their better condition these men were among the first to be transported to various labor camps around the Japanese empire, and Cabanatuan No. 3 was then closed.

Although life in the camps was bad, it is this shuttling of prisoners by ship from one point in the Japanese domains to another that stands as the worst abuse of the captives. The POWs were crowded into the holds of cargo ships without much in the way of sanitary facilities and with inadequate food and water. Worse still, these ships were not marked in any way as prisoner transport vessels, and many were sunk by Allied submarines, unaware that they were drowning their own compatriots. It is estimated that some 3,800 American prisoners died in these hell ships.

For weary prisoners who actually arrived safely the destination could be one of several places. One large draft went to Manchuria to occupy a camp that supplied labor to a complex of factories. Some shorter trips were to various outlying islands in the Philippines. Some Americans, and even more British, were sent to work on railways in Burma and Sumatra, places where the death toll was atrocious. Eventually, many were shipped to Japan itself.

If the Philippines-to-Japan route was the most common POW experience of Americans in the Pacific it was far from the only one. Some 1,500 men — Marines and civilian construction workers — were captured at Wake Island after a fierce battle. They were shipped to a camp near Shanghai, China. Smaller numbers of Americans were rounded up in places like Guam, Java, North China, and the Celebes islands. Japan was not the only destination. In a confusing diaspora, the American prisoners ended up in Korea, Formosa, Burma, and Thailand as well.

The experience of the civilians was a bit simpler. They were mostly imprisoned close to where they were rounded up. This happened fairly quickly in Manila, more slowly in the rest of the Philippines, and only after many months had passed in China. Some Americans in Shanghai were never interned at all. Most of the civilian internment centers were in some sort of school. The rules were numerous and restrictive, but life in general went on with a semblance of normalcy. Schools were organized, newspapers were circulated, and there was recreation of various sorts, including baseball.

Later, as Allied forces approached, life in the internment camps of the Philippines took a turn for the worse. Army guards replaced the previous consular police, rations were cut to near-starvation levels, and there were some summary executions of internee leaders considered troublemakers.

In an environment as hostile as that faced by the captives of the Japanese it might seem remarkable that there was any ballplaying at all. But there are other factors to consider.

Baseball has a long history in Japan. It was introduced by missionaries in the 1870s and popularized by a series of tours by college teams and barnstorming major leaguers. Developing first as a college-level sport and later as a professional game with leagues modeled on the American system, *beso-boru* enjoyed a wide popularity in prewar Japan. Of course, the Japanese approach to the game is a bit different than the American one. Individual effort and achievement is downplayed and made subservient to collective effort and team unity. Discipline was absolute. It is unlikely that any American ballplayer of 1941 (never mind of the current era!) would tolerate the degree of verbal and physical abuse that Japanese players were expected to accept from their coaches. Still, it would seem that any contact between the two great baseball-playing nations of the day would from time to time touch upon this small patch of common ground.

It is surprising that the Japanese did not use baseball more for propaganda purposes. There were a few occasions where photographers would show up to take pictures of happy prisoners playing a game, but very few. There do not seem to have been any instances of film crews attempting to capture a game, although on one occasion in Batavia there was a movie taken of British prisoners playing cricket. Mindful of the chance, albeit a small one, that the film would make it to the West the Brits took ridiculous liberties with the rules of the game, playing out of position and in a manner that made a mockery of both the game and the circumstances under which it was being played. Their hope was that anyone actually familiar with the game would get the message.

In Germany it was necessary to improvise fields and equipment, at least until the Red Cross could come through with gear. In the Philippines and to a certain extent in China there was an infrastructure for baseball already in place. Several of the places where Americans were held had nice ball fields on the premises, and equipment could often be located.

It also bears remembering that the prisoners of the Japanese were in almost all cases held longer than those of the Germans. A Kriegie might have been in captivity for one, two, or quite rarely three ball seasons. A serviceman captured in the Philippines ended up spending the better part of four summers in captivity.

In some instances the climate in the Pacific was more conducive to playing ball. Unlike the northern climes of Germany, you could in theory play ball year 'round in the tropics. But there were problems with long rainy seasons and with oppressive heat, which tended to concentrate ball playing into certain months of the year. Some of the places where camps were located, such as Mukden in Manchuria, were subject to nasty weather at both extremes of the thermometer.

Japanese attitude played a big role in what kind of treatment American prisoners received. Early in the war, before the major Japanese defeats at Midway and Guadalcanal, there were more instances of lenient treatment. But the POWs could never really be sure. The marked degree of unpredictability of Japanese behavior, to Westerners, confounded every attempt to understand it, then and now. In a general sense the farther away from the center of the prison system a prisoner got, the more the treatment varied. Out on the fringes of the Japanese realms or on a work detail far from headquarters a prisoner might actually be treated well at times. Or executed without an explanation.

In most of the German stalags ball was played often and with a high participation rate. Even those who did not play followed the games and helped pass the time by cheering their favorites. It was probably the most popular athletic activity, and along with card playing, theatrical productions, and reading, one of the most popular leisure activities overall. In the Japanese camps baseball did not have so central a role. The conditions were so bad that often there simply was not enough food, energy, or time. That it got played at all is remarkable, and generally this happened with detectable frequency only in those camps where conditions for one reason or another were just a bit better than the dismal norm. As to the other camps, the players were in some instances just about dead on their feet. Part of the history of baseball in the Pacific has been lost this way. It was a game played by near-ghosts, with few spectators able to rouse themselves from their hunger- and disease-induced apathy to even take notice.

The Philippines, Part I: Life in the Camps

The Cabanatuan Camp complex was located north of Manila at the site of a former Philippine Army training base. In addition to being the largest camp in the islands for military POWs it also was a transit point, a place to which prisoners were taken on return from other duties and from which drafts of prisoners were assembled for transport elsewhere. More former POWs, therefore, have memories of Cabanatuan than any other camp in the system, so it is remarkable that while baseball was played at both of the Cabanatuan branches, memories and records relating to it are quite scarce.

The prisoners taken when the island fortress of Corregidor was surrendered on May 6, 1942, were put into Cabanatuan Camp No. 3. Conditions were fair, with the quality of organization on the part of the Marine officers, the better sanitary conditions, and the superior physical condition of the men compared to the Bataan survivors all playing a part. Cabanatuan No. 3 was only occupied for about six months, after which the men were either transported to Manchuria or sent to Cabanatuan No. 1. During that time it is recalled that there was a single baseball game played.

One of the participants was a Marine named Willis A. Johnson. He was a player of some ability, having at one point before the war been given letters of recommendation for a minor league tryout. In June 1942 an idea circulated — nobody knows where it originated — for a ballgame. Some equipment was located, and permission from the Japanese was obtained. Two teams were mustered, one from the Navy and Marines and the other an Army and Army Air Corps squad. The pitchers were "Ding" Campbell and a man named Loverux, who had been a former professional mid-dleweight fighter. Being a good Marine, Johnson says that "of course" the Navy-Marine squad triumphed in a 3–1 game. Johnson later played soft-ball in the camp at Mukden in Manchuria. Campbell was one of the unfor-tunate men to perish in a prison ship.[1]

The story at Cabanatuan Camp No. 1 is harder to picture. A drawing of the camp shows a baseball diamond on the premises, but it lies within the part of the complex reserved for the Japanese guards. The camp is divided into a hospital section and a duty section, and contact between the two halves seems to have been loose.

The provost marshal report on Cabanatuan compiled in 1945 is a flawed document. It seems to reverse the numbers for Camps 1 and 3. The report on Camp 1 is only two pages, while that on 3 runs to 17 pages and covers dates after Camp 3 had in fact been closed. So the following com-ment from the Camp 3 report presumably relates instead to Camp 1.

> Some of the men had brought decks of playing cards with them, with which they whiled [sic] away many a heavy hour. Several ingenious devotees of cribbage contrived boards on which to play their favorite game. There was almost no athletic equipment in the camp, but on a few rare occasions the Japanese provided baseball equipment and permitted the prisoners to indulge in a baseball game.[2]

Traces of baseball at Cabanatuan 1 are scarce. In a diary entry dated October 11, 1942, a medic named Ernest O. Norquist recorded: "Also this afternoon there was an attempt to put on a program in the dysentery sec-tion but it was rained out as was the baseball game also scheduled."[3] As the dysentery area of the hospital was just across Hospital Road from the ball diamond it is possible that either equipment could have been obtained for play in the limited spaces near the hospital complex or, less probably, the Japanese allowed an American group onto the field. On the other hand, it should be noted that this was a reference to a scheduled ballgame that had to be canceled. Perhaps the opportunity never came again. A clear-minded former POW who was on the hospital side from June 1942 to Jan-uary 1943 asserts that during his time there, no baseball whatsoever was played.[4]

The picture of baseball on the duty side of Cabanatuan No. 1 is also murky. There was an open area called Times Square, where some sort of game could have been played, but the general impression of former Cabanatuan inmates is that the camp administration was far too strict to allow this to happen. In fact, for a while even religious services were prohibited. As time went on things got a bit more livable; there were even some movies shown and some amateur theatrical productions. As to baseball being played, one of the few accounts found to date comes from the memoirs of Bernard Fitzpatrick.

Fitzpatrick remembered Major Thomas Smothers being at Cabanatuan. Smothers had played ball at West Point, and had an interest in the game. Fitzpatrick was working under Smothers in a highly sensitive area of camp administration: ration detail. This was work entrusted only to officers of the highest reputation, as any irregularities in the handling and distribution of the food would have been destructive to morale. Many years later, when visiting with the children of Major Smothers, he was asked about baseball in the camp. "I responded that Major Smothers had played baseball in prison camp, but the field was so small and bumpy that even running was difficult."[5]

Major Smothers did not survive the war, perishing on one of the transport ships that attempted to leave the Philippines once the American command of the seas was well established. He was never to be reunited with his two young sons, Tom and Dick, who would eventually become famous as the Smothers Brothers.

There were several kinds of diaries kept at Cabanatuan during the war. Those kept by officers tend to be closely typed documents produced on one of the several typewriters that the Japanese issued to the American officers involved in running the camp. Those kept by the lower ranks are incredible masses of crumbling scraps of paper, including cigarette packs, labels from tin cans, and Japanese propaganda leaflets. They have almost illegible handwriting that has faded over the years. These are slow going for the modern reader, but are especially poignant artifacts. Some of them were buried by their owners before transport to Japan, a trip from which there was sometimes no return. In the diary of Major William H. Owen appears the following entry from the Fourth of July 1943:

> Some of our most ardent patriots celebrated the nation's birthday just as did some of the more devout Christians celebrate Christmas, by becoming stuffy or raring drunk on Bamboo Gin. By a happy coincidence our weekly holiday is effective today, changed back to Sunday, so we have a holiday on the 4th. Baseball games and indoor football."[6]

Owen seems to have served as some sort of paymaster, helping administer the trivial sums of money that the imprisoned officers received in pay at this time.

An entry by a lieutenant from August 17, 1943, relates: "Baseball and volleyball games have been going on for the past week or so and are getting a lot of support."[7] Yet another diary entry from a medical officer dates to sometime in the January to October 1943 time period: "Volleyball nets were provided with balls so each camp unit could play after evening mess. Softballs for playing catch and even a Ping-Pong set were brought."[8] These improvements were apparently courtesy of the Philippine Red Cross, which had been allowed to provide some minimal support to the Cabanatuan prisoners at this point in the war.

The overall picture of baseball at Cabanatuan is that it was an uncommon event and that the participants were generally those who had some proximity to crucial supplies of food and medication. This is not to disparage any of the men mentioned, all of whose reputations are untarnished. But sometimes the margin between survival and death, and between health and illness might be a few pills of quinine, or a ration call that was made or missed. Only those who had the energy to pick themselves up and look beyond the survival of the day could have had the ability to play baseball under these desperate conditions.

Most of the Cabanatuan baseball references date to 1943, which most prisoners remember as the "best" year of imprisonment. The camp had started out as an overcrowded, disorganized place run by Japanese administration that was at best indifferent and often hostile. But as time went on the numbers of men at Cabanatuan were reduced a bit by transports elsewhere, and the daily running of the place was to some extent turned over to the Americans. By great exertions they built an efficient sanitary system, established several messes to distribute such food items as could be obtained, and even opened a small commissary. Even the Japanese expressed admiration for some of these accomplishments.

By 1944 things had changed for the worse, with the American blockade of Japanese sea lanes creating food shortages, and the threat of invasion hardening Japanese attitudes toward their prisoners.

Cabanatuan probably represents the absolute extreme at which POW baseball could exist. If conditions were just a little bit worse it would not have happened at all. Just a little bit better and the POWs might have played it on the larger scale seen at a few other camps. On a high mountain there is a level called the timberline. Below it, plant life is rich and abundant. Above lies only sterile rock and snow. Right on the line, plants struggle to survive, like baseball at Cabanatuan, and can only manage to exist in a scattered and stunted form.

There were many other camps in the Philippines. Some were large and permanent like Bilibid prison. Others were work camps, at places like Lipa

Batangas, Las Pinas, and Pasay. At none of them were conditions good enough to permit baseball, although there is one known reference to POWs at Bilibid at least playing a bit of catch for recreation.

One highly unusual exception to the general pattern of Japanese prison camps in the Philippines was the Davao Penal Colony. Beginning in October 1942, some 2,000 American prisoners were transported to Davao on the southern island of Mindanao. There they were housed in the Davao Penal Colony, a prison camp for civilian criminals. On taking possession of the place the Japanese freed the prisoners, most of whom had been convicted of serious crimes such as murder and rape. In the interest of their "Asia for the Asians" policy the Japanese made these men trustees and kept them on to help run the camp.

Davao sits in the heart of a rich agricultural area, so food should not have been scarce, and at least in the early days of the camp it was not. The camp seems to have been fairly well run, with the prison regime imposed by the Japanese being relatively lenient. There was even a camp library and a store at which food and tobacco could at times be purchased by those few Americans who had squirreled away a bit of currency.

Reactions among the Americans varied. The roughly 1,000 who had previously been held at Cabanatuan and sent south by ship to Davao rightly considered it a move up in the world. But the other 1,000 men were those who had comprised the original garrison of the island of Mindanao. They had gone into captivity without seeing any significant combat, and prior to their concentration at Davao they had been allowed to stay at their posts and to keep their personal possessions. After months of this comfortable captivity they did not find Davao such a nice place.

A diary kept by a medical officer named Calvin Jackson at Davao contains a few interesting entries on ball play at the camp:

> Thurs. Dec. 3 [1942]:
> Slept good. Today is a Sunday according to Nips. They organized a baseball game at 9 A.M. between U.S. prisoners and Philippine trustees. Philippines won 6–3. Trustees have a band and it played. First band I heard since Ft. McKinley. Sounded real good. Band played "Onward Christian Soldiers." I had never heard that at any other game. The trustees were former Philippine government prisoners as this was a government prison. They live outside fence in nice little homes, families are with them, even have a little barrio outside fence. Most of prisoners were liberated but there is still one prisoner with his ankles chained together. We see him walking at times.[9]

The choice of a pregame song may not have been traditional, but it would be reasonable to assume that the Japanese would be familiar enough with the "Star Spangled Banner" to make that an unwise selection. Or perhaps this band of recently unchained convicts just had a limited musical repertoire. A few days later on December 13 there was another game, this time Japanese versus Filipinos.

A second diary exists from this period at Davao, that of Major Lloyd Moffit. He describes an especially remarkable Christmas Eve 1942:

> Andy at hospital and stayed for lunch. Beef with cabbage, green onions, and bananas! We got weighed, me 143 pounds. 5 men caught stealing some of meat issue. Were punished but not severe enough! Went to ballgame between hospital and barricks [sic] #4, and #4 won. Nips umpired. After there was tug-of-war and weight lifting, then rain called off rest of program. For supper had rice, beef stew with plenty of beef, cabbage and onions (better and more than hospital) and good pumpkin pudding with ginger and sugar in it. After chow went to Xmas show. Americans, Filipinos, Japs, Mexicans, and American Indians participated. Excellent show. Large attendance. After show Filipinos gave all rice cakes, then came Midnight Mass.[10]

Ball playing continued into the New Year. According to Jackson:

> Sat. Jan. 2 [1943]
>   Rain during the night. There was a softball game outside the fence. We were allowed to go. Japs 8 — our camp 4. Dinner: fresh fried fish. Supper: a vegetable mixture soup. Another show at the chapel. I did not go. It was reported that it was all Japanese.

Moffit does not give the score, but does provide a little more detail and a view of life in general in the camp at this time:

> Jan. 2 Another holiday. Played Japs a game of baseball and they best us. After the game they were practicing for program tonight and quite a few stopped to look on. Japs soldiers and Americans were mixing and having a good time. Both were playing games with each other. It is certainly a far cry from O'Donnell and Cabanatuan. Seems their attitude has changed a lot lately. We now practically tell the guard on details to go mind their own business. Some of them even do go off and go to sleep and if their captain comes we wake him in time. There are two or three who are still kinda tough but we are softening them up. On a wood cutting the

other day the guard was feeling kinda tough and he wouldn't give us a chance to do any quaning. [*Quan* was a word in a Philippine dialect that in the POW vernacular meant food or the process of obtaining food.] Well, come time to go in and he wanted us to ride in a truck but just for meanness we refused to ride and made him walk in with us. Some do not even carry bayonets with them anymore.

Had a program in evening. Both crowd and program was mixed, Jap, Filipino and American. Was much better than the one at Christmas. Japs had Filipinos singing Jap songs and performing Jap dances. The subtle propaganda could be seen. Seems as if they tried to show the vulgarity of American entertainment as compared to Oriental as well as show that the Japs could do anything Americans could."

Both the Moffit and Jackson diaries concur that another game was played on January 3, between the Americans and the Filipinos. Jackson records the score as 21–19 for the Americans. Moffit adds the detail that there was a very good sermon being preached by Chaplain Dawson at the time, with the ballgame going on to one side of him and the bustle of a kitchen on the other side.

With these two diaries agreeing so closely on the events it cannot be doubted that there was a brief period at Davao where ballgames were common enough to merit only passing references among the more pressing issues of food and work. On the whole the winter of 1942–43 seems to have been an easy time for the POWs, certainly better than any comparable period at any of the other Philippine camps. The frequent rest days, the recognition of Western holidays, the seemingly decent diet, and the participation of the Japanese in athletics and entertainment along with their captives are all quite remarkable.

Unfortunately the good times were not to last. The American contingent at Davao was there to provide agricultural labor, and when the planting season started in earnest they were worked hard indeed. Also, the climate at Davao was especially unhealthy, and the suffering from malaria in particular was intense. Finally, there was a rare successful escape from the penal colony, with the two escapees linking up with the local guerrillas and eventually reaching Australia with some of the first reliable accounts of the horrors of O'Donnell and Cabanatuan. Nobody was actually shot in retaliation for the escape, but the regimen became much more oppressive, and the rosy view of Japanese attitudes mentioned in the Moffit diary soon had cause to be changed.

As a cruel bit of historical irony, the prisoners at Davao, who experienced relatively lenient treatment under the Japanese, actually were rather less likely to have survived their captivity. In 1944 the camp was disbanded; some of the prisoners were sent to a nearby island to perform particularly grueling labor building an airstrip, while others were shipped back to Manila. This late in the war the Japanese transports both between islands and on the longer haul to Japan were being sunk with great regularity, and many of the Davao prisoners died in this fashion.

17

The Philippines, Part II: The Work Details

When the Japanese found themselves with an unexpectedly large number of American POWs on their hands after the fall of the Philippines they had to decide what to do with all of them. Being a rather pragmatic people they concluded that the best thing to do would be to put them to work. This was in keeping with the Bushido concept that these dishonorable prisoners surrendered not just themselves, but all right to direct their destiny. So why not get at least some work out of them, since in furthering the progress of the Greater Asian Co-Prosperity Sphere there lay at least some minimal virtue.

Work details were organized as soon as the fighting ended. Some prisoners even stayed on at Corregidor and on the Bataan battlegrounds to help clean up the mess and recover munitions for their new masters. Other details were drafted out of O'Donnell and later out of Cabanatuan.

Treatment on these details varied enormously. On some details the POW was considered no better than a shovel or some other piece of equipment, a thing to be used roughly and disposed of when it broke under the strain. On others the Japanese concept of loyalty to employees was stretched to loosely include the POW workers, as a sort of very junior employee to whom firmness must be shown, but in the context of benevolent paternalism. There was no predicting just how an individual detail might turn out, but distance from the main prison camps, proximity to pilferable food items, and the personality of the individual Japanese boss, or *honcho*, were all factors.

On a few of the better work details there was the occasional chance to play baseball or softball. This was a more common event on work details than in the main POW camps. Of course, it would be a mistake to assume that most of the work details were anything like the favored few on which there was a chance to play ball. These are the exceptions, the rare occasions where the Japanese and their captives interacted on something akin to a normal, human level. Flickers of light in a dark and disturbing world, they show how the Pacific war could have been, but not in general how it really was.

Manila Port Detail

Ray LeClaire Makepeace lived a roustabout life in the prewar years. After graduating from DeLaSalle High School in Minneapolis in 1932 he tried out for a job with a Northern League team in Duluth, Minnesota. Failing to make the cut he joined the Civilian Conservation Corps, spending two years in northern Minnesota logging camps. Eventually he got an offer from a low-level St. Louis Cardinals farm club and made his professional debut in 1935 with Union City, Tennessee, in the Class D Kitty League. But his pitching arm went sore. He continued in amateur ball as a player and manager, along the way attempting a comeback with a Nebraska League team in Sioux Falls, South Dakota.

Just prior to the Second World War he was working in a defense plant when he saw an ad looking for men to join the U.S. Army and serve in the Philippines. It seemed an appealing notion, so he signed up. He actually had a couple of offers for assignment to noncombat units at stateside bases where Army ball teams were always looking for fresh talent. But he turned them down and insisted on going to the Philippines. He got his way, and arrived in "The P.I." in April 1941.

His posting was to the 60th Coast Artillery based on Corregidor island. After the Japanese sneak attack on the Philippines things were fairly quiet at Corregidor for a while, but following the surrender of the Bataan garrison the island came under continuous bombardment and had to eventually be surrendered in early May 1942.

Through plain dumb luck Makepeace ended up on one of the best work details to be found anywhere under the Japanese flag. Avoiding a couple of drafts of men being sent off to Cabanatuan he got temporary duty repairing boats in Manila harbor and then was assigned to the Manila Port Detail. This group of 400 men was made up mostly of naval personnel and was housed in buildings adjacent to the docks. Their duties consisted of loading and unloading ships, with cargo ranging from food to munitions to horses. It was prized duty for a simple reason — there was food to be stolen.

The Japanese knew that the prisoners were stealing food, but did not work consistently to prevent the practice. Indeed, a few years later when Japanese POWs were doing similar work for their American captors they practiced thievery on a wide scale themselves. A somewhat dimmer view was taken of the concurrent practices of damaging military cargoes and of simply dumping stuff into Manila Bay when the opportunity presented itself. The one cardinal sin was stealing any of the personal possessions of the Japanese. That was a death sentence anywhere under Japanese control.

The work was long and hard, but the combination of fresh air, sufficient food, and physical exercise had the men physically fit, if often tired. But occasionally there was a *yasume*, or rest day. This particularly occurred when a ship containing a moisture-sensitive cargo such as cement was docked. Even a little moisture would ruin the cargo, so work was postponed if there was any rain. When indoor duties were not provided the men sometimes had a chance to play softball.

Makepeace recalls that the games were played on an empty lot next to their quarters, which were in the Port Terminal Building. It was a dreadful patch of ground, being composed of silt dredged from the bottom of the harbor: "coral, seashells, and crud." The POWs referred to it as Yasume Park.

For purposes of work assignment the men were divided up into sections alphabetically A–D, E–L, and so forth. When at rest the men would form teams based on their work sections, and some spirited games were played. The equipment was a mixture of improvised and acquired, and the uniforms were the loincloths they wore in their daily work. They played barefoot, barehanded, and more or less bare all over in the tropical heat. The quality of play was pretty good under the circumstances. There were several athletes of some skill, including a couple of boxers who had held national ratings not long before.

Makepeace participated in one other baseball-related event during his captivity. He had volunteered for a hitch working in the Japanese galley. This was actually not such a great job as there was some sort of caustic substance in the ashes from the cooking fires that played havoc on bare feet, so few POWs could work there longer than a week despite the obvious advantages of working in such close proximity to the all-important food. Taking a break from his duties he stepped out of the kitchen door. Outside there was a group of Japanese soldiers playing baseball. An errant ball rolled to his feet.

Makepeace recalls that the ball used by the Japanese was different than our familiar baseball, with a more rubbery surface and with seams raised a bit higher. A guard who spoke some English came to retrieve the ball.

Makepeace was asked if he knew Ted Williams. He said he did. He was asked if he knew Babe Ruth. He said he knew him too. The soldier smiled broadly and said, "Fuck Babe Ruth!" In the general levity of the moment Makepeace prolonged his *yasume* break a bit and tried to teach a couple of the Japanese how to throw a curve ball. He was rewarded with a couple of cigarettes before he went back to work.[1]

In July 1944 the port detail was closed down, no doubt in part because the activity of American submarines and aircraft was taking such a toll that few ships were arriving safely at Manila at all. Jammed into one of the infamous hell ships, Makepeace and his comrades were shipped to Japan, where they spent the last year of the war mining lead under brutal conditions of deprivation and malnutrition.

FORT STOTSTENBURG

In a way it was baseball that got Tony Czerwein in trouble in the first place. In August 1940 he was playing for a local Chicago team called the Lawndale Boosters. In one particularly tough game against an archrival he found himself at the plate with a runner on third and two out. With the sign on for a steal of home, Czerwein had instructions to take the pitch. But he just could not lay off a tempting knuckler. Ignoring his coach's instructions he took a cut at it and lofted a fly ball to deep center field, where the outfielder hauled it in with a circus catch. Czerwein took the loss and his role in it very hard and the next day walked into an Army recruiting office and signed up. It seems that the formalities did not take long, and that same day he was on a train heading for basic training with just the clothes on his back. Czerwein was assigned to the Army Air Corps and shipped to the Philippines, arriving on December 5, 1940.

Czerwein was a mechanic in a fighter squadron, helping to maintain an ever-dwindling group of planes after the Japanese attacks began. When the last of the fighters was shot down, the ground crews were issued rifles and formed into provisional infantry brigades. These minimally trained units soldiered on as best they could, finally going into captivity with the rest of the Bataan garrison.

After surviving the Bataan Death March and a couple of weeks in Camp O'Donnell, Czerwein volunteered to be part of a 150-member work detail. Reasoning that anything would be better than O'Donnell the detachment was surprised to find itself transported in early May 1942 to a former American base, Fort Stotstenburg.

Stotstenburg was a former cavalry base and headquarters unit. One of the older American installations in the Philippines, it contained many barracks and a variety of older brick buildings, including a large hospital. There was also a prewar baseball field on the grounds. The work detachment was quartered in six wooden barracks surrounded by barbed wire. The treatment was pretty good by Japanese standards; at least there were three meals a day, if of poor quality. The work was not especially demanding, mostly cutting wood, clearing grass from the runways of nearby Clark Field, and general salvage and scavenging duty in the cluttered base complex. This work detail had some experiences uncommon to prisoners of the Japanese. As Czerwein tells it:

> In the early years when the Japs were more victorious, they tried to show some soft-heartedness towards us. Our troops previously at Clark Field had created a baseball diamond which was still in place when the Japanese took over. They challenged us to form a team and to play a hardball game against them. We accepted their smirking bluff. Little did they know that a surprise was in store for them.
>
> In my prewar days I was a semiprofessional baseball pitcher and could throw a hardball at a speed of 90 miles per hour and my battery mate, Bud Helms, was a minor league catcher. I had been starved for over two years, now weighing only 110 pounds, it would be fortunate if I could just pitch. Bud and I agreed to use our American moxie. I would pitch mainly a hinky-dinky round-house curve and knuckle-ball. This way I could preserve my strength.
>
> There was sufficient baseball equipment at the athletic house in Clark Field for both of us. The Japs were the fielding team, but they could not hit a barn if they had been on top of it. The game lasted seven innings and we stuffed a 3–1 defeat down their throats.[2]

Czerwein relates other stories, such as a Japanese-sponsored track meet where a former decathlon runner named Woody Hutchinson won all seven events for a purse of 21 packs of cigarettes. He also claims to have gotten out of several days of work detail by scavenging a couple of golf clubs from somewhere on the base and engaging the camp commander in impromptu rounds on an improvised course. After apparently spending two years at Stotstenburg Czerwein was shipped to Japan, where he ended the war working in a lead mine.

This story of POW-versus-guard play at Stotstenburg has a convincing ring to it, but corroboration from other sources has not turned up. There was a POW compound at Clark Field a bit later than the May 1942 date that Czerwein gives for his arrival. But POWs at that camp were unaware of any POWs being stationed at Stotstenburg, which was about three miles away. These two groups could not have been working on the air strip at the same time without being aware of each other, although perhaps the Stotstenburg group was no longer sent there once the work camp at the field proper was established. Prewar photographs do show the numerous brick buildings that Czerwein describes, as well as the baseball diamond. When contacted some years after publishing his book Czerwein, then living in a Veterans Administration long-term care unit, stood by the account, although he recalled that the score had actually been 4–3 in favor of the prisoners.

Fort William McKinley

Information on ball playing at this location is sketchy. One former POW who was held there from October 28, 1942, to December of that year recalls that some of the prisoners formed a team and played against the Japanese. He was of the opinion that this was before formal work assignments for the POWs had been established. He himself was not in good enough shape to play. Other than the fact that there was a prewar baseball field available at this site no additional information has surfaced.

Calauan Bridge Detail

While the prisoners working on the Manila Port Detail and those at Fort Stotstenburg clearly enjoyed better-than-average conditions, there was another work detail that unexpectedly labored under even better conditions. This group of about 150 men was drafted out of O'Donnell. Some of them literally got up and left the special ward reserved for dying men, reasoning that anything was better than lingering in that miserable place. Most were members of the 192nd and 194th Tank Battalions. These men were selected in part because of some supposed mechanical ability and in part because most of them were in slightly better physical condition. They had served under a resourceful commander, and generally having fought as a rear guard they had suffered less of the starvation endured by troops trapped in the Bataan peninsula.

These men under a Lieutenant Colonel Wickord were transported to the town of Calauan, some 40 miles southeast of Manila. They were housed in the *cabildo*, or town hall, supplied with old U.S. Army blankets, and served regular rations three times a day. The town doctor was allowed to help the prisoners and even to suggest the addition of citrus fruits to the diet to help treat the scurvy many had acquired.

This work detail was under the command of a group of Japanese Army engineers, under the command of a Captain Wakamori. This officer was a graduate of an elite Japanese university, spoke excellent English, and issued orders that the prisoners were not to be abused. Even such rules as did exist were gradually relaxed. Although no contact between Filipinos and American POWs was supposed to occur the engineers would look the other way so long as some minimal face-saving tricks were allowed. For instance a cart loaded with pineapples could be driven over the bridge they were working on and the pony whipped at just the right moment so that part of the cargo would tumble out. With grins all around the guards would motion to the Americans to dig in. Later direct gifts of food were allowed, so long as the gifts were offered to the Japanese. With protocol satisfied the engineers would then share the food with their captive workers.

The relationship between the engineers and the POWs actually seems to have evolved beyond this mere exchange of decencies into a sort of friendship. Captain Wakamori would sometimes make a courtesy call on Colonel Wickord in the evening or suggest that some of the Americans might like to take a walk around town with him. On occasion the captain, something of a music lover, might ask the prisoners to sing to him.

Near the end of May 1942, the mayor of Calauan paid a call on Captain Wakamori. He explained that the town was planning a fiesta in honor of its patron saint, San Isidro. Would the captain, perhaps, be interested in attending? Both parties seemed to understand that this was a stratagem to give some additional aid to the Americans, so the invitation was accepted, with the provision that he be allowed to bring some of the POWs with him. A rest day was declared, and a fortunate group of prisoners attended mass in the old Spanish church of Calauan. After the service they went and sat in a nearby schoolyard, talking with the Japanese engineers as local townspeople served them a light lunch. Later, as participant Bernard Fitzpatrick remembers:

> The Japanese soldiers and some of the more healthy Americans played softball. Captain Wakamori played one inning with each team. He pitched for the American team, and one of his fast throws hit the batter, one of his own men. He walked directly to the man and bowed in apology, before the Filipino umpire sent him to first base. At the end of seven innings the mayor called the game to a halt. I can't remember who won. We cheered both sides.[3]

After that followed the main meal of the day. Given the opportunity to eat as much as they wanted the prisoners gorged themselves. It is unlikely that they thought too much of their previous starvation diet at O'Donnell as they packed away the roast suckling pig, roast chicken, fried rice, and fresh fruits.

Later this work detail traveled to a smaller town called Candelaria, where the prisoners were quartered in an old copra warehouse. Conditions here were not quite so idyllic, food was less plentiful, and both prisoners and Japanese fell ill with malaria in some numbers. Fortunately help arrived in the person of Dr. Marfori from Calauan, who actually traveled to Candelaria to check up on the prisoners and was able to arrange the delivery of some additional foodstuffs. Also it seems that the idea of holding a feast day was shared with the townsfolk of Candelaria. But it did not turn out well. As Fitzpatrick tells it:

> There was a fiesta in honor of the town's patron saint. But the presence of Colonel Kamia, down from Manila on an inspection tour gave an edge of military restraint to the joyousness usual at a Filipino fiesta. A baseball game was interrupted by Colonel Kamia's arrival. Everything came to a halt while the fawning interpreter Suzuki rushed up to bring him a chair. The game resumed, but suddenly Kamia gestured and said a word to one of his staff, and all the American war prisoners were ordered off the field. Horyo were unworthy to compete with the Japanese imperial soldiers. Filipinos, prisoners, and engineers stood frozen for a moment, and then the few American prisoners who had felt strong enough to play walked off the field. The game went on for one more inning. Then Captain Wakamori, stiff and embarrassed, announced that it was time to eat. Kamia sat in his chair and glowered at us."[4]

After a few more weeks of work the prisoners on the bridge detail were returned to the camps. They showed up at the gates of Cabanatuan with their kit bags full of food, but they were sealed with the *chit*, or seal of authority of the engineers, so they were passed through the gates unsearched.

Quite clearly the story of the Calauan bridge detail represents the most benevolent treatment of prisoners anywhere under Japanese control. Some former prisoners who had a much harder time of it doubt its details. But there is at least confirmation from other sources that a Colonel Wickord did take a work detail out of O'Donnell at the appropriate time. By some accounts Wickord was one of the few officers from the tank battalions who was actively disliked by the men, who felt that he was far too accommodating to the Japanese and always on the lookout for his own best interests.

Helpfully, a second member of the detail, Ken Porwoll, has recorded his memories of these events. He also described the lenient treatment by the engineer officers, the fairly open supplying of food by the Filipinos, the assistance of the town doctor, and the attendance of the POWs at the feast. His brief memoirs do not mention the baseball games, but when contacted he recalled that the game at Calauan did occur, that Wakamori did pitch for the American side, but that it only lasted three innings.[5]

18

The Philippines, Part III:
Civilian Internments

As a latecomer to the game of colonial acquisition the United States had fewer citizens and business interests in harm's way during the Second World War than some other nations. So the only place where American civilians were captured on a wholesale basis turned out to be the Philippines.

The Philippines were a Spanish colony until 1898. After that point the country existed in a sort of pseudocolonial status under American control. During the roughly 40 years under the Stars and Stripes a substantial community of expatriates developed. Some were old soldiers, who stayed on after the Spanish-American War. Others were business executives, with interests in mining, shipping, rubber plantations, and sundry other pursuits. Still others were members of various religious orders, both established Catholic and newly arriving Protestant. At the outbreak of war no small number were people on the move from elsewhere, fleeing China and other threatened areas for the presumed safety of Manila. With an agreeable climate, no major native unrest, and available, cheap domestic help, the Philippines were considered a good place to have a family, so a significant percentage of the civilian internees were children. This differs a great deal from the internees in Germany, virtually all of whom were adults.

Civilian internees under the Japanese lived a life that was Spartan by the standards of their prewar existence, but was downright luxurious compared to the miserable lot of the military POWs. At times the lines between these groups were blurry. For instance a group of Army and Navy nurses, clearly military officers, were held in the civilian internment centers. And those courageous civilian men of military age who took up arms to help defend the Philippines went straight into the military prison camps.

The civilian internment centers of the Philippines occupation were generally schools. Although they did have a tendency to become crowded the accommodations were usually substantial buildings that provided decent shelter from the elements. If sanitation sometimes became problematic with large numbers of internees, there was always at least a supply of clean drinking water to help stave off the dysentery that was the defining feature of the military prison camps. Most of the civilian centers had sufficient doctors and nurses, and medical supplies arrived in quantities that allowed something like modern medicine to be practiced. Food was a constant concern, but at least for the largest of the internment centers, Santo Tomas, proximity to the sympathetic population of Manila and a Japanese administration that was more disinterested than malicious allowed crucial supplies to enter the camp.

Being on school grounds there were generally athletic fields available, and sometimes even a store of athletic equipment. Baseball, or more commonly softball was played at all of the internment centers, and provided a much-appreciated diversion from the drudgery of prolonged captivity.

Each of the internment centers has its own history, but the story of the largest, Santo Tomas, is the best documented, and the experiences there largely reflect the general experience of being a civilian captive under Japanese rule.

SANTO TOMAS INTERNMENT CENTER

Santo Tomas University was established in 1611, making it the oldest university in Asia. Located in Manila the campus in 1941 was made up of buildings of newer vintage spread over a 60-acre campus. Under peacetime conditions it had a student body of 6,000. The appeal of the facility as an internment center was enhanced by the eight-foot-high concrete wall that surrounded the campus on three sides. Within these walls were a massive main building, a gymnasium, dormitories, classroom buildings, a Dominican seminary, and considerable open spaces, some of which were quickly converted into athletic fields. This became the Santo Tomas Internment Center, sometimes abbreviated as STIC.

By January 1942 the roundup of enemy nationals in Manila had filled Santo Tomas with upwards of 3,000 people. The demographics of the foreign community were such that about one quarter were children under 16, and another quarter men and women over 60. A roster of internees compiled about this time lists 2,339 Americans, 875 British, 27 Dutch, 36 Poles, and an assortment of others to make a tally of 3,290. About 40 percent were female.

Perhaps reflecting the strong presence of the business community, the internees quickly assembled a highly organized government, with committees for almost any conceivable function, including medical services, sanitation and health, work assignment, education, and recreation. There was even a Discipline Committee, whose job it was to enforce rules put into place by internee and Japanese authorities. Some of the latter were peculiar, for instance, the Japanese forbade any public show of affection among the internees— even those married to each other. Men and women lived separately, and although births did occur at Santo Tomas the official policy was to discourage any conjugal intimacy, regardless of marital status. Offenders of various rules could suffer the indignity of being placed in a jail run by the internees, in essence imprisonment of those already inside a prison.

The Recreation Committee was active from an early date. A mimeographed "Basball Program and Schedule" printed inside the internment camp gives the following history of the early days of ball at Santo Tomas:

> Softball was our first organized outdoor sport. A number of regular Manila B.I. [before internment] teams formed the nucleus of a league, to which were added several new teams. Games were played in the morning, then double headers and finally the interest became so great that two leagues were formed. The Senior Loop became the twilight league, and the new organization became the morning league.
>
> Interest in baseball grew by leaps and bounds, doctors challenged Central Committees, rooms challenged rooms, and buildings challenged buildings, until the deluge came and players and playing fields were all washed up.
>
> Late in August a census of those interested in playing ball was made and it was decided to form one eight-team league. A committee on baseball was drawn up, which chose the players for eight teams. Much thought and consideration was given to the selection of the players so that the teams would be as well balanced as possible.
>
> The Committee gives you the STIC National League composed of 8 teams, each named after one of the National League teams, and each capable of just as much baseball talent and clowning as their namesakes. The Committee hopes that although this may be slightly slower baseball, that it will be more interesting and better balanced than the previous baseball set up.[1]

Cover of "Baseball Program and Schedule," Santo Tomas Internment Center, Manila, Philippines, 1943. Mary Alice Foley Collection, William L. Clements Library, University of Michigan.

The first phase of softball at Santo Tomas is documented in great detail in the pages of *Internews*, an internee-run paper. It came out three times a week, and was produced in quantities sufficient for each roomful of internees to receive two copies. Like the *Bad Nauheim Pudding* it was well run with a staff that featured professional newsmen. Editions of the *Internews* from January 1942 to early summer were taken out when a group of internees was repatriated on the liner *Gripsholm* in an exchange for Japanese diplomatic personnel.

Internee softball was already up and running in January, while fierce fighting was still going on in Bataan. The teams probably were based on pre-internment squads, with the Polo Club fielding two teams, Pan American Airlines mustering an entry, along with a team of uncertain origins known as Nomads. A team designated Shanghai and made up of refugees from that city was another early squad, along with a team referred to as Independents, or Indies. Even in January the schedule called for play seven days a week.

League play at Santo Tomas was characterized by numerous, short rounds of play, some lasting only four to six weeks. By the end of January 1942 the first round had already ended with Polo Club One and Nomads sharing top honors. A second round began immediately, with two new entries: Youngsters and Nineteen. The latter designation probably referred to a room number where some of the players were housed, rather than the age of the players.

There was a recurring problem in the early days of ball at Santo Tomas. Some teams were just better than others. The Nomads and Independents tended to dominate successive rounds of play, while lowly entries like the Youngsters and Nineteen would play a round or two and disband after achieving a dismal record. Eventually the "major" softball circuit condensed down to a five-team field, with a single Polo, Pan American Airlines, Nomads, Indies, and a generally cellar-dwelling Shanghai. Lesser clubs presumably dropped down into a seldom-mentioned afternoon league, with the Youngsters finding a more congenial home along with the Clippers, Limeys, Fog Cutters, Ringers, Outlaws, and Nosox. An April edition of *Internews* stated that 168 players were active in softball leagues, which existed alongside programs for football, basketball, volleyball, and soccer. Boxing was also an active sport, with "smokers" being held with some frequency and lessons being given to children down to the age of five by a former professional.

It was not long before special games began to sprout alongside regular league play. In an intentionally taunting article from the *Internews* of February 14, 1942, one such game is announced:

EXECUTIVE COMMITTEE TO BRAVE BASEBALL WRATH OF GARBAGE MEN

The muscled mighties of the garbage department will hold an indignation meeting on the baseball diamond Sunday at 2, with 10 alleged ballplayers from the executive committee as incidental guests. A large and unappreciative audience is expected to witness the athletic unveiling of the brain trusters.

Earl Carroll will duck at short stop. A. F. Duggleby will hear complaints at rover. A. E. Holland was demoted to starting pitcher, after a long committee meeting. Other prospective victims: Bob Cecil, c, Hank Sperry, 1b, Meade Raleigh, 2b, Frank Groves, 3b, Hal Hertz, lf, V. H. Masefield, cf, Clyde A. DeWitt, rf.

Chuck Bratton will name his excess lunch department team just before the slaughter.[2]

The garbage men ultimately went on to victory just as predicted, on the top side of an 18–3 score.

The same article also announced a proposed game to be undertaken by a team of medical personnel, the Carver's Unit. They were supposed to meet an unnamed opponent "in an attempt to better their previous record, when they lost to several hangers-on, 15–32."

League play was also going on at this time, with a proposal that the winner of the second round play the winner of the first round for the Internee Cup, an award that appeared to be an old tin can if a contemporary cartoon is an accurate rendering. League play still suffered from serious mismatches; one Polo Club–Youngsters game was canceled by "elephantitis of the score."

One of the better written features in *Internews* was a column by an anonymous writer entitled "Behind the Sawali by Golly." (Sawali was a material made of woven bamboo and palm fronds, which served to fashion makeshift walls in the shanties put up by many internees.) The February 17, 1942, "Sawali" gives a lengthy dissertation on sports fandom that gives some feel for the place of athletic competitions during a tedious confinement:

> The camp sports program has settled into the groove; every man is either an athlete or a heckler. The sports are varied and diversified, and the razzing is surprisingly uniform. In fact some people would be shocked to learn the extent of the boos allowed in this teetotaler's paradise.
>
> Hecklers work on a farm system, like the St. Louis Cardinals. Rookies try out with the bridge and cribbage circuit. If they make enough people mad in the minors, they are moved to girls' basketball, a very tough assignment because girl athletes can out scream any number of fans, two to one.
>
> A picked chorus of 100 voices can be heard any morning at the baseball diamond. These are the topnotchers, the men who can

make you laugh or cry, simply by twisting a tonsil. They do a surprisingly thorough job, considering the total absence of pop bottles. Actually, it's good to hear from Brooklyn again.

It's good to know that another form of heckling has disap-
peared, now that the distribution of jobs has been dignified with
red tape. No more does the head garbage chaperon circulate choice
remarks about those who, fleet of foot or mouth, manage to escape
to the diamond. He's out there first. Justice wins the first round!

The last paragraph seems to make reference to an occasionally sur-
facing complaint on the part of the Executive Committee, that playing and
watching softball sometimes interfered with assigned work. All able-bodied men were expected to put in two hours a day on work necessary to the
running of the camp, including sometimes unpleasant tasks such as remov-
ing an old landfill to make arable land for internee vegetable gardens.

Ball diamonds were maintained despite some unusual difficulties.
Early in the internment the baseball diamond had to be relocated when
the original site was lost to an expansion of the barbed-wire fence that
enclosed the one open side of the campus. Routine maintenance was carried out by the occasional appeal for able-bodied volunteers to work on
repairing the field, efforts later coordinated by Ed Powers, who served as
grounds chief.

Various other special games seem to have come along with some regularity. There were challenges put out by a Polo Club all-star team to take
on any challengers. The men living in Room 37 offered to take on any
"room baseball team." A game was played between the "shorties" and the
"elongated all-stars." This contest between those under five foot seven and
those over six foot resulted in a narrow victory for the "behemoths." A
game between bachelors and married men was proposed, but the outcome
is not recorded.

There was also a special game between Stew Raab's Leftovers and
Wally King's All Stars. King and Raab were neighbors, living in a shanty
community conveniently near an isolated stretch of the north wall. This
proved useful in their various business enterprises, which included smuggling prohibited liquor and importing construction materials for building
shanties. They also ran a high-stakes poker emporium.[3]

Not all athletic activity at Santo Tomas was organized. An announcement also appears designating an open field time for anybody interested
in playing pick-up games.

As spring waned the level of softball activity declined. The pages
of the *Internews* carry much discussion of weather proofing the camp for
the coming monsoon season. This along with the intolerable heat of

midsummer seems to have reduced ball playing to pick-up status for a number of months. Statistics published in May do list the leading players, with Joe Yette leading the league at a .489 clip. One hopes that the fact that Yette was also the chief statistician is only an innocent coincidence. Most of the better batters seem to have been from the Indie and Nomad teams.

Play continued at least into August, when the Nomads were described as winning a "rain-spattered softball pennant." Soccer teams were having their difficulties at the same time; the five-team league often played in ankle-deep mud.[4]

By September 1, 1942, the *Internews* announced the formation of an eight-team National League, which was supposed to start play by mid-month. The games were to be held daily at 5:30 P.M., except on soccer nights, when the games were held at 3 P.M.

With a reorganized league, ball returned to Santo Tomas. But there had been a few changes. Mindful of the dominance of a few teams, there had been a diligent effort to draft a group of evenly competitive squads. And, breaking with the pre-internment names that must have seemed less appropriate with the passage of time, the squads were named after National League teams. The first few weeks of play may have been informal practice for the new teams, as the Santo Tomas baseball program lists the first round of play running from December 5, 1942, to January 13, 1943, on which date a Fans All-Star Game was to be played. The baseball program preserved in the Mary Alice Foley collection also contains an all-star ballot and a scorecard to keep track of the results of league play. Appearing in the back pages of the program are a number of small advertisements, actually more a series of well wishes by fans of the various teams. Hometown loyalties are much in evidence:

> The Cubs are a cinch.— Ben Edwards
> The Room Team, Cincinatti [*sic*] Reds— Paul Howard
> The Dodgers, the Bums— A. D. Calhoun
> It looks like the Cincinnati Reds, because they shortened left
>   field.— Mr. and Mrs. John Brush
> In the Old Country the game is rounders, a girls game.— Joe
>   Benedict
> The Boston Braves are nearest my heart.— Alice Zwicker

This last salutation is a sign of another change at Santo Tomas. Alice Zwicker was one of a group of Army and Navy nurses imprisoned at Santo Tomas beginning in the summer of 1942. The largest contingent, 54 Army nurses captured when Bataan and Corregidor fell, came in on July 2. Earlier groups from Manila and later arrivals from the outer islands brought the number of female POWs, virtually the first in American military history, to 99. By all accounts they were a spirited group. After laboring under combat conditions at improvised jungle field hospitals, or deep underground in the embattled fortress of Corregidor, to the nurses, Santo Tomas at first seemed like a great improvement in their life. As to why these Army and Navy officers were held in a civilian camp rather than a military one, it appears that female military officers were a concept so alien to the Japanese that they simply did not know what to do with them. So they did the easiest thing, which was to put them where the other American women were held.

Alongside the official National League at Santo Tomas there was a women's softball league. Four teams made up the field: Manila Ladies, Bureau of Education, Hospital Kitchen, and STIC Nurses. Although the nurses' team had some talented players, including one whose brother had played in the minor leagues and had taught her much, the best team was from the Education Department, whose teenaged players dominated the game. Women showed up elsewhere in the Santo Tomas baseball world. Katy Roberts is recorded as being not only the girls' coach, but also the chief umpire.

Boys' and girls' teams were also fielded, with several of each in existence. One former Santo Tomas internee who was in his early teens at the time recalls that for his age things were a bit informal; players just showed up at the field and teams were picked from those on hand.[5] Other accounts have children's athletics a bit more organized, with formal leagues for softball at various ages, touch football, basketball, soccer, and even an Olympics.

Some memoirs of life at Santo Tomas suggest that the participation of guards in softball games was not uncommon. Anthony Arthur recalled that during one such game an American youngster named Mark Todd went deep into the outfield in pursuit of a fly ball. Not watching where he was going he ran headlong into a pole and was knocked out. In an unusual show of concern, the Japanese soldier coaching third base went to aid him, cradling the unconscious boy's head in his lap.

Christmas 1942 was a cheery occasion at Santo Tomas. The women's and men's choruses had a joint Christmas program, Christmas music was played over the loudspeaker system, Red Cross parcels were distributed, and there were handmade toys for the children. There was a game of soccer featuring the English against the Scots in a civilized version of their ancient conflict. There was an American-style football game between the Green Bay Packers and the Chicago Bears. Taking advantage of the fine tropical climate there was a softball game between the Pittsburgh Pirates and the Philadelphia Phillies. On Christmas Day itself there was roast chicken, cake, and ice cream, treats that the digestive systems of the internees had difficulties handling after having become unaccustomed to such things.

The Japanese authorities interfered little with the life of the Santo Tomas internees during the first year and a half of imprisonment. But this was to change. In the spring of 1943 the Japanese announced plans to move some of the internees to a remote internment center to be opened at Los Banos. There was much suspicion with respect to Japanese motivations, especially as the transferees were mostly to be the younger, more able-bodied men of the community. Protests were to no avail, and the first batch of 800 internees left for Los Banos on May 14. The day before their departure there was a ballgame played between those who were leaving and those who were staying. It is doubtful that the "home" Santo Tomas team enjoyed its 2–1 win very much.

After the departure of the Los Banos group the feel of the Santo Tomas community changed. So many of its more energetic members were now absent. Of course the numbers did not stay down for long, as 819 new internees were shipped in from other locations to fill the empty spots. But it was not the same: 325 were men over 50, and 198 were children under five. The loss of so many of the athletic, younger men had a major impact on baseball at Santo Tomas. Of course, games were still played. One of the newly arrived internees recalls a British-American series. But the intensity and quality of play that was so evident at Santo Tomas from January 1942 to May 1943 was gone forever.

The other major change at Santo Tomas did not happen until early 1944. The camp had previously been under civilian authority, but Japanese reverses in the field had brought the war close to the Philippines. So Santo Tomas was taken over by military authorities, who imposed a harsher brand of discipline, and severely curtailed the vital flow of food and medicine from the citizens of Manila. Soon hunger and disease were a part of the daily life of the internees. Against this grim backdrop one of the last chapters in the history of baseball at Santo Tomas would be comically played out.

On April 25, 1944, a new military commander of the Santo Tomas Internment Center arrived. He was called Colonel Yoshie, but he sometimes claimed that his name was too long and difficult for the internees to pronounce, and preferred that they refer to him as "uncle." Yoshie let it be known that he was a lover of sports, especially baseball.

On the emperor's birthday, the colonel ordered that a baseball game be played the next day, April 30. It was promised that the director-general of prison camps would be there as the commandant's guest. A couple of all-star teams were assembled and were warming up on the field. When it became evident that the director-general was not going to show up, Colonel Yoshie went onto the field and began pitching to one of the internees. His technique was not good, and he had to start out standing fairly close and gradually increase his range until he was at something like a normal pitching distance. To the amazement of the assembled internees the colonel then announced that the scheduled game would not be played, but that he would put together a team of Japanese to play an internee team. Various members of his staff and soldiers from the guard company were drafted for the Japanese squad, which featured Yoshie as captain and pitcher. An internee team was hastily assembled.

Accounts of the game can be found in several sources, but all agree that the colonel was pitching overhand, contrary to the general rules of play at Santo Tomas. Most also agree that his pitching was terrible. The Americans delicately attempted to avoid hitting his marshmallow tosses too hard or too often. When the ball was put into play the Japanese fielding was ragged. Internee Peter Wygle recalled:

> They looked great, but *man* did they stink as baseball players. The third baseman would boot a dribbling ground ball, then pick it up and throw it all the way over the spectators behind first base. The commandant would go storming over all bluish yellow in the face, throw his glove at the poor guy, stick his face up against his and yell at him at the top of his voice for about five minutes. Then he'd storm back to the pitcher's mound and start pitching overhand again. ... Our people were playing like a bunch of jelly-boned goons, trying not to beat the guards by more than about 459 to nothing, because they figured that would be akin to beating the boss at golf. No telling what the camp would be like after that."[6]

Not a young man, Yoshie went to the sidelines between innings and sat in a chair, complaining of the heat. He fanned himself and took off the boots he was wearing to play. Nevertheless, in true Bushido form he did complete the game, which the internees won by a prudent 5–3 score.

Apparently Yoshie managed to participate in another game a few days later, although he was still pretty sore from the first game. He is said to have distributed bananas to the players after this game. Some accounts also have him producing eggs from his sleeve like a conjurer.

Japanese behavior, especially when they were attempting to be friendly, was seldom understood by American prisoners. But one source claimed that Colonel Yoshie had been told by the commandant of Los

Banos that he would have no trouble with the Americans if he just "played ball with them," and he chose to interpret this colloquialism in a literal sense. Another somewhat less plausible version of this story has the commandant being told to "play ball with the prisoners and don't try anything underhanded."

Softball continued to be played at Santo Tomas after that point, without the uncomfortable presence of the Japanese commandant. But hunger, increased Japanese security measures, and anxiety regarding their fate when the Allied attack finally came reduced everyone's energy and interest in leisure activities in general.

Santo Tomas was an early objective for American troops when General Douglas MacArthur finally did "return" in 1945. The camp was liberated and evacuated before the battle, which would level much of Manila, started in earnest.

Los Banos

This internment camp was established in 1943 on the grounds of an agricultural college. It was some 40 miles from Manila in a rich agricultural region. Originally this 60-acre campus contained some 15 concrete school buildings, five large dormitories, and many smaller cottages. Some of the buildings were damaged or destroyed in the Japanese conquest of the Philippines, so additional, flimsy barracks-style buildings had to be added when the number of internees grew.

The initial group of 800 transferred from Santo Tomas in May 1943 and set up housekeeping in a gymnasium, a YMCA building, and several cottages. Football and baseball fields were present on the campus, and the internees were initially allowed their use. Successive transfers from other internment centers eventually brought the total number of inmates to 2,144. Roughly three quarters were Americans, along with British, Dutch, Canadians, Australians, Poles, Norwegians, Italians (once their homeland switched sides), and a miscellany of others.

Conditions at Los Banos were always worse than at Santo Tomas. In part this was due to its isolation from Manila, and in part just to the fact that it was established later in the war. So only a few baseball stories have been recorded out of Los Banos.

On one occasion the camp commandant decided

> that the internees would play softball against a team made up of Japanese office staff. The committee, concerned about the welfare

of the internees, felt that the internees should play to lose; Ben Edwards, one of the players, disagreed and insisted that the team play to win. The players eventually won the argument and agreed to play the Japanese. Even though the game was played with a Japanese ball — the size of a baseball — the internees routed the Japanese through four innings. Thereupon, the Japanese commandant abruptly called the game. The Japanese never mentioned the game again nor suggested a rematch.[7]

One other memorable game occurred in the early days of confinement in Los Banos. Somehow a shipment of Red Cross parcels actually made it to the camp. The internees opened the packages with the greatest of expectations, but soon found that they had been shipped the wrong boxes; instead of clothing suitable for the tropics the boxes held long-sleeved underwear, long British style shorts, and least useful of all seersucker nightgowns. After the initial shock and disappointment wore off the internees decided to make the best of things. In what must have been the most bizarre ballgame ever played in captivity the prisoners organized themselves into two softball teams. One dressed in long underwear, shirts, and ties, the other in long shorts, shirts, and ties. The girls of the camp dressed up in the seersucker nightgowns and led cheers. The umpire wore a top hat and tails that were obtained someplace. After somehow managing to play a serious game for about three innings the players started to ignore the rules, among other things pitching overhand. General laughter overcame the players and spectators and put an end to the game. The Japanese thought their charges were insane, and their opinion is understandable.

Life at Los Banos took a nasty turn in 1944 when a set of particularly brutal Japanese guards took over. Deaths from disease, starvation, and even the occasional execution became the norm. The camp was liberated in February 1945 by the descent — as if from the heavens — of American paratroopers.

BAGUIO

Near the city of Baguio there were two civilian internment centers. Camp John Hay, a small military post, served as a temporary internment center in the first four months of the Japanese occupation. Conditions were crowded, but not harsh. One internee described the following scene on the tennis courts, which seem to have been the only recreational area: "Two Japanese soldiers are playing baseball with the Americans on the court. When they miss three times they roar with laughter. It is all very fraternal."[8] In April 1942 the Americans were moved to a somewhat larger camp, Camp Holmes.

Holmes was also a small internment center, housing only about 500, mostly American citizens. A description compiled in December 1943 for an organization called Relief for Americans in the Philippines describes the camp as being in the old constabulary barracks. Six doctors and one dentist were on hand, and there was an: "excellent school under the supervision of a large faculty from the Bront School also interned there." There were "several baseball teams and games held nearly every afternoon for exercise and the entertainment of the internees."

Contemporary sketches of the camp show a baseball diamond in a prominent location. The few diary entries published from this camp suggest that the game had a youthful flavor, with the youngsters of the community being the main players. Records indicate that the camp was about 27 percent children under 18, with 64 boys and 73 girls. A woman interned there describes the coming of age of her teenaged daughter in these terms: "...blooming, full of pep, gaining, eat anything. Yells her head off at baseball and plays it violently. She is dating two different [boys]."[9] Given the apparent shortage of young men this speaks well indeed for her spirit.

Conditions at Camp Holmes got worse as the war went on, but were never as harsh as at places like Los Banos. Even in the midsummer of 1944 the men of the camp were given a day off from work to celebrate the Fourth of July, with the festivities including among other events a ballgame. This was probably just about the last ball played by any Americans in the Philippines, as Japanese authorities soon had the islands on a war footing, with short rations and shorter tempers. Unlike the liberation of Santo Tomas and Los Banos, the transfer of the internees to American control in February 1945 was without incident.

BACLODOD

War was slower coming to the outlying islands of the Philippines archipelago. It was June 7, 1942, before the Japanese showed up on the island of Negros to round up the Americans there. When they did arrive they imprisoned the Americans and other enemy civilians at Baclodod North Elementary School. The usual segregation of internees by gender was carried out, and the facilities were hardly comfortable ones, but otherwise things were not too bad.

Baclodod had some unusual features even as measured by the peculiar standards of the ad hoc communities that were forced together by the conquering Japanese. The commandant of the facility was a local man of Japanese descent named Yasamori, who had worked as a laborer on an American-owned sugar plantation. The naming of a man of such low station in life to lord it over the fallen Westerners was no accident, nor was the assignment of his former employer to the task of cleaning his office everyday. Such gestures aside, the internees at Baclodod had some remarkable freedoms. Early in their captivity they were given permission to retain the firearms they brought with them into the camp, so as to guard food supplies when on authorized foraging missions. On one occasion there was even a cinema night, featuring *Felix the Cat*, the Yale-Army football game, and a Laurel and Hardy silent movie among other features. Recreational activities included chess, bridge, poker, badminton, horseshoes, and baseball.

A former instructor from a Filipino boys school organized sporting activities. After calling for volunteers to make up some baseball nines he set out to have their first practice. Unfortunately the British and Dutch internees had no idea what they were doing, and attempted at times to round the bases clockwise, or to skip some bases altogether. This provided much merriment for the internee spectators who were variously seated on the grass, on a verandah, and on the roofs of the outdoor latrines. Apparently slow studies, some of the rookies continued to err when a real game was attempted.

An internee named Elizabeth Vaughn kept a diary of her experiences. In an entry for Monday August 3, 1942, she wrote:

> Full Sunday yesterday. 7:15 special mass for Catholics, 9:00 baseball game of six innings (fast and exciting playing). Several Britishers in game had never played before adding to confusion and joy of spectators, many of whom likewise knew nothing of game. One Dutch padre running from third base to home plate saw he could not make home before arrival of ball from field so returned to first base from which he had originally run to third. Could not understand why he was not allowed to return safely there (crossing field from third to first base). The seven padres here are much fun and well liked, as are the two sisters.[10]

The internee community at Baclodod reached just over 200 by late 1942. In the spring of 1943 they were moved to Santo Tomas as part of the consolidation of enemy nationals that began with the opening of the Los Banos Camp.

19

Shanghai

On the eve of war in the Pacific Shanghai was certainly the most cosmopolitan city in Asia, and perhaps on the entire planet. In addition to the native Chinese population there were large communities of stateless White Russians, who fled there after the revolution. There was another large group of more recent refugees: European Jews who crossed Russia, some with passports provided by obliging Japanese officials, in search of a haven from Hitler's racist politics. There were also enclaves of Westerners, the International Settlement, and the French Concession. These little islands of American, Italian, British, and French citizens existed in uneasy truce with each other and with the Japanese Army, which had conquered this area of China in the late 1930s.

It was a city of glamour and illusion. Nightclubs and casinos provided a glittering nightlife. The great British and American trading companies did business on favorable terms imposed on the Chinese after the Boxer Rebellion, and alongside them Chinese gangsters did a brisk trade in opium. The U.S. Fourth Marines kept order in the International Settlement, and kept the Japanese out. They were also there to "show the flag" for parades and other ceremonial functions in this last twilight of colonial rule. Within the Western communities all the functions of ordinary life went blissfully on.

By late 1941 the U.S. military was certain that war was imminent. The general feeling was that it would break out in China or the Philippines. To forestall an "incident" the decision was made to evacuate the Fourth Marines from Shanghai. This was accomplished just a few days before Pearl Harbor. It is bitterly ironic that the Marines would have been much better off staying where they were. They ended up helping to defend the Philippines and suffering all the torments of the soldiers captured there.

About 40 percent of them died. By comparison 96 percent of the military prisoners held at Shanghai survived the war.

Shanghai as the chief port city of southern China ended up as a collection point for prisoners taken by the Japanese over a wide area. The first prison camp of any size in the area was at Woosung. This 20-acre former Japanese Army base had seven barracks buildings surrounded by an electrified fence. In the first few months of 1942 some 1,500 Allied prisoners arrived. About 200 were the famous North China Marines, an elite group that guarded American embassies and consulates in Beijing and Tientsin. A few hundred more Marines were survivors of the fierce battle for Wake Island. Also from Wake were about 700 civilian construction workers who had been helping build defensive works on the island. The remainder of the captives were a mixed bag of Merchant Marine crews and a few British transferred after the fall of Hong Kong.

As prisons go, Woosung was not too bad. The Wake Island contingent arrived in frigid weather while clad in light tropical uniforms. By contrast the North China Marines had enjoyed a relaxed few weeks of their initial confinement, and when they were taken down to Shanghai they were allowed to bring full winter gear and a moderate amount of personal belongings. Still, the camp was built on mud flats, a swampy, unhealthy location, and the guards were often abusive.

The provost marshal report from July 31, 1941 on Woosung describes the recreation facilities as "satisfactory," and mentions that "the prisoners had softball teams and there was a softball diamond." This field may have been the most professionally laid out ball yard in the Far East. With a wealth of engineering talent on hand in the persons of the Wake Island construction crews they made a good job of it.

Approximately 800 to 900 men worked on the project. Surveying equipment was improvised. An even grade was defined, and crews of prisoners with *yo-ho* poles (three-by-eight woven mats on an eight-foot pole carried by two men) moved the dirt, filling drainage ditches and low spots. Sections of tree trunk were attached to handles so that two men at a time could tamp down the dirt. One marine recalls that they "worked several months on that job. Finally, in late summer, the face of that field was as level as the top of a pool table, and firmly packed. Once we were finished with that job, we moved onto another and never used the field for recreation, but then, we never expected to."[1] By several other accounts, however, ball was played at Woosung.

One great advantage experienced by the Shanghai prisoners was that the International Red Cross had regular access to the camp. Along with crucial supplemental food supplies, the organization sent in other items, including sports equipment. Along with softball the prisoners used the field for soccer and touch football.

There seems to be little surviving information on the structure of ball playing at Woosung. The prisoners were kept occupied on work details most of the time and could only play on rest days. Competition seems to have been by barracks. But in other sports there appear to have been games between contingents, such as North China versus Wake Islanders, and it seems likely that this was the case in softball as well.

In December 1942 the entire population of Woosung was transferred to a new camp at Kiangwan. This was built on higher ground, and in general was a better camp. The provost marshal's report mentions that "the prisoners spent their leisure time in improving the camp grounds by planting flower and vegetable gardens, and laying out a sports field."[2]

Less has been recorded about ball playing at Kiangwan, although it seems that there was a field large enough for baseball and other sports to go on simultaneously. One interesting document relating to play at Kiangwan is a letter written home by a Marine prisoner William Chittendon. Under a very attractive letterhead from "Shanghai War-Prisoner's Camp" the text reads in part, "We have a good softball field and a summer schedule will soon be under way with games being played each Sunday."[3]

Another letter from a civilian construction worker dates to September 1944. It relates, "One of the main sporting events is a series of baseball games (Big League Soft-Ball) between the civilians and the service groups, which I always watch. The standing in this series is 3–2 in favor of the service."[4] This would seem to imply that ballgames had become somewhat infrequent by that point in the war, if indeed only five games had been completed by that late date.

A hint of playing conditions at Kiangwan comes from a photo that appeared in the *Sporting News* on September 13, 1945. It is one of the few photographic records of POW ball in the Pacific, and shows a Japanese officer in full uniform conversing with two healthy-looking American officers. In the background can be seen an infield and backstop, with prisoners sitting on what appear to be bleachers. Under the headline "Yank War Prisoners at Ball Game," a paragraph reads:

> A MUTUAL INTEREST IN BASEBALL helped to alleviate the lot of some American prisoners of the Japanese, this picture indicates. An unidentified American colonel talks with the Jap commandant at a prison camp in Shanghai, China, before the start of a ballgame, according to the caption accompanying this photo distributed by the YMCA War Prisoners' Aid. The picture was received from the organization's Swedish representative. However, the YMCA said it

"had no means of judging whether the comparatively favorable conditions shown would be found in other camps," because conditions in Japanese camps varied widely.

The picture is undated and could have been taken at either Kiangwan or Woosung. Kiangwan would seem to be more probable. An International Red Cross inspection report from September 1944 mentions that a "good supply of sports equipment, donated by the YMCA" had been delivered by the Swedish minister in Tokyo, who had visited two months earlier. This would seem to tie in with the reported visit of a "Swedish representative." In any case, by the time this picture appeared in *Sporting News*, the Kiangwan camp had been almost completely evacuated by successive drafts of prisoners being taken to Japan.

The war years in Shanghai also saw civilian internment camps, but they developed in a fashion very different from that seen in the Philippines. There were simply too many potential enemies of Japanese rule to lock them all up. The White Russian and European Jewish communities together may have totaled close to 200,000. Quite a few of the Chinese citizens had no reason to love their new masters, and there were various groups, such as the French and Italians, who had ambiguous status. Despite warnings to evacuate there were still some 6,000 British and 1,000 American citizens in the city.

With so many potential internees the Japanese at first did the only reasonable thing: they left almost everybody at liberty. After a time they did impose a curfew and required the wearing of identifying armbands. Finally in November 1942 the gradual process of rounding up Westerners began, with the opening of the first internment center on the grounds of the former Marine headquarters building.

Among the largest internment centers was that at Pootung, across the river from Shanghai. Here an old British-American Tobacco Company warehouse was used to lock up some 1,100 American, British, and Dutch men. The buildings were substantial but run-down, surrounded by a high concrete wall topped by barbed wire.

During the winter of 1942–43 there were few recreational opportunities for the prisoners beyond walking around and around the interior of the building. Off to the north there was a wasteland of several acres of rubble, the ruins of a village demolished by bombing in the Japanese conquest of 1937. One morning in May 1943 the Japanese guards were seen to be fencing in the area with barbed wire. By afternoon a gate had been opened into the area and a sign put up that read "Happy Garden." The commandant even announced over the loudspeaker system that, at the request of several inmates, this area was being provided for recreation. He wished them much pleasure in the Happy Garden.

With considerable effort the prisoners cleared away the debris and built a ball diamond as the first improvement to the property. A ball was made from fabric scraps, and bats whittled from boards. Soon ballgames were being played with enthusiasm, even by some internees who had previously wallowed in apathetic sorrow. A tennis court and areas for cricket and soccer were also set up, which along with garden plots for vegetables made the entire area a center for the internee community — and a place not undeserving of its name.

Later in the war several other internment centers were opened, and ball was no doubt played at some of them. The camp at Chapei, on a former college campus, had a large American presence and seems a likely site for ball play, but there have been surprisingly few accounts of life in these camps.

20

Mukden

The camps near Mukden (since renamed Sheng-yang shih) in Manchuria, or northern China, were unusual in the Japanese system. They existed to provide labor to a complex of factories, and therefore the POWs were treated with some consideration of their value as laborers in the Japanese war effort.

The main factory was the Manchurian Machine Tool Company, an aircraft component plant that had been designed by American engineers and completed in 1940. Attitudes toward Americans were relatively benevolent among the factory managers, and they were sometimes able to arrange humane working conditions and extra food rations. Of course, their influence did not extend into the actual prison camps to which the men returned each night.

The first draft of men destined for Mukden left Manila in October 1942. Many came out of Cabanatuan No. 3 and were former defenders of Corregidor. Some 2,000 made the trip in the soon-to-be-commonplace crowded cargo holds of Japanese ships, with the constant threat of torpedo attack. After a contingent was off-loaded in Japan there were about 1,200 Americans who arrived in Mukden around November 11. Most were sick, malnourished, and just plain cold in their tropical uniforms. They were soon joined by a small contingent of British troops, whose senior officer was the charmingly articulate Major Robert Peaty.

Penned in a temporary enclosure with the chill Manchurian winter descending upon them there was not much to do except huddle and wait. The diet was inadequate, with a blue-tinged cornmeal mush as a staple. Work duties in the factory were welcome, as there was at least some heat there. Men, especially those who had endured the additional suffering of Bataan and Camp O'Donnell, died in large numbers.

But eventually spring came. Prisoners went to work clearing an athletic field between the officers' barracks and a storage shed. After much brick and rubble had been moved there was a fairly good playing surface. As Major Peaty recalled many years later:

> When the thaw came after the winter deep freeze — down to −34C — we began to revive and, as the Manchurian sun began to warm up, so did we. It wasn't long before those who had sporting inclinations got things going. The Americans produced some baseball equipment and the British and Australians produced some cricket gear. We started to teach each other these national games and it amused me greatly to see the American baseball players throw down the bat each time they scored a run in a game of cricket, and how our chaps would run around the baseball diamond hanging on to the bat.[1]

As the summer of 1943 progressed so did construction on a new camp adjacent to the factory complex. A move was imminent when three Americans, two Marines and a Navy man, made the only escape attempt from Mukden. They had been stockpiling food for months and no doubt realized that they would never be able to sneak it along when the camp moved house. According to a fellow Marine named Willis Johnson the plan was to strike out northward until they reached a river that they felt would take them into Soviet territory. There they were planning on building a raft. Johnson was supposed to join them in the attempt, but landed in the hospital at the time of the escape.

The plan failed. Somewhere they ran into a group of Chinese border police and were apprehended — by Japanese accounts after killing one of the policemen. The three were returned to Mukden, questioned, and eventually executed for "stealing." What they stole was not specified, but presumably it was the labor owed to their Japanese captors.

In July the prisoners were moved to the new camp, and work soon began on a new athletic field. But they were to be given little opportunity to use it, as the Japanese administration refused permission for most athletic activities as punishment for the escape attempt. Baseball was quite specifically banned, as the Japanese claimed that the escape attempt was planned at a baseball game. It may have been true since Johnson, one of the conspirators, was an avid player.

It should be mentioned that while most accounts of ball playing at Mukden refer to baseball the actual game played was with underhand pitching, using an improvised ball cobbled together out of boot parts. While there were some scant Red Cross supplies that reached Mukden through Russian sources, little of it was ever seen by the prisoners, and any athletic supplies they had were improvised.

Major Peaty kept a diary of his time at Mukden, and some of the entries cast a bit of light on the Mukden League:

> 22.7.43
> Special holiday "with amusements" for the benefit of the propaganda corps, who took photos and recordings of concert, baseball, and a memorial service held at the cemetery, organized by the Japanese camp staff.
>
> 29.7.43
> Move to new camp.
>
> 7.8.43
> Started leveling the yard to make parade-cum-sports ground.

According to the postwar provost marshal report on Mukden, this became "a fairly large sports field, one end was for baseball and the other end for volleyball and basketball."[2] Some former Mukden vets recall that the downfall of basketball occurred when the Japanese discovered that an inflatable basketball was being used to smuggle alcohol from the factory into the camp.

The Peaty diary continues into the late summer of 1943:

> 26.9.43
> First outdoor games permitted since the escape, when we had football and volleyball to-day. The Japanese have steadily refused permission, as they say that the escape was planned at a baseball game, but persistence seems to have gained our point.

A Red Cross delegate inspected the camp on November 13, 1943, and reported that outdoor activities included "baseball, association football and American football on full size sports grounds. On separate smaller grounds—volleyball and basketball." Of course, the Japanese were noted for dressing up camps just prior to the infrequent Red Cross inspections.

After enduring another dismal Manchurian winter, the POWs were finally given permission to play baseball in August 1944. There seem to have been eight teams participating in a round-robin tournament. Alas for the pride of America, a British team dominated league play. According to another British Mukdenite named Arthur Christie, the British team was captained by Lieutenant A. B. Griffen,

> a New Zealander who lived and breathed Cricket. Referring to all the positions on the diamond in Cricket terms, confusing to say

the least. He was our fifth column, for instance the catcher was the wicket keeper, first base was mid on, third base was square leg, the pitcher the bowler, the outfield and the other bases given their equivalent cricket terms.

The confusion amongst the Yanks, they hadn't a clue when instructions were shouted to the fielders. The Referee just could not understand when the cry went up, "How's that umpire" as a man was tagged on base.[3]

Games were already being played when Major Peaty made the following diary entry:

> 6.8.44
> Discharged from hospital. I have noticed that these air raid warnings have all been on cloudless days, and think photography may have been the object. Kit inspection. To-day was a notable day for the "Limeys," as we won our first baseball game in two years, … beating the U.S. Navy 5–3, which resulted in much good-humored chaff. Very hot, but so far we have not reached last year's peak of 106F.

Arthur Christie goes into a bit more detail about the "good-humored chaff":

> 6th August 44. We won the game, what a shaker for the Yanks 5 to 3, the Navy spirits must have been in Davy Jones' Locker. Afterwards in the barracks, the raging was unbelievable, especially from the Air Force our next we were to play. Bins were filled with water, boats were sunk, airmen were paddling away all over the place showing no commiseration to the Navy, they had been sunk by the Limeys, and were singing "down goes the fleet the Limeys sank you" or words to that effect. We had to wait a few weeks for the next match, the whole series was a sort of round robin. I was in hospital when this took place and only saw some of the fun, when the Limeys shot down the Airforce, we beat them too.

Peaty's diary entry for August 8 accurately reflects the priorities of the hungry captives: "4 oz. Ham and Eggs issued. We beat the American Officers' team at baseball 10–6. 65 men in hospital, the most since January. Nearly all with diarrhea."

The Limeys went on to beat a U.S. Marine team on September 8. According to Christie there was once again a fair amount of ribbing involved in the postgame festivities:

The Baseball-English-Cricket team had gone on in the series, to beat those Montezuma heroes the Marines. When this happened it was as if the American way of life or even the world had come to an end. Everyone singing the Marine Hymn, very dolefully with the following words. "From the hills of Montezuma, To the shores of Tripoli, the Marines were victorious, Till they met up with the Limeys."

The Brits went on to beat an Infantry team in a semifinal, then a British Officers' team beat the American Officers. This was intolerable, and there was talk of the Americans seeking revenge at rugby. But watching the ferocity with which the British practiced that game persuaded the American officers to leave well enough alone. Remarkably, the Limeys made it all the way to the finals of the baseball tournament. Supposedly even the Japanese camp staff came to watch. According to Peaty:

> 15.9.44
> We have had a great cleaning of barracks, and the Japanese graciously donated one tin of insect powder for the whole camp. "The Limeys" actually got into the final of the Baseball League, but we suffered a defeat at the hands of the U.S. 60th Coast Artillery, being beaten 10–3. Still, it was a good effort to reach the final in a game which we have only just learnt. The nights are getting cold; last night was the first three blanket night.

American veterans of Mukden have varied memories of softball at the camp. Many do not remember it at all, and some find the idea inconceivable. This is a case where all I can fairly do is report both sides of the argument and accept that the story will generate some controversy. This is not the only contentious point in the Mukden story. Much more seriously, there are also widely differing opinions on the subject of whether the Japanese carried out germ warfare tests on the prisoners.

Willis Johnson remembers that there was a six-team league. On one occasion as a game was just about to start a Japanese interpreter named Noda stopped play with no explanation. Somebody muttered a mild oath, and Noda heard it, but could not tell who had said it. He demanded to know who had spoken in this fashion in his presence, but nobody would admit to it. The equipment was confiscated, and the players, or perhaps the entire camp, were placed on half-rations. Finally after about a week an Army sergeant named Dumont Wade, who was among the organizers of the league, confessed to the deed to spare his comrades the continued punishment.

Johnson also recalls the hazards of playing with minimal equipment: one Navy chief was injured fairly severely when he was hit by a thrown bat.[4]

By late 1944 it was evident even to the fairly isolated POWs at Mukden that things were not going well for the Japanese. The appearance of Allied planes in the sky underscored this point. On December 7, 1944, in a fitting remembrance of Pearl Harbor, the Manchurian Machine Tool factory was bombed by American B-29s based in China. Unfortunately the Mukden camp was adjacent to the target, and the POWs, having one of their infrequent *yasume* rest days, were on the parade ground in large numbers. Several errant bombs landed among them, killing 19 and wounding 35. In the mad scramble the football goal posts were torn down to make improvised stretchers.

After the raid athletic activities were much reduced. Slit trenches were dug in the parade ground for protection from future raids, reducing the available space for play. Captives from other areas of the shrinking Japanese empire arrived to worsen crowding. But there still seems to have been play on a minimal scale. Arthur Christie, for instance, recalls that one of the Americans wounded in the bombing raid was a fellow named Baum Gardner of the 60th Coast Artillery. He lost a leg and had a piece of shrapnel hit him above the right ear and exit above the left eye. Funerals of the other men were delayed three days with the expectation he would also die. But he recovered and was said to have umpired a ballgame on crutches a few months later.

On August 17, 1945, a few American officers parachuted in plain sight of the camp and, with considerable chutzpah, convinced the Japanese that the war was over and that they should surrender the camp. At about this time the Russians declared war on Japan, and Russian troops arrived in the area a few days later. The Japanese were rounded up and either summarily shot or shipped to a captivity in Siberia from which many would not return.

Several higher-ranking American officers were transferred to Mukden late in the war. They were able to keep detailed diaries, and there are a few hints in those documents that indicate that the trenches in the athletic field were filled in, allowing it to be put back into service. But most of the liberated captives had other priorities at that point. There was food to be consumed, Japanese souvenirs to harvest, and a brewery in nearby Mukden with nobody particularly minding the stock.

In the Boondocks

The experience of the Americans taken in the Philippines tends to dominate accounts of the Pacific POW experience. But strictly on the basis of numbers this should not be so. Collectively British, Canadian, Australian, and Dutch troops were captured in greater numbers than Americans, but these accounts are not easily available to American readers. Their stories are sometimes in other languages, or at a minimum not widely circulated in this country.

To a certain extent the main direction of the Japanese advance in 1941 and early 1942 was not even directed at the Philippine islands. They just happened to be in the way. The real prizes were farther south, where Indonesia and Malaysia held rich amounts of rubber and oil. The Allied prisoners taken in this southward lunge were a mixed lot of nationalities, including some from baseball-playing nations.

The story of their war is not widely known, as defeats are always less heralded than victories. But they deserve credit for delaying the Japanese advance long enough for Allied forces to check it short of Australia. Many of them paid a high price and passed through the gates of prisons less noted than Cabanatuan and O'Donnell. The treatment they encountered there ranged from savage brutality to surprising leniency. On a few rare occasions when the treatment was not too harsh, they even had a chance to improvise a ballgame or two.

JAVA

Given the thousands of miles separating the European and Pacific theaters it was rather remarkable that a handful of Americans found themselves prisoners of *both* the Germans and Japanese. George Duffy was one such prisoner.

Duffy was a junior officer aboard the American merchant ship *SS American Leader* in September 1942. When it was some 850 miles west of Cape Town in the South Atlantic it came across another merchant ship. Or so the sailors thought. It proved to be the German auxiliary cruiser *Michael*, a merchant ship equipped with armaments and designed to masquerade as a harmless cargo vessel to lure its victims in close. After a brisk one-sided fight the *Michael* picked up the 47 surviving American merchant seamen. At this point in the war there was some degree of coordination between the German and Japanese navies, so after a few weeks the Americans were transferred to a German tanker on a supply run and taken east to Japanese-occupied Java. Describing his captivity many years later, Duffy recalled:

> After the German Navy turned me and my surviving crew members over to the Japanese on Java we were lodged in a camp near the docks. These buildings had been used by native dock workers and their families and surrounded a large open area which was probably a soccer field. It became a sports field for us. Each barrack sponsored a soccer team and a regular league was set up with schedules and standings. Also, the Australians used the field for their "Australian Rules" games. Nearby was a smaller open area where basketball was played.
>
> So, we Americans decided to show our Allied friends how baseball was played. Somehow or other a bat and a ball were requisitioned and we put on pick-up games from time to time when the field was available. This went on for a few months until the camp was abandoned by the Japs and we were moved into the nearby city of Batavia.
>
> One other athletic event was the organized track meet held on either Christmas or Boxing Day of 1942. I made note of it in my journal and the fact that I won a bar of soap in the 440–yard dash.
>
> In none of these activities did the Japanese participate.
>
> Now another story comes to mind. In the second half of 1943 and the first six months of 1944 I was in a camp south of Batavia where we were employed in growing vegetables. We also cultivated a large area for the growing of castor oil beans. By this time an American Liberty ship captain had joined us. He came from 'way down Maine and had played some organized baseball in his youth. Even then (in '43 or '44) he had a great arm and would entertain us— and the Japs—out in the castor oil beans by finding baseball-sized stones and simulating a throw from center field to home plate.

Then one day, someone pointed out to the Japs that many Americans could throw baseballs in the same manner, but now they were throwing hand grenades! The Japs had a straight-armed hand grenade throwing motion that had a range of 90 feet and the lesson was not lost on them. No more rock throwing.[1]

George Duffy ended up being part of a working party on Sumatra that was detailed to build a railway across the island. British intelligence officers parachuted into Sumatra at the end of the war and liberated what were by then walking skeletons. Nineteen men of the 47 who survived the wreck of the *American Leader* died in captivity, half of them drowning when their unmarked transport was torpedoed by an Allied submarine. Duffy survived the war and went on to a long career as a Merchant Marine captain.

The stone-throwing ship captain was a fellow named Owen H. Reed, who had been captain of a Liberty ship sunk by a German U-boat off Durban, South Africa. Reed died in the sinking of a Japanese transport in which 1,600 Allied prisoners and some 4,300 Javanese labor conscripts perished. Details of Reed's baseball career have not come to light at this time.

MAKASSAR

At the onset of the Pacific war the United States did have a small fleet in Far Eastern waters. This Asiatic Fleet was stationed in the Philippines, where their bases were early targets of Japanese bombing raids. Thus left without supply and repair facilities the Asiatic Fleet was forced to withdraw southward, where most of it was sunk in a series of running battles with Japanese forces invading Indonesia.

Several American ships went down near the Indonesian island of Celebes. One of these was the destroyer *USS Pope*. A Japanese warship picked up the surviving crew members, and they were treated quite well on board. Perhaps there was some sense of sympathy for fellow mariners, or perhaps in the Bushido world view bedraggled men clinging to floating wreckage were considered to have done about all that could be expected for their president.

American, British, and Dutch troops, both European and native, were confined in a compound near the city of Makassar. There was sufficient food, the quarters were adequate, and the climate was mild. There were, however, some instances of Japanese cruelty, including guards beating prisoners with baseball bats, which suggested an idea to the POWs:

In addition to our occasional bits of excitement in the camp, we had long periods of monotony, varied only by the fact that we read different books. The enlisted men, who felt the monotony more than the officers did, suggested getting baseball equipment from the Japanese, reasoning that if baseball bats were available for beatings, there might be some available for baseball.

After several tries we were able to get bats and leather with which to make a baseball. Because no gloves were to be had, it was decided that a softball should be made. Before long a team from the *Pope* and a team from the *Perch* [a scuttled American submarine] took the field, with Fisher and Haines as the opposing pitchers.

I have never determined who enjoyed the baseball games more, the Americans or the British. Whenever the Americans had a game, the British would line the fence of the athletic field to listen to the "chatter" of the players. To the British this was the main attraction, for they did not understand the game played on the field. (Nationality dictated the game played on the field. The Dutch and British usually played soccer, and the British occasionally played cricket."[2]

MALAYA

British and Commonwealth troops defending the Malay peninsula and the city of Singapore did not put up an especially commendable fight. Far from fighting with the suicidal bravery that characterized Japanese soldiers, Allied forces numbering by some estimates over 100,000 were roundly defeated and forced to surrender to a Japanese invasion force of about half that size. Some 80,000 prisoners were taken in what Winston Churchill called the worst defeat in the history of British arms. The fall of Singapore was a severe blow to Allied confidence and appears to have even surprised the Japanese.

One of the defenders of Singapore was a young Australian artillery man named Russell Braddon. When news of Pearl Harbor actually broke he and his mates had been detailed to go "upcountry" to the city of Malacca to play the Army Service Corps in rugby. Either the British forewarning of Japanese intentions was inadequate or the priorities of the officers commanding the Malayan garrison were dubious.

Captured in jungle fighting, Braddon was imprisoned at Kuala Lumpur, in a civilian lockup called Pudu Gaol. He had about 1,000 other British and Australian POWs, many of them wounded, to keep him company. Baseball as a sport has always enjoyed a measure of popularity in

Australia, especially as a college sport. So at Pudu there were a few prisoners with some familiarity with the sport. Using a small triangular patch of ground inside the walled compound the prisoners organized teams and played baseball. These games came to an "abrupt halt" when the prisoners defeated a team of their Japanese guards. Eventually Braddon ended up on one of the infamous railroad building crews, which took so many lives—and futilely so, as the rail lines so constructed proved to be of no military or economic importance.

A second account of the games at Pudu comes from another Australian, a fellow named Kenneth Harrison. He was a good friend of Braddon and considered Braddon's talents in the production of ribald musical shows to be of the highest order. Harrison recounts the usual stories of bad food, rampant disease, poorly treated wounds, and abusive guards. But he still found Pudu to be one of the better camps in which he spent time. The guards were frontline soldiers rather than the sorry specimens of Japanese, Korean, and Formosan soldiers who generally drew the inglorious duty of prison camp work. The camp regimen must not have been too strict: there were concerts held and Harrison was even allowed to put out a single issue of a camp newspaper called the *Pudu Presento* (*presento* being a pidgin word that means approximately "please give me" or "may I have that?"). As for ball playing Harrison tells the following tale of a baseball-cricket hybrid:

> As another concession the Japanese allowed us to play baseball [with a soft ball] in the big prison quadrangle on the afternoon of each yasume day. This soon developed into an organized competition with teams representing the English, the Welsh, the Scots, and the Australians, all taking part. For several yasume days, the bored Japanese guards on duty watched with obvious interest and then asked if they could field a team. We could hardly refuse and so the I.J.A. entered the competition. The Japanese showed a natural affinity for the game, and, being much better fed and healthier than we, were very worthy opponents. Despite our initial misgivings, all seemed to be going smoothly until their national obsession with "face" brought disaster.
>
> Leadership lay clearly between the Japanese and the Australians, and we played them one hot afternoon in September 1942. I was catching for the Australian team and we noticed that the second Japanese batter was heckled all the way to the plate by the other guards. From what we could gather, he claimed to be a star player in Nippon and much *sake* had tempted him into a great deal of boasting about his prowess. Rod McLeod hurled down the first ball, our little friend swung mightily, there was a loud and distinct

snick, the ball stuck in my fingers, and under Pudu rules our Nippon warrior was out.

The other guards were almost helpless with laughter and several had tears streaming down their cheeks. This was just too much for our little friend who, with many threatening growls of "Kurra" and swishes of the bat at me (for catching him), refused to heed the umpire. Finally, like a petulant little boy, he went to the guardhouse where he locked himself in one of the toilets and sat on our only bat. An appeal was made to the guard commander in an effort to regain it and the final result was that, from then on, all baseball was banned at Pudu.

This also ended a rather unique example of the Japanese fraternizing with POWS.

But these diversions were interludes only, and all the time we were playing baseball and arranging concerts, the "happy feet" men* were wearily walking the corridors, and sick men were dying. And if the Japanese despised us for being prisoners, they were at least consistent, for they had proved over and over again that they would rather die than surrender.[3]

SINGAPORE

Most of the British and Australian troops captured at the fall of Singapore were confined in and around Changi Prison. The prison proper was a large Western-style penitentiary designed by American engineers who used Sing Sing as a model. When the Japanese took over Singapore in February 1942 they first used the prison for civilian internees and put the military prisoners into a large compound surrounding the prison. Warehouses, barracks, and other structures were pressed into service. Later the civilians were moved to a camp on Sime Road, and the prison structure was opened to hold some 10,000 POWS. The number of prisoners was so large that by necessity the Japanese allowed them to largely govern themselves.

The camp at Changi may seem familiar to readers of the James Clavell novel *King Rat*. Clavell was an ex-POW, and had spent time at Changi. But he merely used the camp as a backdrop, a setting for a work of fiction. In reality conditions at the camp were significantly better than those depicted in the novel. Rations were delivered, and there was decent sanitation, electricity, and clean drinking water. Work details were generally not too

*Many of the prisoners had beri-beri, a vitamin deficiency that caused a very painful, burning sensation in the feet due to nerve damage.

arduous and afforded opportunities to scavenge food and to trade with guards and natives. Prisoners who had experience at several camps tended to describe Changi as a "low-budget holiday camp" or even as "POW heaven"! Of the 87,000 prisoners who passed through the camp only 850 died, and many of those succumbed to wounds suffered in the battle for Singapore rather than from ill treatment.

Sports at Changi tended to reflect the makeup of the place, which was mostly British with a strong Australian presence and a smattering of Americans. There was boxing, cricket, and basketball, with the latter sport involving the occasional competition between British and American teams or even between the British and a team made up of Korean guards. Baseball was played on occasion, but documentation is sketchy. The basketball games concluded in February 1945, and a British POW involved commented in his account that this was the last organized athletics at the camp, football and baseball having been previously banned by the Japanese.

One of the few definitive mentions of baseball comes from a July 1942 newsletter published in the civilian portion of the complex, and the reference is probably about activity in the civilian compound: "DID YOU KNOW? That some enthusiasts have actually begun baseball in the Camp? They may be seen in the main yard of an afternoon with a stick whittled down from a thick branch and a tennis ball, pitching, hitting, throwing and catching. One of the boys, incidentally, sports a Yankee gob's headgear."[4]

ON THE BANKS OF THE RIVER KWAI

Most of the prisoners working on the so-called Death Railway through Burma were British and Australians, many captured when Singapore fell. But there were a few Americans as well, including Kyle Thompson. Thompson had joined the Texas National Guard in 1938, at the tender age of 16. His unit was called to active duty in November 1940 and eventually was designated the 2nd Battalion of the 131st Field Artillery Regiment. This unit, which would become known as the "Lost Battalion," was shipped to Australia soon after the outbreak of war, and was shortly detailed to Java to help defend that Dutch possession from an anticipated Japanese invasion. They did not have long to wait. The Lost Battalion acquitted itself well in the early fighting, providing artillery support to the Australian infantry that engaged the enemy. But after a few days of conflict the soldiers were told to lay down their arms, as the Dutch governor had surrendered the entire island.

After a stay in a former Dutch Army base, which became known as the Bicycle Camp, the prisoners were shipped to Singapore. After a brief sojourn at Changi they were sent upcountry to Thanbyuzayat, a base camp for the construction of the Burma Railroad on the banks of the River Kwai. (There was no actual "bridge on the River Kwai," despite the name of the famous film. The railroad ran along one bank. After the war obliging locals "found" a bridge to satisfy the tourists.)

The year 1943 was spent in back-breaking labor in disease-ridden jungles. A series of temporary encampments were laid out in places so far removed from human habitation that they had no proper landmarks and could be defined only in relationship to the focus of their miserable existance, the railroad. Most of these wretched places, like 80 Kilo Camp and 114 Kilo Camp, needed no fences or actual guarding. There was simply no place to which one could escape. Of the original 500 Americans on the work detail, 133 perished. Eventually the railroad was completed. But as if to make the sacrifices of the prisoners even more futile it never carried any useful traffic, being all too easy for Allied air raids and guerrilla raids to disrupt. After the war the rails were torn up and sold as scrap.

Once their work was done the prisoners were returned to Thanbyuzayat. Some were sent to other details but others, including about 100 Americans, stayed at the base camp. Like tools for which no work could be found they just sat there, seemingly forgotten for a while by the Japanese.

Remarkably, conditions at the camp improved, although to men who had survived the Death Railroad almost anything would be regarded as several steps up in the world. There was a functioning hospital, and a theater was built where Broadway-style shows were put on. In his account of captivity Thompson recalls:

> On the Emperor's birthday, in the early months of 1944, the Japanese declared a holiday and gave us extra rations. Following what would have been an unimaginably sumptuous lunch back in the jungle, our captors decided to challenge the American POWs to a baseball game. Our group was somewhat reluctant to get involved, but when the Japanese issued a challenge, acceptance was automatic — to refuse would have brought their wrath down on our heads.
>
> After laying out the diamond, the Japanese sergeant asked, "Who umpire?" Nobody moved a muscle. Again, in a sterner voice, the sergeant asked, "Who umpire?" Still no response. It was obvious he would soon lose his cool, so I reluctantly moved up a couple of steps and "volunteered" to serve as umpire.

My legs were wobbly and my disbelieving brain shouted, What are you doing here dummy! as I stepped behind home plate. The game was fairly routine for an inning or two; then, as a Japanese guard stepped up to the plate, our pitcher appeared to have gotten a second wind and began hurling the ball with impressive speed and accuracy. The Jap swung and missed, then hit a foul for his second strike. I held my breath as the third ball whizzed toward the plate. The guard just stood there, and I weakly hissed, "Strike three!" This fellow, who literally had the power of life or death over me, whirled and began gesticulating wildly and jabbering away in Japanese. His brown face became a darker brown as he bulldozed me backward with his chest. I thought I had had it, but fortunately, the Japanese sergeant intervened. I have no idea what he told the guard but he must have said that when the ump calls a batter out, he's out. I don't remember who won, or even when the game ended. I did determine, however, that this would be the end of my umpiring career.[5]

Hong Kong

In addition to the unfortunate Canadians at North Point Camp there were at least two other collections of Western prisoners in Japanese-occupied Hong Kong. British military prisoners along with some Canadians were held at a camp called Shamsuipo, on the site of a former British barracks. It was a bad camp. It is a wonder that there was a sports program at all after the sports officer, Flight Lieutenant "Dolly" Gray, was taken into town one day to buy athletic equipment, but was instead beheaded for his supposed knowledge of a secret radio. Nevertheless, volleyball, softball, and cricket were played at the camp.

One of the guards at Shamsuipo was a Canadian citizen of Japanese descent nicknamed the "Kamloops Kid" because of his hailing from the British Columbia town of Kamloops on the Canadian west coast. It seems that he experienced a great deal of racially motivated discrimination as he grew up, including taunts, insults, and beatings. He developed a raging hatred of all things Canadian and of all white men. Having been sent back to Japan in the prewar years to continue his education he eagerly enlisted in the Japanese Army as a way to wreak his vengeance. The Kamloops Kid spoke perfect English, with the accent and vernacular of western Canada. He was the most cruel and sadistic of all the guards, administering ruthless beatings for the slightest offense. And yet, he still on some level identified with the Canadians and at times seemed to be making a sincere attempt to befriend them, to fit into their society in a way that he had been unable to as a child.

One day the Kid came upon two prisoners playing catch with a baseball. He demanded that he be included. The prisoner and the guard tossed the ball back and forth, easily at first, then harder and harder, as if the intent had become to challenge or even injure each other. Finally the Canadian POW threw a looping curve ball, which struck the Kid square in the face. Enraged, the Kamloops Kid beat the prisoner severely.

Kamloops figured prominently in another baseball story from Shamsuipo, in which the familiar practice of dressing up a camp for an inspection visit backfired on the Japanese:

> It was one of the strangest days of our prison life. Truckloads of shiny new sports equipment came zooming into camp one morning. Baseball gloves, bats, balls, boxing gloves, sports togs. Ration trucks arrived with meat and other exotic food supplies. Crews set up a baseball diamond on the parade square. We were ordered to clean up, shave, organize teams, sports squads. The Agony Ward was cordoned off with barbed wire to look as though it was outside the camp.
>
> The mystery was soon solved. That afternoon a party of Red Cross officials arrived to inspect the camp — our first living contact with the outside world. We were full of cautious optimism. At least we were not forgotten! Apparently stories of this "hellhole of the Pacific" had finally gotten out. Tokyo had bowed to international pressure.
>
> Emaciated prisoners donned boxing gloves that felt too heavy to lift and were ordered to swing them at each other under threat of severe reprisal. Baseball players, their bony shapes swathed in bright new jerseys and shorts, were set in motion hitting and chasing a ball. Volleyball teams seemed to be having a fun day at a holiday resort as the party passed. The inspecting party was accompanied by our officers, who were warned by Kamloops to keep their mouths shut. He would do all the talking, thank you, and God help anyone who dared utter a false note. Good health, happy games, jolly sports, general contentment all around. A heartwarming picture to take back to the outside world and silence all the malicious calumnies circulated to give Japan a bad name. Shame on those nitpickers.[6]

As the inspection came to a close a courageous Captain Norris edged his way close to the inspector and blurted out the news that all that they had seen had been a fake and that a hospital full of dying men was to be found just on the other side of the barbed wire. The Kamloops Kid was furious and denied it all. But the Swiss inspector would not be deterred and insisted on seeing the Agony Ward. A tour of its grim confines revealed skeletal men who lay in their own diarrhea and stared back at the inspection party with maddened eyes. The inspector was livid and left the camp promising a complete report to the International Committee and a formal protest to the Japanese government. Almost immediately the sports equipment and rations were packed and trucked away. For his courage Captain Norris was singled out at roll call the next day and beaten nearly to death.

Some of the more thoughtful Canadians regarded the Kamloops Kid with a measure of something that came close to sympathy. They recognized that the bitterness that he harbored came in part from the racism of their culture, and they recognized that he was caught in between, unwelcome and uncomfortable in both Canadian and Japanese cultures. But they never forgave him for his brutality.

Far too many Japanese involved in the atrocities of the camps escaped judgment. But the Kamloops Kid was a Canadian citizen, and victors are seldom merciful to turncoats. After the war the Kid was tried, convicted, and hung for his crimes.

The Shamsuipo camp itself lives on after a fashion. In recent years it has become an internment center for Vietnamese refugees.

STANLEY PRISON

When the Japanese took over Hong Kong there were still 5,000 or so Western civilians who had been unable or unwilling to leave in the months preceding hostilities. The largest group, some 2,500, was British although there were also 300 Americans. The Japanese set out in their customary fashion to publicly humiliate them in the eyes of the native populace, first boarding them in several large brothel/hotels, then parading them through the streets on the way to their place of captivity. This was to be the grounds of Stanley Prison.

The prison complex was built on a narrow peninsula, allowing the place to be made secure by the erection of a small section of barbed-wire fence. The area so enclosed was about 50 acres and included the prison, housing for the prison staff, and a large school called St. Stephen's College. The actual prison was off limits to the internees. This internment center had no fewer than three recreation fields, although two were pragmatically converted to vegetable gardens. Softball was played there as was soccer. In what I think to be the earliest published account of baseball under Japanese captivity, Gwen Priestwood wrote:

> To keep in physical shape, although they were weak from malnutrition, some of the police cadets and young Hong Kong socialites used to play a mild sort of softball. One afternoon they were playing when three or four Japanese officers came up, watched the game for a few minutes, and then indicated that they wanted to play, too. The white men didn't care much for this, but they submitted gracefully. A Jap went to bat.
>
> He lifted the ball high, and a young English girl who was playing managed to catch it. "Out!" she sang triumphantly. The Jap stayed in there, grinning. Other players ran over to him yelling: "You're out-out-out!" The Jap shook his head. There was another chorus of "Out!"
>
> The officer collected his wits. "Not out, no," he said in broken English. "Singapore broken — not out."
>
> He swung his bat again. There was nothing to do but humor him. Most of the afternoon was spent pitching to him and catching his drives. Every time, all the white folks would yell "Out!" and the Jap would grow angrier and angrier and retort, "No, not out. Singapore broken!"
>
> We gave up after a while. No one could win against that sort of oriental logic.[7]

Although interesting because of its early date, the Priestwood account has a few difficulties. In her foreword Gwen Priestwood admitted that she was omitting or changing some details to protect those who were still imprisoned at that time. Even her nationality was not stated, although the implication was that she was American. If there were a Mr. Priestwood, we are told nothing of him or of his fate.

The largest section of the book deals with her escape from Stanley. It is a stirring tale, with a plucky upper-class lady cleverly hiding her jewelry, then exchanging it for currency and assistance for her and her fellow escapee. Eventually they link up with friendly guerrillas and make it to Allied territory, where she is feted at dinners at the British and American embassies. It is all a bit too Hollywood.

The account also grates on modern sensibilities. The distinction between "white folks" and "Japs" is only a milder form of the racist rant current at the time, which depicted all Japanese as buck-toothed, myopic, evil little monkeys. Propagandizing hacks who turned out the stuff would have had no difficulty producing Nazi *untermensch* drivel for a different employer.

To be fair, the Priestwood escape is mentioned in other accounts from Stanley. In one of them she is described as a "very pretty English girl." If her escape was perhaps a bit less heroic than she makes it out to be it was still a rare feat. As to her tale of "Hong Kong socialites" playing ball, it has the sort of goofy surreal quality that happens more often in real life than in poorly written propaganda. I cannot help but wonder if the "young English girl" mentioned might not have been Gwen Priestwood herself.

22

Shantung Compound

At the beginning of the Pacific war there was a substantial Western community in North China. In addition to the diplomatic corps there were business interests drawn by the favorable trade conditions imposed on China in the previous century; there were missionaries of all stripes, drawn by the prospect of converting some of the vast sea of humanity that inhabited the place; and there were diverse men and women in all walks of life united only by their citizenship in one or another of the Western nations that now found themselves at war with Japan.

For the military, represented mostly by a small contingent of American Marines, captivity came immediately. The diplomatic personnel were rounded up soon thereafter, and exchanged with their Japanese counterparts in accordance with accepted protocol. But for the Western civilians in places like Peking, Tsingtao, and Tientsien the future was uncertain. The Japanese were not eager to feed and house them, so they were simply placed under house arrest under the watchful eyes of Japanese security forces.

That changed in February 1943, when orders came for all Western civilians to report for transportation to an internment facility. The facility turned out to be Shantung Compound, three miles from the Chinese city of Weihsien.

The civilians, some 2,000 in total, were marched under a gateway lettered with Chinese characters that read "Courtyard of the Happy Way." They found themselves crammed into a former Presbyterian mission compound, which measured only 250 yards by 150 yards, little more than the size of a large city block. A six-foot wall surrounded the compound, which contained a church, a hospital, school buildings, and numerous small shacks closely packed together where once lived students boarding at the school. And there was a ball field.

It was onto the ball field that each new group of arriving internees was led to listen to the standard speech from the Japanese commander extolling the virtues of Japanese rule and warning of the dreaded penalties for any infraction of the rules. A speech along these lines appears to have been inflicted on all prisoners of the Japanese at all camps under their control for the entire duration of the war.

The initial population of the camp was made up of some 800 British, 600 Americans, 250 Dutch, and 250 Belgians, these last two groups being mostly Roman Catholic clerics. There were also a few Cubans from a touring jai alai team caught in China by Pearl Harbor, some Palestinian Jews, an Indian translator, a "Negro and Hawaiian jazz band," and a contingent of White Russian women, spouses of British and American men. There were also merchants, evangelists, teachers, tourists, adventurers, and those on the run from miscellaneous political, legal, or personal complications.

With commendable dispatch the internees turned the camp, which had been abandoned and badly looted, into a home. Willing if not always capable hands were turned to cooking, plumbing, laundry, and the many other tasks for which this privileged caste had previously relied on native labor.

The chief chronicler of life at Shantung was a young American teacher named Langdon Gilkey, who had been employed as an English teacher at Yenching, a privately owned Anglo-American university near Peking. He relates with pride the accomplishments of those first few months, which soon allowed time for a few diversions. Lectures and theological discussions were organized. Theatrical and musical performances were put on in the church. And "the culmination of these early forms of 'culture' came, surely, when a baseball league (e.g., the Peking Panthers vs. the Tiensin [sic] Tigers) started in earnest on the small ball field, exciting the whole population two or three afternoons a week."[1]

The baseball league was a center of community life. Cut off as the internees were from outside communication, the performances and prospects of the various teams were major topics of discussion. In a camp where the gender ratio amazingly was about 50:50 the games became a popular social venue for the new couples that formed.

Gilkey's main focus in writing his story was not to catalog all the activities of the place, but rather to describe the workings of a community under stress yet allowed to find its own solutions. *Shantung Compound* is an excellent piece of work in this regard, easily in the front rank of captivity stories to come out of the Second World War. But Gilkey is rather lax in reporting useful information, such as number and names of teams, and he certainly is not going to give us box scores. But he does include a few scraps of information on the players and their game.

No doubt it was primarily softball despite persistent references to baseball. A map of the compound shows a small diamond with the compound wall forming the boundaries of the outfield. It appears to have been only 90 feet to each foul pole, with "deep" center field jutting out to about 150 feet, where a guard tower kept a watchful eye on the proceedings. They most certainly could not use a "live" ball in this park. How cooperative the guards were with retrieval missions is not recorded.

Of the players a few are mentioned. While listing the inhabitants of a typical dormitory Gilkey writes "And finally at the end of the row was an American, formerly of the 15th Infantry, a very tough and bitter character — though a very good softball player — and his rather sullen, slatternly but probably once sensual Russian wife." Also among the players was "Karl Bauer, tall, straight, strong and sour, an ex-marine and ex–pro baseball player. Karl was never known to smile; for him everything that happened was an irritant, and everyone hostile. As we came later to know, he was capable of generation with less reason, more unhappiness in himself and others than anyone I have encountered before or since."

The summer of 1943 seems to have been the golden season for ball playing at Shantung. For late August of that year 200 Americans were repatriated on the liner *Gripsholm*. Additional Americans left a short time later when most of the Roman Catholic priests and nuns were released. The 200 or so Americans left became a small minority as the camp population was filled out with additional British internees and, to the surprise of all concerned, with a contingent of Italians who suddenly found themselves enemies of Japan when their wavering homeland switched sides in the war. In a population to whom baseball was foreign the popularity of the league must have suffered.

The Shantung internees certainly should have had enough energy for recreation; it would be difficult to find any camp under Japanese control where the prisoners ate better or got along better with their guards. In addition to regular rations that were delivered daily from the surrounding agricultural lands there was a thriving black market.

This camp was under the jurisdiction of Japanese civilian authorities, specifically, a police force attached to the consular service. They generally left the internees alone to run their affairs and did not watch the walls too closely. Soon an active trade over the walls was carried out between local Chinese farmers and any internee sufficiently fluent in the local tongue and able to haggle over price. In this regard the Catholic priests stood out. One Trappist monk was given special dispensation by his bishop to suspend his vow of silence to aid in the transactions! At one point some 1,300 eggs were being smuggled over the wall *per day*, with equally large amounts of other foodstuffs. It is fortunate that the military POWs elsewhere in Japanese control could have had no way of knowing about this state of affairs.

Eventually the Trappist monk was caught black marketeering. After due deliberations the Japanese sentenced the cleric, used to long spells of silent contemplation, to a brief stay in the cooler. The Chinese farmers involved were lined up against the compound wall and shot.

One notable inmate of Shantung compound was Eric Liddell, a British runner whose refusal at the 1924 Olympics to compete on a Sunday became the basis for the movie *Chariots of Fire*. Described by Gilkey as "a living saint," Liddell was instrumental in organizing athletic events to keep the idle teenagers in the compound out of mischief. Although his interests seem to have understandably run more toward track, field hockey, and soccer, one former Shantung internee does recall Liddell teaching the youngsters "rounders." Tragically, Liddell died in February 1945, apparently of a brain tumor.

Life dragged on at Shantung throughout the war, with no diversions other than improvised athletics, theatricals, and musical entertainment. With no radio, news from the outside world was minimal. One day a plane flew over and seven American paratroopers dropped into a nearby field. In a scene that would have been considered hopelessly corny in a B-grade John Wayne movie, their leader, a tall major with pistols strapped to each hip, marched into the office of the Japanese commander and with guns leveled announced that the war was over and that he was there to take over the camp. An uneventful transfer of power was carried out.

Tall, muscular, and confident the paratroopers strode among the threadbare internees like gods. Prompt repatriation was promised. Small children and most of the single women in the camp trailed after them in an admiring retinue. Ten days later the paratroopers were relieved by a regular GI unit. The letdown was significant. These were ordinary Joes, their job to maintain order and keep the camp where it was, repatriation being impossible under the chaotic conditions in the surrounding countryside.

They did the best that they could, but the internees were in no mood to be forgiving. In particular a captain named Spofford was the object of their scorn. He was placed in charge of camp morale. His first move was to string up a powerful PA system, which blared popular music into all corners of the camp. The internees, used to peace and quiet or perhaps the music of their small camp orchestra, were most displeased.

At one point he made a speech promising to get "as soon as humanly possible" baseball bats and balls and to organize checkers tournaments and track meets. The tired internees were longing for home and were in no mood to listen to a bustling den mother. But one of Captain Spofford's ventures carried a risk greater than bored derision.

After the liberation of the camp an airlift began. Unable to deliver supplies by land the Army Air Corps resorted to packing supplies into improvised containers made by welding two 55-gallon oil drums together. Packed solid with tin cans these behemoths were attached to parachutes clearly marked MAXIMUM LOAD 350 POUNDS. They were then dropped in the general vicinity of prison camps.

At Shantung the initial drops were made in fields surrounding the camp, where a magically appearing horde of Chinese peasants would scramble out of nowhere to try to scavenge what they could. A slightly more cautious group of internees would venture out soon thereafter. There was enough to go around for all parties, even though many of the cans were flattened by their high-speed impact. There were several close calls, with containers plummeting down within feet of their petrified recipients.

One day the none-too-bright Captain Spofford arranged to have a children's party on the ball field. In a festive moment he decided to drape a bright yellow parachute over the backstop. The pilot of the B-29 making the supply run mistook this for a drop marker and let fly the load of supply drums directly on target. With mothers and children fleeing in panic the field and surrounding buildings were bombarded with potentially deadly missiles. Fortunately nobody was hurt, and Spofford entered the annals of military history as perhaps the only officer to ever order an air raid on a baseball field — and a friendly one at that.

Soon after that comic episode the camp was evacuated and the internees returned to civilian life. Of course China had changed radically in the interval, and most of them no longer had a place to which they could return. Langdon Gilkey went on to a distinguished career as a writer and theologian.

Japan

For many Allied prisoners of war in the Pacific their final destination proved to be the Japanese homeland. About 11,400 Americans, along with numerous British and Commonwealth prisoners, were liberated there at the end of the war. Of course many died before liberation. It would seem logical that this captive army of Westerners would have had many chances to come into contact with baseball, which was in the prewar years the most popular team sport in Japan. But this was not to be, for after Pearl Harbor all was not well with baseball in Japan.

Baseball had been introduced into Japan during the 1870s by American teachers and missionaries. It caught on quickly, but in a fashion subtly different from the American version. In Japan the game took on martial arts overtones, with emphasis on collective effort and the development of physical and mental stamina. It was not uncommon for coaches to make their teams drill until they dropped from exhaustion.

The foundation of baseball in Japan was not the sandlot, as was the case at that time in America, but rather it was a sport for high school and college athletes. While the Japanese High School Baseball Tournament was started in 1915, the first professional league was not launched until 1936. The impetus for a Japanese league was in part due to the successful tour of an American all-star team through Japan in 1934, the players including Babe Ruth and Lou Gehrig.

If the coming of the Second World War hit the American professional leagues hard, it devastated the Japanese equivalent. In addition to the drafting and often dying of many of the professional players, Japanese baseball had to contend with a cultural backlash against all things American. Uniforms were changed to replace Western-style logos and numbers with Japanese characters. Team names were altered a bit as well. The Giants and

Senators were transformed into the Kyojin and Tsubasa. Some accounts of the era also have the name of the sport switching from *beso-boru* to *yakkyu*, a Japanese word meaning "field ball," but this appears to be an incorrect oversimplification.

Baseball found a way to get by during the early war years; the schedule was even expanded in 1942. But by 1944 the Japanese professional league was down to six teams and the season significantly shortened. The 1945 season was cancelled altogether as bombing raids and the threat of invasion put the entire country on a war footing. Even baseball stadiums were pressed into national service, one serving as an ammunition dump and another as a military hospital where medical experiments on POWs were reputedly carried out.

American prisoners arriving on Japanese shores in the last two years of the war would have come at a time when that nation had little enthusiasm or resources to devote to baseball. Most of the prisoners had little opportunity to encounter it.

Allied POWs were taken to Japan for the purpose of providing slave labor. They were held in many small camps associated with mines and factories. Rest days were infrequent, and while prisoners were seldom killed outright they were often worked to death. These prisoners working in basic industries, such as coal and copper mining, were being used in a manner somewhat more in keeping with the spirit of the Geneva Convention. But the work was harder, and because they had fewer opportunities to trade with Japanese workers they lived a more desperate life than those POWs employed in such directly war related industries such as shipyards.

On special occasions such as the Emperor's birthday there were a few instances where prisoners from the various Allied nations were lined up against Japanese competitors in track and field meets, with the intent of proving Japanese superiority. Despite the obvious unfairness of pitting starving men against healthy ones the POWs often did quite well. But any POW involvement in baseball in Japan has to be considered a great rarity.

There were some Americans who arrived in Japan very early in the war. There was a diplomatic contingent that was actually in the country at the time of Pearl Harbor. In a fashion similar to the Bad Nauheim experience, these civilians were put up in hotels under close scrutiny and repatriated after various bureaucratic delays. Being held in an urban environment there apparently was no opportunity to play ball even if they had wished to.

One group of American prisoners reached Japanese shores before all the rest. There was a small contingent of military and civilian personnel stationed on the island of Guam. Being this far out in the Pacific the island was considered to be indefensible, and no serious fortifications or reinforcements were in place by December 7. After putting up a token resistance these men were captured and shipped directly to Japan. The civilians from Guam were not placed in military POW camps as were their equivalents from Wake Island. Instead these 27 men ended up in the Hyogo Civil Internment Camp No. 1, near Kobe. When visited later in the war the camp held 61 prisoners, including 29 American and 24 British citizens. The facility was a compound of some 1,300 square meters, which had formerly been the dormitory of the Canadian Academy. The grounds contained a baseball field; this game, along with horseshoes and walking, appears to be the available outdoor recreation during a benign confinement.

In January 1942, the military captives from Guam, along with an assortment of British and Dutch captured about the same time, were confined at Zentsuji, the first Japanese POW camp to hold Western prisoners.

The Zentsuji camp had a long history of use. It had held prisoners during the Russo-Japanese War in 1904, then German civilian internees during the First World War, and finally POWs again during the Sino-Japanese conflict in 1937. Between uses as a jail it had served as a barracks and warehouse complex. It was located in the middle of one of the Japanese Army's largest training areas, directly adjacent to an elaborate Shinto shrine dedicated to Japanese war dead.

Zentsuji was intended to be a "model" POW camp, the sort of place where the Red Cross and propaganda corps could go and report back on the humane treatment prisoners could expect under the Japanese flag. It does not seem to have entirely lived up to its billing however, and most first-person accounts of the place describe life there as one of monotony and inferior food.

Compared to the camps in the Philippines, however, it was a paradise. During the entire course of the war only ten Americans died at Zentsuji, a number that would be reached by breakfast time at O'Donnell or during the worst era of Cabanatuan. The Americans at Zentsuji had the good fortune to have workable sanitary facilities and a capable medical staff. Food was in short supply but never quite dropped to starvation levels, and the prisoners had a few unique advantages, including free access to English-language Japanese newspapers through much of the war.

The Red Cross did visit Zentsuji with some regularity, and official reports mention that a significant amount of recreational equipment, including baseball and volleyball gear, was delivered. There are existing propaganda photos of the latter in use. But in general sports equipment was not provided to the prisoners when the Red Cross was not around. The official provost marshal report on the camp compiled after the war states:

> Books, playing cards, chess and checker sets were received from the YMCA and were expeditiously distributed. Athletic gear such as volley ball and baseball equipment was restricted by the Japanese. The items were used by the Japanese during the most desirable times of the day and the same was true of the musical instruments furnished by the YMCA.[1]

Although baseball did exist at the Zentsuji camp it was more or less a sham, put on for appearances at this propaganda camp.

The Tanagawa Prisoner of War camp was a different sort of place. The POWs at Tanagawa were there to work, mostly on a nearby construction site where a dry dock for submarines was being built. One of the prisoners there was Kary Emerson, who had endured the usual sequence of combat on Bataan, the forced march to O'Donnell, and a stay at Cabanatuan. He seems to have endured these hardships better than most, and so was selected as one of the relatively healthy men sent on an early transport to Japan. He arrived there on Thanksgiving Day 1942.

Tanagawa camp was a mixed experience. The guards could at times be reasonable, but at least by the end of the war the treatment had deteriorated to the point that the Japanese commander reportedly was seized by liberated POWs and put to death in a summary judgment. Disease claimed many American lives, and the work schedule was six days a week of hard labor. But on occasion the seventh day, the *yasume* day, could be memorable. As Emerson recalls the summer of 1943:

> The Japanese were avid baseball fans. After the weather warmed up, it became their favorite pastime. Japanese camp and guard personnel ate lunch at 1100 hours at which time we started carrying food to the outside work details. After we returned, then we would eat and be about our jobs at 1300 hours. The Japanese asked us to eat in a hurry and join them in baseball practice, which we did. On the diamond, prisoner-guard relationships were forgotten. However, after a few days we realized that the daily game required energy we couldn't afford. Nevertheless, they demanded that we play baseball with them instead of resting during our lunch period. This routine continued until it dawned on us that we had won every game. So one day we very carefully planned our play so that they could win. Thereafter we were not required to play baseball

each day. We finally realized that survival takes some thought in addition to luck, determination, and many other factors.

We convinced the Japanese to let us have a holiday on July 4. A normal holiday meant that we didn't have to work on that day, but could mend and wash our clothing, and read or generally relax. Recognizing that July 4 was a special holiday, after lunch the Japanese walked us about four miles to a golf course that was not being used because of the war. Many relaxed in the sun and watched others play baseball. A few Japanese played on each team, so the prisoners interpreted the rules differently for the Japanese. For example, if the Japanese batter got a hit, before he could score a run we always found a way to call him out, usually it was for turning the wrong way at first base. The Japanese were so excited they didn't notice the inconsistencies of the umpire's decisions.[2]

Do not conclude that life at Tanagawa was any sort of holiday. At about the same time as the above events, Emerson recorded that 22 officers and 47 enlisted men had already died. But it did turn out to be the best of the several Japanese camps at which he spent time.

By the summer of 1944 the number of Americans held in Japan had risen significantly as the Japanese tried to evacuate their captives from the Philippines ahead of an anticipated invasion. The Japanese mood was grim and the faltering economy geared totally to war production. As the least industrialized of the major belligerent nations Japan still relied on manual labor to do tasks that elsewhere would have been at least partially automated. William Chittendon, who we encountered earlier at Shanghai, was now put to work manhandling scrap metal at a steel mill near Tokyo. As he describes his favorite war story:

One warm day during the summer of 1944, I had just finished the well watered noon ration, and walked a few feet outside the workshed door to get a breath of "fresh" air. In the adjacent street a pickup baseball game was in progress. These were Korean or Japanese kids, maybe both, probably 12 to 14 years old, who were also employed in the Japanese war effort to please the emperor and better the "Greater East Asia Co-Prosperity Sphere." They were playing with a bat that had seen better days, and the kind of ball in use in Japan in those years. I watched them hitting out fly balls and enjoyed their delight in the sport. Being the out-going sort of character that I am, at one point I asked them in pantomime and broken Japanese if I could take a turn with the bat. They giggled among themselves, and handed the bat and ball to me. At the time my weight (normally about 150 pounds) had dropped to 115. But of my own making, I had a challenge on my hands to represent well the American way, Old Glory, and the honor of the United States Marine Corps! I had to "JUST DO IT" as the TV ads say. I breathed a silent prayer and tossed the ball in the air. The gods were with me! The "sweet spot" of the bat made a perfect connection with my target. The ball took wings! It sailed over the shortstop's glove, then began to soar. As I recall the event in 1993, in my mind's eye I still see the ball forcing the outfielders back, but not far enough. The baseball returned to earth well past anyone in the outfield. I felt like Babe Ruth after just hitting one over the fence at Yankee Stadium. The kids gave me a standing ovation. It had made my day, and the world was still safe for democracy.[3]

For Allied prisoners in Japan the end of the war was heralded by a remarkable series of events. First came rumors, tales of a new bomb of unspeakable power. Then came a sudden increase in food rations and an unusual number of *yasume* days. Finally there came an official announcement, usually from the camp commander, that the emperor had ordered an end to hostilities. (The concept that they had been completely beaten and that it was a surrender was not acknowledged at the time and is still a difficult notion for some Japanese.) In some locations the guards just left. At others they dutifully turned their guns around and dedicated themselves to protecting the Americans from the largely imaginary threat of the civilian populace. In either case, the prisoners were left in a sort of twilight captivity, officially free but still all alone in the enemy homeland. The first contact with the outside world came from above, with squadrons of American planes dropping containers of supplies on known POW camps. Sometimes the results were tragic: at least two prisoners were killed by a direct hit on their hut.

In these final days and weeks of captivity the physical condition of the prisoners improved rapidly, and some started giving thought to a bit of recreation. By this time Chittendon was working a dock detail near Nigata. By August 18, 1945, the prospects of peace seemed so certain that the commanding officer there, Major Quinn, called for volunteers to make a ball diamond. But Quinn was not well liked, and most of the men were more interested in resting. But Chittendon did find time to play a bit of catch and some volleyball before he was liberated by Allied occupation forces.

Ernest Norquist records one of the later days of his imprisonment in Japan in the following entry for August 26, 1945:

> We have three volleyballs here now. I got out and played yesterday, finding I'm pretty rusty in the joints, but managing to have some

fun and exercise. There is a baseball and some gloves here, too. The men made a net for volleyball out of pieces of old rope. Incidentally one Japanese came out and played with us a while. Why not? He was good at it.[4]

Understandably not all of the liberated prisoners had such a philosophical attitude toward their former captors. But with the cold war looming and Japan soon destined to stand as our chief Asian ally, attitudes were soon to change.

Axis Prisoners of War

One reality of losing a war is that a large number of your soldiers become prisoners—with the obvious exceptions of those who are killed in action and the less obvious exceptions of those stationed in areas that the war bypassed. Certainly this was true for Germany, Italy, and Japan, which had millions of their men captured during the Second World War.

The conditions of captivity varied enormously. Many of the war monuments, or *Denkmals*, to be seen in Germany bear a list of names below the inscription "Dead or Imprisoned in Russia," and indeed there was little perceived difference.* But many Axis soldiers who were captured by the Western powers received care that was exemplary. The Geneva Convention was almost universally honored, including Article 17, which states: "So far as possible, belligerents shall encourage intellectual diversions and sports organized by prisoners of war." From time to time this even included baseball.

About 500,000 German prisoners of war spent time in America. Significant numbers were also held in Canada. At least in America the prison camp system was decentralized, with over 500 small camps, often organized around work assignments. Camps and subcamps were located in every state, although there was something of an effort to keep prisoners away from the coastal regions so as to hinder escape attempts.

Life for the German POWs had some features in common with the universal experiences of prisoners of war. There was boredom. There were occasional escape attempts, mostly more comic than dangerous. There were educational programs, camp newspapers, and sports programs. In the

---

The last POW of the Second World War, a Hungarian captured in 1944 while serving with the Wehrmacht, was discovered in a Russian mental hospital in the summer of 2000.

latter, soccer was by far the most popular game, with a form of volleyball known as *faustball* playing a minor role alongside various track-and-field events. Baseball was an alien concept, another strange feature of a foreign land.

There was a facet of life in "Stalag USA" that Allied prisoners did not encounter in their captivity. There were significant political divisions within the German POW community, which were a constant source of strife with occasionally fatal consequences. Many of the early captives were from the Afrika Korps, tough professional soldiers with high morale and a strong belief in eventual German victory. After the Normandy invasion a huge wave of mixed captives poured west across the Atlantic. There were some SS troops who were utterly fanatical and who had a dark history of violence against all perceived enemies of the Reich. There were also low-grade troops scraped together as the weight of Allied forces began to crush the German war machine: 15-year-old boys, grandfathers, and former Russian POWs who had volunteered for or had been dragooned into German service.

In the American POW camps all these groups were lumped together at first, and the results were disturbing. Pictures of the Fuhrer were displayed prominently, and the Nazi salute was retained. Those who dared to question Nazi war aims and principles were sometimes tried by secret "order courts" and executed. As prospects for an Allied victory in Europe became more and more assured, farsighted officials in the Pentagon began to wonder what sort of victory it would be. Determined to avoid the mistakes made at the end of the First World War there began a secret effort to reeducate the Germans who would soon be repatriated, to somehow instill in them the principles of democracy, which were seen to be deficient in German history. There was a strong wish to avoid if possible the prospect of a Nazi revival that might result in another war in a generation or so. There was also a growing concern about the Russians, whose vigorous efforts to reeducate "their" German POWs in the ways of Communism might create a postwar Germany hostile to the West in a different fashion.

Attempts to "Americanize" the German prisoners got underway in 1944, supposedly prompted by Eleanor Roosevelt's concern about reports of Nazi atrocities, murders, and forced suicides within the camps. The headquarters of this effort was a facility known informally as the Factory, which was set up on a former coastal artillery post on an island in the middle of Rhode Island's Narragansett Bay. Here specially selected Germans were brought for further education and to advise the Americans on ways to influence the rank and file of the captive Germans. Some of the major efforts included reviewing films for possible showing in the camps, monitoring the content of the many camp newspapers, transcribing radio broadcasts, and eventually producing a prodemocracy periodical called *Der Ruf* (the Call) that was distributed to all the camps.

Less obvious measures were also employed. Religious activity was encouraged, as a counterforce to Nazi fanaticism. To occupy the idle hours: "The Factory devised methods to use other recreational activities as well. Equipment was provided for both German and American games, and as time passed, the programs leaned toward all American games like baseball, basketball and horseshoe pitching."[1]

The effort to steer the Germans to the American national pastime was no doubt well intended. It certainly would have been a propaganda coup to have been able to report on an "Afrika Korps World Series" or similar event. But the effort was a dismal failure. To put it plainly, the Germans were uninterested. The pages of their camp newsletters have extensive sports sections, which describe their soccer leagues with all the passion and detail that their American counterparts in the stalags lavished on baseball. The few mentions of baseball among the Germans use terms like "halfhearted."

The work camp at Montgomery, Minnesota, is a fair example. In June 1944, 30 German prisoners of war arrived under guard to help set up a work camp adjacent to a cannery. Barbed wire was strung around some existing buildings, and two guard towers were built. Later in the month 228 more prisoners arrived, along with a contingent of 32 soldiers and one officer to guard them. Additional prisoners arrived later in the summer. The prisoners were paid 60 cents per day to work in the cannery and in nearby fields and vining stations. Howard Hong, who was the area Red Cross representative, dropped in on them on July 24 and reported: "The men have prepared jumping pits and a fist ball court or small soccer field. Soccer balls are unavailable locally. Nearby is a city playground which they may use for tennis had they racquets and tennis balls. The dearth of equipment has led them to improvise out of nothing and to try playing baseball a little."

The prisoners may have picked up some rudiments of the game from their guards. Baseball had been a dead issue in Montgomery through much of the war years due to the military service of most of the young men of the community. But within two weeks of the opening of the Montgomery POW camp the game was revived when the guards of the camp organized a team and began playing a series of games against local teams of high school students and oldtimers. After one of these games the German POWs took the field to play "soccer ball" against a team from a POW camp at nearby Fairbault. Unfortunately the local paper does not enlighten us on

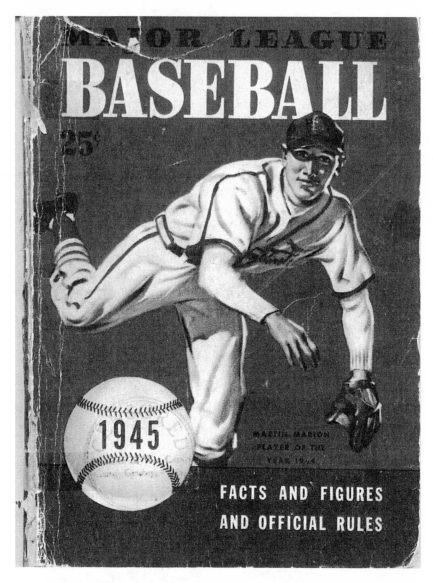

Cover of 1945 *Baseball Handbook*. (Note censor's stamp, Camp Gruber, near Muskokee, Oklahoma, 1945.) Courtesy Royce Parr.

just what the Germans thought about the baseball game, nor on what the townsfolk of Montgomery thought about the soccer contest. But as relations between the camp and the town appear to have been amicable it might be assumed that they were pleased to see the Montgomery camp prevail in a 6–4 decision. At the end of the harvest season the cannery stockade was closed down and the prisoners returned to their base camp.[2]

PAUL TROUT, (left) and HAL NEWHOUSER, *Detroit Tigers* Leading E.R.A. Pitcher 1944—A.L. Most Valuable Player

Photograph from 1945 *Baseball Handbook*. Courtesy Royce Parr.

Howard Hong kept excellent notes, and there is mention of a low level of baseball activity at several other camps within his district. At branch camp number 401 near Remer, Minnesota, there was a five-acre athletic field with baseball equipment available. The camp was located at a former CCC camp in the north woods and had a fairly informal regimen, which included swimming privileges for the POWs in a nearby lake. A similar camp at another CCC facility was located at nearby Deer River. This camp also had a recreation field, volley ball field, full-sized baseball field, recreation hall, stage, and piano. After a while the American guards did not even bother to accompany these prisoners to their work sites. Perhaps this contributed a bit to their delinquency, as several of them were picked up by local game wardens for fishing without valid licenses.

The overall picture that emerges of the attempts by the Factory to teach German prisoners baseball is that it was a flop. It seems to have vanished with scant records and no known photographic images, although POW camp guards did have locally successful teams at several camps, including Camp Clinton, Mississippi, and Camp Concordia, Kansas. One surviving artifact does give a glimpse of what was attempted. It is a 1945 edition of a paperback book called *Major League Baseball Facts and Figures and Official Rules*. It contains statistics and articles on the 1944 season, the World Series, military baseball, and even the All-American Girls

League. Stamped on the cover are the words CENSORED WAR PRISONER CAMP CAMP GRUBER (a POW camp within a large army base near Muskogee, Oklahoma). On the first inside page, stamped over a photograph of Paul Trout and Hal Newhouser, are the following words in both German and English: "NOT TO BE RESOLD Purchased through the POW Fund for Barrack Distribution." If resale of items of this sort was in fact a problem then the brass back at the Factory cannot have been entirely displeased. The captive Germans may never have grasped the concept of the infield fly rule, but their capitalistic tendencies seem to have been sufficiently developed to keep them from slipping into godless Communism.

The baseball-playing nations involved in the Second World War were the United States, Japan, Canada, and debatably Australia. The casual and perhaps even the serious student of this era of history may be surprised to learn that of the four, Japan actually had the most of its soldiers taken prisoner — and by a wide margin, approximately tenfold.

This fact is at first hard to reconcile with the famous Japanese aversion toward being taken prisoner. Indeed, in the early stages of the war Japanese prisoners were quite a rarity. For instance during the Burma campaign Allied forces supposedly killed 17,000 Japanese soldiers while only capturing 142, and most of them were too badly wounded to have had much choice in the matter. As the tide of battle turned against the Japanese, prisoners began to turn up in larger numbers, notably during the Philippine campaign. But the greatest number of Japanese prisoners were scooped up during the last two weeks of the war, when the Soviet Union declared war on the then-helpless Japanese empire and invaded Manchuria. Up to 1.5 million Japanese soldiers and civilians were carted off to forced labor, mostly in Siberia.

There were of course many Japanese who were bypassed during the American island-hopping campaign in the Pacific. Some of these soldiers are very particular about drawing a distinction between themselves, who ceased to fight by imperial command, and those unworthy Japanese who actually surrendered during active hostilities.

As will presently be seen, Japanese POWs were clearly the last World War II prisoners to play baseball. And they may well have also been the first.

World War II is generally said to have begun with the German invasion of Poland in 1939, but this designation is arbitrary. Japan had by that point already invaded China several years earlier and had also fought a brief but savage border war with Russia over Mongolia.

The Chinese conflict was a muddled three-way fight with the Japanese capturing and holding Manchuria in the north and most of the southern coastal cities. They were opposed by both Communist and Nationalist forces, which each hated the Japanese marginally more than they hated each other. Ultimately, of course the Communists prevailed and took over China (exclusive of the stubborn island of Taiwan). One of the leading figures of the People's Liberation Army in this era was Marshal He Long. He was said to be an illiterate peasant who organized the first platoon of the PLA, arming them with vegetable knives.

Baseball had been known in China since the early 1880s, brought by early railroad builders and missionaries. Somehow Marshal He had become a fan of the game, although he was not held to be much of a player himself. The marshal felt that it provided ideal training for soldiers: the throwing skills helped with grenade tossing, the sliding and base running helped train assault troops, and the batting improved their aim. He was once quoted as saying, "Baseball and sports are the pillars of national defense and development." For coaches the marshal decided to give preferential treatment to Japanese POWs, who would help teach his troops baseball. Given the nature of the war in China preferential treatment probably meant that he let them live. At one point, perhaps after the war, Marshal He even built a special factory just to supply baseball equipment for the army.

After the war Marshal He was a revered figure in Chinese society and among other honors was appointed commissar for national sport. Baseball seemed ready to flourish in China, with He Long as its founding father. But it was not to be. Marshal He imprudently criticized some of the economic policies of Chairman Mao tse-tung, and was an early victim of the Cultural Revolution of the 1960s. Baseball in China more or less died with him, as the Red Guards denounced it as Western decadence. A few brave souls still played the game in secret, awaiting a revival of the game that in recent years begins to look more hopeful.

The report of Japanese POWs being pressed into service as baseball coaches is undated, and it is worth mentioning that both Communist and Nationalist forces held onto large numbers of Japanese prisoners after the official end of the war in 1945.

The United States entered the war abruptly on December 7, 1941, and captured its first prisoner of war the same day. After participating in the attack on Pearl Harbor Ensign Sakamaki abandoned his damaged midget submarine and swam ashore on an Oahu beach. He was taken in February 1942, to the United States, where he remained the *only* Japanese POW in American hands until late summer of that year. Eventually other prisoners joined him, mostly those individuals who were felt to have some potential as sources of military intelligence or who might aid in propaganda campaigns.

After initial interrogation on the West Coast most of these prisoners were held at either Camp McCoy, Wisconsin, or at a camp in Clarinda, Iowa. Research so far has uncovered no evidence of baseball being played at either facility. At McCoy, where the largest group of Japanese were held, they were confined to an isolated part of the sprawling facility and were unpopular with both the American troops training there and with their supposed allies, the German POWs held at the same base.

One group of Japanese POWs in America apparently did get to play baseball on a limited basis. The same Special Projects Division that was responsible for the Factory also undertook a program of re-education of Japanese prisoners of war. Beginning in the summer of 1945 a group of "potential converts to democracy" was culled from the main group of POWs and sent to one of three reorientation centers in Texas. Here they were given a series of lectures by the faculty of nearby Sam Houston State Teachers College and given "a heavy dose of American music, newspapers, movies and cartoons, and such recreational activities as softball, table tennis, and baseball."[3] The subsequent careers of these men have unfortunately never been traced to determine the degree of their conversion into democrats.

Most Japanese prisoners never made it near the shores of America. Some were kept in camps on various Pacific islands, near where they were captured. One Marine officer had an unusual experience in a rear echelon area during the Pacific war:

> Our regimental team took on the Island MPs. Our boys had just returned to a rest area after the New Georgia battle and commanding officers were trying desperately to eradicate the picture of dead Japanese and watery foxholes from the minds of our soldiers. Our regiment had several good softball teams. In spite of rules against officers playing on enlisted men teams, I accompanied the team I organized to their games, both as manager and as third baseman.
>
> The island MPs had a topnotch team, and we traveled a few miles by 6'6 truck to their well-kept diamond. Both sides warmed up a bit and then settled down for the ballgame. Private Gaines was up first and drew a base on balls. I was up second. I took a good hefty swing at the first ball, missed, and it was just then that I noticed *them*.
>
> They were sitting behind some chicken wire fences about twenty yards away, parallel to our third base line. Our team bench was between the line and the chicken wire. About twenty laughing,

cheering, jabbering Japanese were watching our game! The same species of men that we had killed in New Georgia and whose maggoty bodies we had smelled soon after they died. The identical features, builds, skin. Just better fed and a lot more jovial.

Needless to say, trying to watch the ball with one eye and these Japanese with the other didn't work. I fanned. One of my men forgot himself for a second and called out disgustedly, "Keep your goddam eye on the ball ... sir." I walked back to the bench and pointed out my discovery to the rest of the men. They ceased to be interested in the game. We gawked at these Japanese while they smiled back at us and cheered us, unconcernedly. Later we learned most of them had been prisoners for about a year, having been captured at the Canal. As far as we knew, these were the same as the enemy who had shot at us from trees in the Munda fight, who had ambushed our medical trucks on the Jeep Road, and who had held grenades to honorable stomachs when the jig was up.

We lost the game 1–0. The third baseman bobbled two easy grounders, and the Japanese screamed lustily. The louder they screamed the more he bobbled. It was an odd experience. One week ago we had shot our last little yellow brother, and this afternoon he was cheering us on to victory at his favorite game, baseball.[4]

Although this group of Japanese numbered only 20, there were enough of them to form their own teams and play baseball, in addition to rooting for American teams from their front row seats along the third base line.

Another Marine, who served with an interrogation and translator team, encountered a group of Japanese prisoners in a camp on Guam. There were some 300 of them, and in their leisure time they played baseball, volleyball, chess, and a Japanese game called go. The Japanese prisoners on Guam were avid baseball fans, playing almost every day after work. One day in 1945 something unusual happened:

A group of prisoners arrived from Iwo. They were dirty, ragged and frightened as were all POWs when first admitted to the camp. As they walked down the main street one tall POW seemed to be attracting a great deal of attention. The prisoners were bowing to him and talking about him. I asked a young Jap sailor who spoke some English about this newcomer. He said, "He Japanese Basu-Baru; he Japanese Babu-Ruthu."

Later when the famous ballplayer became accustomed to captivity, he would pinch-hit at ballgames. He always had a runner. I never saw him do anything but hit. Of course, he was a major.[5]

Japanese prisoners playing ball at Cowra, Australia, summer of 1944. Courtesy Australian War Memorial.

The identity of this illustrious prisoner is not known with certainty. The most tempting candidate would at first glance appear to be Minoru Yamashita, who was a player of some prominence at Keio University and later professionally was an outfielder for the Hankyu Braves in the prewar years. Yamashita is a member of the Japanese Baseball Hall of Fame, and was known as the "Babe Ruth of Japanese Baseball." Unfortunately there is little known of his military service beyond the fact that he did serve (a picture of him in uniform seems to confirm this) and that he survived the war. But Professor Massy Ikei of Keio University responded to my query with information that suggests that Yamashita was never a POW, so the prisoner on Guam could have been some other early Japanese player of prominence. A search of prisoner rosters from the Guam camp would probably not be productive, as a high percentage of Japanese prisoners of war did not give their true names when captured.

One reason that so few Japanese prisoners were held in camps in the United States was that there was an agreement among the Allies to share the expense and inconvenience of housing prisoners. For instance, America took a large contingent of German and Italian prisoners who had been previously under British control so as to lessen the burden on the food supply of the British isles. There was a similar understanding in the Pacific. Japanese prisoners were usually housed in camps in Australia and New Zealand, with the United States contributing food and supplies for their upkeep.

One of the two major POW camps in Australia was Camp No. 12, near Cowra, New South Wales. Various captives had passed through Cowra during the war years. One group was Italian prisoners of war captured in the Middle East. They spent their time working on local farms and were generally considered ideal prisoners. Approximately 1,200 Indonesian civilian dissidents were also briefly imprisoned at Cowra at the request of their government, which felt that they were likely to become Japanese collaborators. The Australian government chose instead to view them as political prisoners who had been imprisoned for years without reasonable cause. They were quickly set free.

By the summer of 1944 the camp held something in excess of 1,100 Japanese prisoners, along with various Koreans and Formosans who had been captured while serving unhappily under the Japanese flag. Conditions of captivity were luxurious by the standards of army life that the Japanese had previously known. There was good food, physical fitness training, modern medical care, and ample recreational opportunities. Life should have been good, but there was widespread discontent. In part it was due to the Japanese sense of shame at being captured. Interrogators routinely found that hints of physical violence or withholding of privileges had no effect on the Japanese. But the threat to inform their families back in Japan as to their true status often shocked the prisoner into cooperation.

On the surface all was calm at Cowra. The Japanese prisoners held outdoor parades and Shinto services. They built a baseball backstop and had rather informal baseball games. Curiously, given the rabid nature of Japanese baseball fandom in general, there were few if any spectators at the games. An extensive series of photographs was taken in the summer of 1944 for inclusion in propaganda leaflets to be dropped on Japanese-held islands. Baseball teams or partial teams appear in the photos, but no fans. With the benefit of hindsight one wonders what this implied about the morale of the prisoners and their feelings about their captivity.

On August 4, 1944, an announcement was made that some of the Japanese were to be moved to another camp to relieve overcrowding of the facility. In the early morning hours a bugle sounded, and the Japanese prisoners rushed the fences in the largest mass escape attempt of the war.

Japanese prisoners playing ball at Cowra, Australia, summer of 1944. Note the backstop and benches. Loose grouping of the players suggests that this was a practice session. Courtesy Australian War Memorial.

Baseball gloves were used to scale the barbed wire, and then blankets were tossed over the top so that others could climb over. Bats were among the improvised weapons used to assault the guards.

Since the Japanese were running directly into gunfire the casualty toll was high. When the count was complete, 243 were dead, including several escapees who committed suicide by stabbing themselves or later throwing themselves in front of trains. Another 334 prisoners did manage to escape briefly, but they were rounded up in the days that followed. Four Australian soldiers were killed in the incident. Contrary to popular fears, civilians who came in contact with the escapees were not harmed, and in fact were treated with respect.

Since there was no plausible hope of actually crossing the Australian desert and the surrounding oceans to reach Japanese or neutral territory, the incident at Cowra has generally been viewed as a mass suicide attempt.

Baseball bats and other weapons used in mass escape at Cowra, Australia, summer of 1944. Courtesy Australian War Memorial.

Interestingly the small contingent of Japanese officers at the camp never left their huts, and about 50 of the enlisted men "escaped" to the relative safety of the officers' compound. This appears to be the only instance in which baseball equipment was utilized in a violent incident in any prisoner-of-war camp.

Japanese soldiers fighting in Burma upon their surrender at war's end were confined to prison camps for up to another two years. While in captivity they developed the usual camp institutions, including musical and theatrical groups, as well as baseball teams. There were even games played against their guards—but only against the Indian troops, never the British, who maintained an aloof and disapproving distance from their prisoners.

For the last few months of the war the Japanese government was actively trying to work out terms for an honorable surrender. As an intermediary the Japanese chose the Soviet Union, which had maintained a neutral stance toward Japan. But the Russians were not an honorable partner in this role, as they were already planning their own "Pearl Harbor."

The morning after the mass escape at Cowra. The body of a Japanese prisoner lies at the base of the fence, with what appears to be a bat across his knees. Courtesy Australian War Memorial.

On August 8, 1945, Russian troops attacked the Japanese forces in northern China. At one time the Japanese Kwangtung Army had been an elite force, but the demands of the Pacific war had stripped away the best men and materiel. They were no match for the seasoned Red Army troops and surrendered after a brief fight. Over a million Japanese soldiers and an unknown number of civilians were marched oto captivity in Siberia. The actual number of Japanese captives taken is something of a mystery. When the number of Japanese known to be in Manchuria is compared with the numbers known to have died in Soviet hands or to have been later repatriated, there are several hundred thousand soldiers and civilians who simply vanished. Many of them probably died in the Soviet gulags. The Russians were desperate for laborers to help rebuild a crippled economy and were not particular about whom they enslaved or how badly they treated them. German POWs were viewed with a degree of hostility that can be understood in light of the damage the German Army had done to

Mother Russia. The Japanese, on the other hand, dug coal, cut timber, and harvested crops under close guard, but with no greater degree of oppression than the political dissidents and ethnic minorities who worked alongside them.

For most of the Japanese captured by the Russians there was little time for recreation. But officers seemed to fare just a bit better. A contingent of officers numbering up to 10,000 was held at Izhevsk on the Kama River east of the Ural Mountains. It was a bleak place, 80 kilometers away from the nearest railroad station and essentially cut off from the outside world once the Kama River froze in late October. Some prisoners were held in the A Camp, a three-story cement building that had obviously been a prison for a long time. Rooms had low ceilings and small windows. Dotting the surrounding brick walls were ominous groups of bullet holes. Somewhat more fortunate prisoners found themselves in the B Camp, which had previously been a theological school during czarist times.

The concerns of the Japanese prisoners were predictable: food shortages, illness, and homesickness. And they coped in the usual ways. A small number of books were shared, although both book reading and camp newspapers were subject to close ideological scrutiny by the Soviet captors. Game boards were made for go, shogi, and majan, although the latter was discouraged since it involved gambling. Those with inclinations toward arts and crafts did carvings, with a likeness of Stalin being especially popular with the German POWs held at Izhevsk. They would sometimes give the Japanese a bowl of rice for the privilege of taking a couple of whacks at the bust when the Russians were not looking! There were active amateur theatrics, including a "baseball-based love story" written by a Takushoku University graduate.

In the spring of 1947 there spontaneously arose a desire to play baseball. There were some 300 graduates of Waseda University and Keio University among the captives, and it was resolved to play a game between alumni of these two schools. On the Waseda squad were Goro Taniguchi, Masuo Noshimura, Shigeru Machiya, Rihachi Abe, and others who had played for the university team. The Keio squad included former baseball team members Seiichi Sakai and Keiji Narita, rugby player Yutaro Nemoto, judo club member Kenichi Ishiwatare, and several other former Keio men with baseball experience.

Equipment was improvised. Three baseballs were made by wrapping stones with old cloth and threads, then covering them with leather from the lining of insulated boots or jackets. According to Taniguchi, "They were not perfectly spherical. But it was interesting because I could throw screw balls and curve balls."[6] As a pitcher he probably also approved of the composition of the balls—surely balls formed with stones at their centers would be the ultimate "dead" balls. A bat was made from white birch wood, and gloves were fashioned from insulated gloves and blankets. Outfielders just used their bare hands.

A Tokyo University graduate who served as translator approached the Russians and obtained permission for the game to be played on a small open area. Special ground rules were created to deal with the trees and flower gardens in the playing field.

At Cowra baseball games were played without spectators. Not so at Izhevsk. A large crowd turned out for the game, lining the first and third base lines and leaning out of the windows of the buildings. Cheering sections were organized. The Waseda boosters made a flag out of a reddish brown blanket with a *w* fashioned out of bandage material. The Keio rooters countered with a tricolor pennant formed from a valuable clean white sheet that had red and blue stripes tinted with bengara and iodine. The amateur theater members made an imitation brass band. Cheering sections sang "Young Blood" and "Northwest of Tokyo."

The starting pitcher for Waseda was Taniguchi, formerly a great player, but now 46 years old. His control was good, but speed was lacking, and several of the Keio players were able to successfully hit off of him. Among the general festivities the actual score of the game was of little importance, but for the record Keio won by a 5–3 tally.

The Russians were interested in the game, although ignorant of the rules. One was puzzled by the apparent unfairness of having a single offensive player face off against nine defensive players. Another announced his intentions to watch the game from a less-crowded perspective. Taking his chair he set it up behind second base and observed the proceedings from what must have been the best seat in this or any ballpark in history.

The effect on morale among the prisoners was so dramatic that the entire mood at Izhevsk changed. As the Japanese got more cheerful, the Russians got more suspicious.

There were high hopes that the experiment could be expanded upon, and a six-university league was planned. With some difficulty teams were recruited to bear the standards of each of the major Japanese universities. Rikkyo University had to scrape up a group that included some men who had never touched a ball before. But the plans did not bear fruit. After just a game or two a typhus epidemic struck the camp, and the remaining games were cancelled.

The Prisoners of Tashkent

American servicemen, most seeing the world for the first time, found themselves in some odd situations. But perhaps none was odder than the assorted Army and Navy aviators who found themselves interned by Russia, our staunch ally. Of course, as young men with time on their hands will do, they found a way to play baseball. In Russia. In December.

The roots of this historical oddity lie in the fact that while beginning in 1941 Russia was locked in a fight to the death with Germany, it still remained officially neutral with respect to Germany's ally, Japan. The reasons for this are complex. First, Japan never declared war on Russia. The Axis was in theory a defensive alliance, and various partners had no absolute obligation to come into the war when one of their allies attacked somebody. No doubt there were many occasions when Hitler wished that Mussolini had continued Italy's neutrality beyond the first six months of the war.

It would be laughable to assign any scruples or ethical principles to Joseph Stalin. As has been seen, once the war with Germany was over, he had no problem repaying Japan for its helpful neutrality with a sneak attack. But in the early stages of the war he had his reasons for not picking a fight. When the German Army was at the gates of Moscow in the winter of 1941–42 the Russian state was saved not only by winter but also by the arrival of reinforcements from Siberia, which were freed up only by a peaceful frontier with Japan. Even after the crisis had passed and Japan could pose no significant land threat, there was a compelling reason to stay friends.

In one of the quietest large-scale operations of the Second World War the United States sent millions of tons of Lend Lease material through Japanese-controlled waters to Russia's Far East port of Vladivostok. There was an understanding that no actual munitions or weapons could be sent, but massive amounts of noncombat equipment, especially trucks, went through, along with the raw materials that Russian factories used to make weapons. This lifeline was invaluable, especially as it allowed Russia to concentrate its industry almost exclusively on munitions, counting on fleets of American trucks and vehicles. What Germany thought of this situation has never been ascertained. So, even when Russia had stabilized the Eastern Front to the point where Japanese land action need not be feared, there was the realization that Japanese air and sea power could cut this economic lifeline at will. The end result of this strange situation was that if an American crew flew into Russia from German air space, they were welcomed as comrades and allies. If they flew in from Japanese air space, they were locked up.

The first of the American internees arrived on Russian soil a mere four months after Pearl Harbor, when a single plane from the Doolittle raid was forced to land in Kamchatka. The crew had hopes of being able to simply refuel and leave, but instead found themselves the focus of a diplomatic crisis. Shuttled to the west the four men found themselves in the path of the German attack on Stalingrad and had the unusual distinction of having to flee both Japanese and German forces on the same mission. Finally, they were lodged in a camp near the Russian border with Iran. In a pattern that was to be repeated several times they were allowed to escape, aided and abetted by a succession of serendipitously appearing helpful citizens, who all but pointed them toward the border and gave them a shove. Quite obviously the entire affair was put on by the NKVD, which was the ancestor of the KGB.

From that point forward American fliers began to descend on the Russian Far East in bunches. The usual greeting for an American bomber limping along with battle damage or running on near-empty tanks was anti-aircraft fire. At least one plane was brought down with its crew in this fashion. But most landed safely, their crews rounded up and confined at a variety of local sites, including a school and a weather station.

There was not much to do in captivity. Relations with their Russian hosts were sometimes strained, but there were a series of basketball and volleyball games between Russians and Americans. It was not unheard of for the Americans to play against the anti-aircraft gunners who had been shooting at them days previously.

Volleyball was the most common game there, and the fortunes of the Americans varied. At first the Soviets dominated but close study of their game plan offered the Americans a chance to get even. Tiring of a string of losses the Russians eventually had two Red Army athletes specially flown in for a Fourth of July celebration in 1945. Winners of many medals in the sport, the two had no difficulty taking on American squads of any size.

The stay in temporary quarters in the Russian Far East lasted for weeks or months. When a sufficient group of internees was assembled they were transported by rail or air. Traveling either in unheated, louse-ridden train cars or in casually maintained transport aircraft, the men were subjected to frequent vodka-soaked gatherings of local Red Army officers during which their health was toasted to rather unhealthy levels.

The ultimate destination was Tashkent, an ancient caravan city near where Russia borders India and Iran. Here they were cooped up in a former school building with two-foot-thick adobe walls. There were grounds consisting of several acres enclosed by adobe walls and water. Under the supervision of the Red Army and with the NKVD in the background they could only sit and wait. Just under 300 Americans would mark time there, with the smallest group being 43 and the largest 130.

In short order parts of the grounds were prepared as a ball field. The first group to arrive in Tashkent in 1943 carved a bat from a willow tree trunk and made a softball from unraveled woolen stocking yarn wrapped around a wine bottle cork and covered with boot leather. A backstop was made of woven reeds. Bases were made from handsewn bags filled with sand. Play commenced on December 1, a remarkable opening day made possible by the temperate conditions in the extreme south of Russia.

The 1943 internees were moved into Allied territory by the same sort of "wink and nudge" operation as the Doolittle raiders. But others took their place.

In 1944 another group occupied the Tashkent internment camp. Unaware that their predecessors had done the same thing, they set out to improvise softball equipment. A rubber heel from a flight boot was used as a core for the ball, which was wrapped with yarn from worn-out stockings. A goatskin hanging in an outbuilding was stolen for the leather coating. Major Putakana, the Soviet officer in charge, was outraged. He assembled all the internees and railed at them, demanding to know the identity of the thief. Nobody said a thing. Soon thereafter the scene was repeated. While the previous internees had procured a suitable tree limb without difficulty, this time Major Putakana stormed and raged because somebody had had the audacity to cut down a tree to make a bat. Again, the Americans kept mum.

Fortunately for American-Soviet relations the next month a team from the embassy in Moscow arrived bearing gifts: reading material, a short-wave radio, and proper softball equipment. Left behind by subsequent batches of departing internees it served for the duration of the war.

Upon its "escape" from Russia, each group of internees was required to destroy any diaries or other materials that would indicate where they had been and to sign a pledge to never speak of it. Thus this odd chapter of history vanished almost completely from sight.

Afterword

The first chapter of POW baseball was written during the Civil War, when brother fought brother to determine what sort of nation America was to be. Baseball was a new game then. The war accelerated its spread dramatically as young men from all walks of life and from all parts of the country were forged together into regiments clad in blue and gray. What would become the national pastime of a United States was played in camps when the armies were at rest and in prisoner-of-war camps North and South when conditions permitted.

Baseball remained a part of military tradition in later conflicts. The troopers of Custer's Seventh Cavalry had several active teams and even played while on campaign. The Spanish-American War spread the game to the Caribbean and to the Philippines. There was quite a baseball craze in France late in the First World War, prompting some to predict it would soon become the preeminent game in the Old World as well as the New. Coming into the War to End All Wars as essentially "late relief," there were not many Americans taken prisoner in that conflict, but among them and among the ranks of British and Canadian prisoners there was some baseball played under surprising circumstances.

Much has changed since the end of the Second World War, and these changes make it likely that the final chapter in the history of POW baseball has already been written.* The nature of war has changed. Since Hiroshima it has become increasingly improbable that we will ever again see a large-scale war between the industrialized nations. What we have instead experienced has been an unpleasant chain of police actions, undeclared

---

*A single instance of softball among Korean War POWs has come to light, but the play was part of a Communist-sponsored sports festival day that was strictly for propaganda purposes. In my opinion it should not be counted as true POW ball.

conflicts, and sundry varieties of modern-day gunboat diplomacy. Our adversaries are increasingly cultures that do not share Western traditions with respect to human rights in general and the treatment of military captives in particular.

Another development of note has been the dramatic shrinking of the planet by modern telecommunications. No longer will families of missing military personnel have to wait months or even years to hear word of their loved ones. The day after their capture it is likely that they will be paraded in front of television cameras for political purposes. Since POWs have become such valuable pawns on the foreign relations game board, they are now carefully guarded, not grouped in open barbed-wire enclosures, but holed up in isolated basements and moved frequently to avoid rescue attempts. Not exactly an environment ripe for a pick-up game of baseball.

The concern for the fate of possible prisoners has even changed the tactics of conflict. Now we wage war with avoidance of taking prisoners as a major concern. One can debate the effectiveness of influencing the course of world affairs by bombing from several miles up, but it certainly will spare us the horrors of another Bataan Death March.

It must also be admitted that we as a people have changed.

Baseball can no longer make an exclusive claim to being our national pastime. If one had to select a single activity common to young Americans from all parts of our country it would have to be — and a prayer for the Republic would not be out of place here — Nintendo.

Even among athletic pursuits baseball shares the stage with basketball, football, and soccer, a sport which would seem to be the definitive POW pastime on a global basis. The U.S. military also no longer promotes athletics to the extent that it once did, and boxing seems to be the only sport that in recent times has still had some quasi-official sanction.

If POW baseball has had its moment on the stage, my efforts will stand as not only the first, but also quite probably the definitive history of the topic. Like all of the members of the World War II generation, the former prisoners of war are now in their late seventies and up. Anyone attempting to revisit the story will have to do so without the opportunity I enjoyed to speak firsthand with many of these gallant gentlemen. The knowledge that this is both the first and last chance to write their story has added a humbling and somber tone to what has in general been a delightful endeavor.

If the number of entries in journals or mentions in the camp newspapers can be used as a guide, baseball ranked somewhat down the list in terms of POW concerns. Food, women, the outcome of the war, and cigarettes would all rank higher. But baseball did spring into life each year just like baseball in the free world, and provided many months of exercise, diversion, and a reminder that somewhere, far beyond the barbed wire, the America (or Canada) that they knew still existed and awaited them.

They played with inferior equipment. They played on uneven fields of irregular dimensions. They played hungry and sick. Frankly, the caliber of play at places like Kriegie Stadium, Yasume Park, and Happy Garden was probably none too high. But the remarkable thing, as has been said on another topic, was not that it was done well, but that it was done at all.

Notes

Chapter 2. Stalag Luft I

1. Report on Stalag Luft I. American Prisoners of War in Germany. Prepared by Military Intelligence Service, War Department, November 1, 1945, p. 5.
2. Correspondence, Bruce Bockstanz. 2000.
3. Greening, C. Ross, and Spinelli, Angelo. *The Yankee Kriegies*, p. 15.
4. Anonymous diary, held at National POW Museum, Andersonville, GA.
5. Vietor, John, *American Airmen at Stalag Luft I*, p. 67.
6. Correspondence, Bruce Bockstanz. 2000.
7. Norman Quast diary, unpublished (diary still in possession of Mr. Quast).

Chapter 3. Stalag Luft III

1. Torres Ferres Wartime Log. Australian War Memorial.
2. Report on Stalag Luft III. American Prisoners of War in Germany. Prepared by Military Intelligence Service, War Department, November 1, 1945, p. 1.
3. Wirebound World. In Torres Ferres file. Australian War Memorial.
4. Sergeant Robert Alldrick. Communication in National Archives of Canada, RG24-C-9-6. Office of the Special Assistant to the Adjutant General.
5. Dancocks, Daniel. *In Enemy Hands: Canadian Prisoners of War 1939–1945*. Edmonton, Alb: Hurtig, 1983, p. 101.
6. Kurt Stauffer Collection. Kurt lives in Seattle.
7. "Spotlight on Stalag Luft III." In Torres Ferres file, Australian War Memorial.
8. Correspondence, Ralph Kling, 1999.

Chapter 4. Stalag Luft VI and Stalag Luft IV

1. Sergeant A. G. Deans. Communication in National Archives of Canada, RG24-C-9-6. Office of the Special Assistant to the Adjutant General.
2. Correspondence, Brice Robison, 2000.
3. Correspondence several ex–POWs, including Joe O'Donnell and Fred Ward, 1999.

Chapter 5. Stalag IIIB

1. Report on Stalag IIIB. American Prisoners of War in Germany. Prepared by Military Intelligence Service, War Department, July 15, 1944, p. 1.
2. Richard K. Varley Diary. Iowa Gold Star Museum, Johnston, Iowa.
3. *POW-WOW* (Stalag IIIB edition), June 25, 1943. State Historical Society of Wisconsin.
4. Greening, C. Ross, and Spinelli, A. *The Yankee Kriegies*, p. 15.

Chapter 6. Oflag 64

1. Report on Oflag 64. American Prisoners of War in Germany. Prepared by Military Intelligence Service, War Department, July 15, 1944, p. 1.
2. *Oflag Item* reproduced in Bickers, James, *Achtung: Oflag 64, 1943–1945*, Evanston Publishing, 1993.
3. *Oflag Item.*
4. Col. George Juskalian, *Ex–POW Bulletin* 41, no. 2 (1984).

Chapter 7. Stalag Bush Leagues

1. Report on Stalag 7A. American Prisoners of War in Germany. Prepared by Military Intelligence Service, War Department, November 1, 1945, p. 4.
2. Report on Stalag 17B. American Prisoners of War in Germany. Prepared by Military Intelligence Service, War Department, July 15, 1944, p. 5.
3. *The Gremlin* Vol. 1, No. 2. Copy in National POW Museum, Andersonville, GA.
4. Correspondence, Martin Parisot, 2000.
5. Report on Stalag 2B. American Prisoners of War in Germany. Prepared by Military Intelligence Service, War Department, July15, 1944, p. 1.
6. Jack Dower, manuscript at United States Army Military History Institute,Carlisle, PA, manuscript collection.
7. Taylor, James. *Prisoner of the Komoran.* 1945.

8. Morgan, Guy. *POW.* 1945.

9. "One Year," an account of the sporting, entertaining, and general activities of Australian warrant and noncommissioned officers at Stalag 383 in Germany. September 25, 1942–1943. Copy at Australian War Memorial.

CHAPTER 8. BAD NAUHEIM INTERNMENT

1. Alvin Steinkopf papers, State Historical Society of Wisconsin.

2. *Bad Nauheim Pudding.* In Alvin Steinkopf papers, State Historical Society of Wisconsin.

3. Burdick, Charles B. *An American Island in Hitler's Reich: The Bad Nauheim Internment.* Menlo Park, CA: Markgraff Publications Group, 1987, p. 85.

4. *Washington Post,* 02/21/81.

CHAPTER 9. STEALING HOME: BASEBALL AND ESCAPE

1. Shoemaker, Lloyd. *The Escape Factory.* New York: St. Martins, 1990.

2. Greening, C. Ross, and Spinelli, A. *The Yankee Kriegies,* p. 12.

CHAPTER 10. MICKEY GRASSO

1. *Washington Post,* 05/15/50.

2. *Ibid.*

3. *Washington Post,* 03/27/50.

4. *Baseball Digest,* July 1951.

5. *Washington Post,* 05/05/51.

6. *Cleveland Plain Dealer,* 04/24/54.

CHAPTER 11. AUGIE DONATELLI

1. *Chicago Tribune,* 05/27/90.

CHAPTER 12. PHIL MARCHILDON

1. *Washington Times-Herald,* June 1950.

2. Marchildon, Phil. ACE.

3. Personal communication, Dwayne Linton, 1999.

Chapter 13. Bert Shepard

1. Snelling, Dennis. *A Glimpse of Fame.* Jefferson, NC: McFarland, 1993, p. 117.
2. *Los Angeles Times,* 06/10/95.

Chapter 14. O Canada

1. Watchorn diary. Imperial War Museum.
2. Page, Charles. Talk titled "Repatriated from Oflag VIIB." Copy in National Archives of Canada. RG24-C-9-6, Volume 8023, File 20-3.
3. Liscombe, W. J. Letter in National Archives of Canada. RG24-C-9-6, Volume 8023, File 19-47.
4. Hobbs, Charles. *Past Tense: Charlie's Story.* 1994.
5. Forsyth, Thomas, fond, National Archives of Canada. R2463-0-8-E.
6. Ebdon, Frank William, fond, National Archives of Canada. R2568-0-3-F.
7. Verreault, Georges. *Diary of a Prisoner of War in Japan.* Rimouski, Quebec: Vero, 1996.

Chapter 16. The Philippines, Part I

1. Personal communication, Willis Johnson, 1999.
2. Report on American Prisoners of War Interned by the Japanese in the Philippines. Prepared by Office of the Provost Marshal General, November 19, 1945, p. 14.
3. Norquist, Ernest. *Our Paradise.* Hancock, WI: Pearl-Win, 1989. Entry for October 11, 1942.
4. Personal communication, Tillman Rutledge, 1999.
5. Fitzpatrick, Bernard. *The Hike into the Sun.* Jefferson, NC: McFarland, 1993, p. 181.
6. William Owen diary. U.S. Army Military History Institute, manuscript collection.
7. Barker, Robert A. *Philippine Diary.*
8. Goodman, Julien. M.D., POW. New York: Exposition Press, 1972.
9. Jackson, Calvin G. *Diary of Col. Calvin G. Jackson, MD.* Ada, Ohio: Ohio Northern University, 1992, p. 88.
10. Moffit, Lloyd. Diary at U.S. Army Military History Institute, manuscript collection.

Chapter 17. The Philippines, Part II

1. Personal communication, Ray Makepeace, 2000.
2. Czerwin, Tony. *POW, Tears that Never Dry*, p. 48.
3. Fitzpatrick, Bernard. *The Hike into the Sun*, p. 132.
4. *Ibid.*, p. 146.
5. Porwoll, Kenneth. *But Not Alone*. Manuscript at Minnesota State Historical Society. Also personal communication, 1999.

Chapter 18. The Philippines, Part III

1. "Baseball Program." Mary Alice Foley Papers, University of Michigan–Ann Arbor.
2. *Internews*. Published by Committee for Relief of Americans in Philippines. 1942. Housed in several archives, including the Wisconsin State Historical Society, Marcia Gates Collection.
3. Johansen, Bruce. *So Far from Home*.
4. *Internews*. This is from a later edition, copy in Australian War Memorial.
5. Personal communication, Peter Wygle, 2000.
6. Flanagan, Edward M. *Angels at Dawn: The Los Banos Raid*, p. 40.
7. Crouter, Natalie. *Forbidden Diary*.
8. *Ibid.*
9. Vaughn, Elizabeth. *The Ordeal of Elizabeth Vaughn*.

Chapter 19. Shanghai

1. Biggs, Chester. *Behind the Barbed Wire*. Jefferson, NC: McFarland, 1995.
2. Report of War Camps in Areas Other Than the Four Principal Islands of Japan. Kiangwan, China, dated July 31, 1946, p. 3.
3. Chittendon, William Howard. *From China Marine to Jap POW*, p. 131.
4. DeTurek, E. B. Letter in Kurt Stauffer Collection, Seattle, WA.

Chapter 20. Mukden

1. Letter accompanying Robert Peaty diary. Imperial War Museum.
2. Robert Peaty diary. Imperial War Museum.
3. Christie, Arthur. Unpublished manuscript. Ms. with Maurice Christie, London.
4. Personal correspondence, Willis Johnson, 1999.

Chapter 21. In the Boondocks

1. Personal correspondence, George Duffy, 1999.
2. Michel, John J. *Mr. Michel's War*, p. 127.
3. Harrison, Kenneth. *The Brave Japanese*.
4. July 9, 1942, edition of apparently untitled Changi newsletter. Stahle file in Australian War Memorial.
5. Thompson, Kyle. *A Thousand Cups of Rice*.
6. Allister, William. *Where Life and Death Hold Hands*.
7. Priestwood, Gwen. *Through Japanese Barbed Wire*.

Chapter 22. Shantung Compound

1. Gilkey, Langdon. Shantung Compound, p. 34.

Chapter 23. Japan

1. Prisoners of War Camps in Japan and Japanese-Controlled Areas. Zentsuji Headquarters Camp. Report dated July 31, 1946, p. 4.
2. Emerson, Kary. *Guest of the Emperor*, p. 55.
3. Chittendon, William Howard. *From China Marine to Jap POW*, p. 151.
4. Norquist, Ernest. *Our Paradise*.

Chapter 24. Axis Prisoners of War

1. Krammer, Arnold. *Nazi Prisoners of War in America*.
2. *Montgomery Messenger*, July 1944.
3. Krammer, Arthur. *Pacific Historical Review*, Vol. LII, No. 1 (February 1983).
4. Frankel, Stanley. *Frankel-y Speaking.*Unpublished.
5. Tillery, A. J. Unpublished manuscript, Chalmette, LA.
6. Ikei, Masaru. *The History of the Tokyo Six-University Baseball League*.

Sources

Those interested in the history of POW baseball, and in the POW experience in general would be well advised to rapidly seek out the remaining ex-POWs, who are the ultimate sources of information. As I complete this manuscript most of them are around 80 years old, and their ranks are thinning quickly. It has been my pleasure to communicate in one form or another with dozens of these gentlemen.

The next best source of information would be the various diaries and other documents compiled during or soon after the Second World War. These are scattered far and wide, but the better collections are worth tracking down.

ARCHIVES

National POW Museum
Andersonville National Historic Site
Route 1, Box 800
Andersonville, GA 31711

The National POW Museum is located on the site of Andersonville Prison of Civil War infamy. Its collection is eclectic, as are all collections that rely on donated material. The staff, especially Fred Sanchez and Eric Reinert, have proven to be very helpful.

U.S. Army Military History Institute
22 Ashburn Drive
Carlisle Barracks
Carlisle, PA 17013-5008

Another valuable trove of documents, these collections are biased somewhat toward preserving the memoirs of rather senior officers, whose experiences were interesting but atypical. There is also an overrepresentation of memoirs from the Pacific war, which, depending on your purposes, can be useful.

National Archives of Canada
395 Wellington Street
Ottawa, Ontario, Canada
K1A ON3

The National Archives of Canada contain some useful information on the topic of POW baseball, including a complete set of International Red Cross inspection reports on Axis prisoner-of-war camps.

National Baseball Hall of Fame and Museum
25 Main Street
PO Box 590
Cooperstown, NY 13326-0590

No look at any aspect of baseball history could be undertaken without consulting the National Baseball Hall of Fame. Scot Mondore was kind enough to help me find a few treasures among the imposing collections.

Australian War Memorial
GPO Box 345
Canberra ACT 2601, Australia

The Australian War Memorial contains a well-organized and extensive collection of manuscripts and photographs and has an extremely useful online catalog.

Imperial War Museum
Lambeth Road
London, SE1 6H2
United Kingdom

The Imperial War Museum is probably the world's single most comprehensive collection of source material on the Second World War. I had the opportunity to spend an all-too-brief afternoon in its reading room in the course of this project. Although obviously oriented toward the history of British arms there is ample material on the contributions of Commonwealth and American troops. The staff is unfailingly courteous and helpful, and thus can be excused for not really understanding baseball.

State Historical Society of Wisconsin
816 State Street
Madison, WI 53706

I was pleased to find some useful information close to home, at the Wisconsin State Historical Society. It has several collections relating to the Bad Nauheim internment, including copies of the *Bad Nauheim Pudding*.

Special Collections
U.S. Air Force Academy Library
2354 Fairchild Dr.
Suite 3A10
USAF Academy, CO 80840-6214

The U.S. Air Force Academy libraries have a collection dealing with Stalag Luft III that is probably rivaled only by material held at the Imperial War Museum. For my research purposes the crown jewel was the carefully preserved copies of the *Gefangenen Gazette*, which the staff was kind enough to make available for my use.

American Ex–Prisoners of War
National Headquarters
3201 East Pioneer Parkway, #40
Arlington, TX 76010-5396

Some basic information on camps where Americans were held can be obtained from the American Ex–Prisoners of War. This organization has mostly compiled the summaries generated by the Office of the Provost Marshal in the immediate postwar period. The relentless passage of time is thinning the ranks of this fine organization, which has done so much both to educate the general population and to advocate for the former prisoners of war. Although their numbers are growing smaller I should think they would prefer it that way, as this reflects the smaller number of American soldiers who have fallen into enemy hands since the Second World War.

Society for American Baseball Research
812 Huron Road, Suite 719
Cleveland, OH 44115

All serious students of baseball history will be aware of the SABR. I cannot conceive of a baseball-related question so arcane that the membership of this organization would be unable to illuminate it. My casual inquiry in a SABR newsletter started the process by which an idle musing became a globe-spanning research project.

The topic of prisoners of war has generated a large number of secondary sources in the form of books and magazine articles. It would be impossible to provide a comprehensive bibliography, or even to list all the books I consulted in the course of this research. In literary quality they span the entire spectrum from scholarly texts to plainly written memoirs. Here are some of the standard sources, which I include for their general utility, along with a sampling of lesser-known texts that I consider to be either of particular interest on a specific topic or to be of superior quality with respect to insights on the experience of being a POW.

SELECTED BIBLIOGRAPHY

Europe

Beltrone, Art. *A Wartime Log.* Charlottesville, VA: Howell Press, 1995.

Bickers, James. *Achtung: Oflag 64, 1943–45.* Evanston IN: Evanston Publishing, 1993.

Burdick, Charles. *An American Island in Hitler's Reich: The Bad Nauheim Internment.* Menlo Park, CA: Markgraf Publications, 1987.

Dancocks, Daniel. *In Enemy Hands.* Edmonton, Alberta: Hurtig, 1983.

Dillon, Carrol. *A Domain of Heroes.* Sarasota, FL: Palm Island Press, 1995.

Durand, Arthur. *Stalag Luft III: An American Experience in a World War II German Prisoner of War Camp.* Baton Rouge, LA: University Microfilm.

_____. *Stalag Luft III: The Secret Story.* Baton Rouge, LA: Louisiana State University Press, 1999.

Greening, C. Ross and A. Spinell. *The Yankee Kriegies.* New York: National Council of YMCA, 1945.

Hobbs, Charlie. *Past Tense: Charlie's Story.* Burnstown, ON: General Store Publishing House, 1994.

Marchildon, Phil. *ACE.* Toronto, New York: Viking, 1993.

Shoemaker, Lloyd. *The Escape Factory: The Story of MIS-X.* New York: St. Martin's Press, 1990.

Snelling, Dennis. *A Glimpse of Fame.* Jefferson, NC: McFarland, 1993.

Spivey, Delmar. *POW Odyssey.* Attleboro, MA: 1984.

Taylor, James. *Prisoner of Concern: Canadian Prisoners of War through the Twentieth Century.* Vancouver: University of British Columbia, 1994.

Vance, Jonathan. *Objects of Concern: Canadian Prisoners of War through the Twentieth Century.* Vancouver: University of British Columbia, 1994.
Vietor, John. *Time Out: American Airmen at Stalag Luft I.* New York: Richard Smith, 1951.

Pacific

Allister, William. *Where Life and Death Hold Hands.* Toronto: Stoddart, 1989.
Barker, Robert A. *Philippine Diary.* Chicago, IL: R. A. Barker Foundation, 1990.
Biggs, Chester. *Behind the Barbed Wire.* Jefferson, NC: McFarland, 1995.
Braddon, Russell. *The Naked Island.* London: Werner Laurie, 1952.
Chittendon, William Howard. *From China Marine to Jap POW.* Paducah, KY: Turner Publications, 1995.
Crouter, Natalie. *Forbidden Diary.* New York: B. Franklin, 1980.
Daws, Gavin. *Prisoners of the Japanese.* New York: Wm. Morrow, 1994.
Fitzpatrick, Bernard. *The Hike into the Sun.* Jefferson, NC: McFarland, 1993.
Flanagan, E. M. *The Los Banos Raid.* Novato, CA: Presidio, 1986.
Gilkey, Langdon. *Shantung Compound.* New York: Harper and Row, 1966.
Goodman, Julien. *M.D. P.O.W.* New York: Exposition Press, 1972.
Gordon, Richard M. *Horyo: Memoirs of an American POW.* St. Paul, MN: Paragon House, 1999.
Harrison, Kenneth. *The Brave Japanese.* Adelaide, Australia: Rigby, 1966.
Hartendorp, A. V. H. *The Santo Tomas Story.* New York: McGraw-Hill, 1946.
Jackson, Calvin G. *Diary of Colonel Calvin G. Jackson, M.D.* Ada, OH: Ohio Northern University, 1992.
Johansen, Bruce. *So Far from Home.* Omaha, NE: PBI Press, 1996.
Kerr, E. Bartlett. *Surrender and Survival.* New York: Wm. Morrow, 1985.
Knox, Donald. *Death March: The Survivors of Bataan.* New York: Harcourt Brace Jovanovich, 1983.
Michel, John J. A. *Mr. Michel's War.* Novato, CA: Presidio, 1998.
Normand, Elizabeth. *We Band of Angels.* Random House, 1999.
Norquist, Earnest. *Our Paradise.* Hancock, WI: Pearl-Win Publishing, 1989.
Priestwood, Gwen. *Through Japanese Barbed Wire.* New York: D. Appleton-Century, 1943.
Thompson, Kyle. *A Thousand Cups of Rice.* Austin, TX: Eakin Press, 1994.
Vaughn, Elizabeth. *Community Under Stress, and Internment Camp Culture.* Princeton University Press, 1949.
Vaugn, Elizabeth. *The Ordeal of Elizabeth Vaugn.* University of Georgia Press, 1985.
Verreault, George. *Diary of Prisoner of War in Japan.* Rimouski, Quebec: Vero, 1996.
Waterford, Van. *Prisoners of the Japanese in World War II.* Jefferson, NC: McFarland, 1994.

Miscellaneous

Carr-Gregg, Charlotte. *Japanese Prisoners of War in Revolt*. New York: St. Martin's, 1978.

Hays, Otis. *Home from Siberia*. College Station: Texas A & M University Press, 1990.

Ikei, Masaru. *The History of the Tokyo Six University Baseball League*. Tokyo: Baseball Magazine Co., 1995.

Iwao, Peter Sano. *One Thousand Days in Siberia*. Omaha: University of Nebraska Press, 1997.

Krammer, Arnold. *Nazi Prisoners of War in America*. New York: Stein and Day, 1979..

Ooka, Shohei. *Taken Captive: A Japanese POW's Story*. New York: John Wiley and Sons, 1996.

Index